PRAISE FOR "I DIDN'T SIGN UP FOR THIS."

"In this inspirational book, Manser shares her vulnerability and authenticity, inviting educators to grow in their self-empowerment, just as she has, within an emotionally challenging profession. Diane's journey and her choice to maintain joy will encourage all aspiring and veteran educators to continue serving with empathy and connection. Insightful, authentic, and uplifting: a must-read for all educators."

—Thomas C. Murray, Best-Selling Author &
Director of Innovation, Future Ready Schools, Washington, D.C.

"Not only is Diane Manser a beautiful and brilliant writer, but her gut-honest transparency and raw vulnerability is a freaking gift. By bringing to light the emotional struggles and exhaustion teachers face—and doing it with humor, joy, and love—she's literally going to change lives. Her words offer comfort and encouragement to disillusioned, burned-out teachers and give them permission to be honest about their challenges and to ask for what they need. She is so unbelievably brave—not because she's fearless, but because she feels the fear and does hard things (like writing this book) anyway. Chapter after chapter, this book absolutely blew me away. I hope it finds its way into the hands of teachers everywhere."

—Marla Taviano, Author of *Whole: Poems on Reclaiming
The Pieces of Ourselves and Creating Something New* As
Well As Other Poetry Masterpieces and Amazing Books

"Manser authentically confronts the emotional and personal toll of teaching, embracing its inseparability not as a complaint of the profession, but an inevitable and beautiful aspect of being a passionate educator. While the emotional labor of teaching is often undervalued, Manser uses stories to take the reader into the mind and heart of a teacher who comes to accept the interweaving personal and emotional aspects of life as an educator and in doing so understands it—and herself—to find joy and gratitude."

—Dr. Scott Eveslage, Superintendent of Schools

"*I Didn't Sign Up for This...* is a must-read for educators seeking validation and guidance in their own teaching journey. Diane fearlessly navigates the turbulent waters of teaching, revealing the raw emotions and profound lessons hidden within this noble profession. Diane's experiences serve as a beacon of hope and practical wisdom that offer invaluable lessons on developing the emotional fortitude necessary to thrive in the classroom.

Whether you're a seasoned educator looking to renew your passion or a new teacher seeking solace and direction, this book will inspire you to embrace the emotional journey of teaching and emerge stronger and more equipped to make a lasting impact on young lives.

Diane's story powerfully reminds us that teaching isn't just a profession; it's a transformative journey of the heart and mind. This book is a treasure trove of inspiration and guidance for anyone committed to the noble pursuit of education."

—Dr. Brea D'Angelo, Director of Special Operations and Systems K-12

"This book provides an insightful and authentic look into the world of teaching and education. The author, Diane Manser, has a talent for capturing the complexities and nuances of the classroom experience, from the hopes and dreams of teachers to the challenges they face on a daily basis. The book offers a mix of emotions, from courage and humor to vulnerability and honesty, painting a realistic and relatable picture of life as an educator. It will resonate with pre-service and veteran teachers alike, who can find solace and connection in shared experiences, as well as outsiders who gain a deeper understanding of the dedication and passion that drives teachers to help their students succeed. This thought-provoking book can help spark conversations and broaden perspectives on the important work that educators do every day."

—Dr. Christy Ridgley, School Administrator

"For those who commit to this profession fully, it can be an emotional roller coaster, and many suffer in silence. The heartfelt and tangible examples of the journey from fatigue to empowerment make this book a must-read for anyone in the field of education. It's an emotionally resonant read that provides hope and reintroduces the joy in this profession. This should be a required read for novice and veteran educators alike."

—Dr. Dennis M. Williams, Jr., Principal

"*I Didn't Sign Up For This...* offers a compelling exploration of the emotional landscape in education. It underscores the importance of teachers' self-awareness and emotional regulation as foundational to effective teaching. By emphasizing that behavior is a form of communication, the book illuminates how a teacher's response can either escalate or de-escalate a situation. Through poignant real-life interactions, it vividly illustrates the profound impact of educator's emotional intelligence on classroom dynamics. A must-read for educators seeking to cultivate joy and understanding, it champions a holistic approach that benefits both teachers and students alike."

—Rose Miele, Coordinator of Teaching & Learning
For Elementary Education, and K-12 Assessment Coordinator

"Diane shares insight throughout the text that take seasoned teachers years or even decades to learn in a way that is relatable and practical. *I Didn't Sign Up For This...* is an excellent resource for beginning teachers, and the experiences shared serve to remind even the most veteran teachers that they are not alone, even on their most challenging days."

—Susan Scherffel, Special Education Teacher and
University Supervisor for Student Teachers

"Diane Manser reveals that teachers are often blindsided by the profound challenges that await them in the classroom. She describes with equal parts honesty and humor the emotional whiplash of a job that builds you up one moment only to tear you down the next. Her hard-won wisdom can help teachers discover that what they've signed up for, while harder than they could have imagined, can also lead to deep personal growth and transformation."

—Seth Gillihan, Phd, Licensed Psychologist and
Author of *Mindful Cognitive Behavioral Therapy*

"As a former teacher, this book is a must read for any aspiring, veteran, or retired teacher. Diane's accounts of her classroom are captivating, and her detailed stories will have you transported right into the scene. Her ability to reflect on her personal challenging teachable moments allows the reader to connect with the experience, which many of us current and former teachers have shared. In this book, Diane mastered the symbiosis of humility, growth, and hope."

—Victoria Geppert, NeuroLogic Specialist, Marriage and
Family Therapist, and Former Special Education Teacher K-12

"Diane beautifully shares her experiences as a teacher with a raw vulnerability that resonates beyond the teaching profession. This book will guide you to reconnect to yourself, and help you create an immovable connection to live in your authenticity. You will feel inspired to find gratitude and joy to truly live engaged in your "one wild and precious life."

—Carrie Henry, Life and Connection Coach

"Manser is as brave as she is insightful. Her book is a tremendous resource for new and veteran teachers. It's what I needed in my first year of teaching and what I now cherish in my 31st."

—Ed Doran, High School English Teacher

"Diane Manser's *I Didn't Sign Up For This...* is a must read. Most of us are somewhere in the journey of wanting to present ourselves to others in a way that maintains our core values to be heard and respected. Diane's journey, rationale, strategies, and communication skills will lead you to feeling empowered as well. Using the teaching lens, Diane's methods can also facilitate growth in many other roles and occupations in life. Her honest, raw accounts and solutions inspire one to examine ways one could incorporate her philosophy and strategies to feel more empowered."

—Meryl Lightstone, Retired Elementary School
Educator and Elementary School Librarian

"The challenge of teaching is often more emotional that we feel comfortable sharing, perhaps because to do so would be to admit weakness or incompetence. Through her honest experiences, Diane invites us to identify the hard feelings that come with our jobs and, more importantly, practical ideas for how we can move forward in them. If you've ever thought, "Boy, I didn't sign up for THIS!" Diane's stories and reflections will resonate with you and give you hope."

—Nalene Hilker, Advanced Placement Language and Composition Teacher

"It's certainly fitting to enter this profession with optimism and high hopes, but if they are not balanced with realistic expectations, we run the risk of losing individuals who may have eventually excelled. The wisdom, heart, and experiences contained in this book will help better prepare future educators and give solace and advice to veterans."

—Sean Deluca, High School English Teacher

"*I Didn't Sign Up For This...* will be immediately validating for teachers and enlightening for everyone else. It's the beacon of light we need in an era when teaching is judged from the outside looking in and teachers are leaving the profession in record numbers. While Diane affirms that yes, teaching is emotional, she also gives us hope."

—Kimberly English-Murphy, High School Gifted Teacher

"A must-read for teachers at all stages of their career, *I Didn't Sign Up For This...* sheds light on the often overlooked emotional side of teaching. Using her own career experiences, Diane Manser provides valuable insight into what emotional challenges educators face and invites us into her journey of finding practical and positive solutions. Whether you are a preservice teacher or a classroom veteran, you will find yourself nodding along to this refreshing take on what really goes on inside the classroom and how we can equip ourselves for what we are not typically prepared."

—Kristina Ulmer, High School English Teacher

"This is a special book that will bring you back to your why: why you teach, why you became an educator. It is empowering, solution-focused, and what the professional development educators need in today's teaching climate. You will live differently after reading this beautiful book, filled with so much inspiration from Mary Oliver, Jim Fortin, Oprah, Mother Theresa, and Diane Manser. This book helps us to lower the volume on the negatives and focus on our higher calling of "bettering the ball," leaving the world a better place one student at a time, one situation at a time. This book is for anyone wanting to live better and reach their fullest potential to inspire others to do the same. You will become immovable."

—Nicole Wagner, Elementary School Guidance Counselor

"This book should be required reading for anyone who wants to better understand what it feels like to be a teacher. Diane bravely, and with humor and grace, helps us understand the best and worst of what our educators experience. If you know a teacher, are a teacher, or think you might want to be a teacher, read Diane's story and gain a vital new perspective on one of the world's most important professions."

—Matthew Ulmer, Award Winning Author, and Husband to a Teacher

"*I Didn't Sign Up for This...* is a refreshing take on facing the classroom in our current world. Diane's message about the emotional impact of teaching is powerful, impassioned, and poignant. This message goes beyond discussing the struggles we face on a daily basis; it empowers us to face them with compassion and integrity."

—Stephanie Clinise, High School English Teacher

"*I Didn't Sign Up for This* presents a facet of the teaching experience that is often overlooked- the emotional impact resulting from educating humans with varying backgrounds, family situations, needs and behaviors. Diane addresses her personal teaching experiences and her own emotion-filled journey as she draws back the curtain in an authentic, enlightened, and loving manner. Her message for teachers, novice and experienced alike, is that we can reclaim our joy within the challenges of teaching."

—Elizabeth Mitchell, Elementary School Teacher

I DIDN'T SIGN UP FOR *THIS*

One Classroom Teacher's Journey Through Emotional Fatigue to Personal Empowerment

Diane E. Manser

teaching is emotional™

Philadelphia, Pennsylvania

The stories and examples that fill these pages are from the author's perspective and are shared from her memory as she revisits them years later. They are from the author's experiences and observations, the experiences of teachers closest to her, and from those she has met along the way. They illustrate a particular truth that happens in teaching. While they come from personal experience and conversation, the stories that are present in this book are universal experiences of teachers everywhere despite location. The individual stories do not represent the whole of the author's school or of the students she has taught. They are shared to encapsulate the emotional impact that teachers experience, so teachers can prepare themselves and can serve as they are meant to serve. Names are removed and identifying features have been changed. All stories and examples that come from the author's fellow teachers are used with permission.

Teaching is Emotional books are available from your favorite bookseller or from www.teachingisemotional.com

Cataloging in Publication data on file with the publisher.

Beautiful and catching cover design as well as amazing interior design by Rachel Moore, The Designing Ninja.

ISBN: 979-8-9899081-3-4 (PAPERBACK)
ISBN: 979-8-9899081-1-0 (EBOOK)
ISBN: 979-8-9899081-2-7 (AUDIO)

Printed in the USA

1 3 5 7 9 10 8 6 4 2

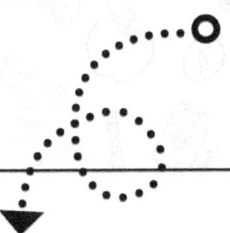

This book is dedicated to my most influential teachers, Leah and Eric. God guided me to you, and because of you, I have grown in the most important ways. I am so thankful for you both.

I love you immeasurably.

CONTENTS

PART I: CONFIRMING THE PROBLEM

····o PART III: EPIPHANY & EMPOWERMENT

SPECIAL ENDORSEMENT

"When I met Diane in the summer of 2023, she was telling a group of us what it's like to be a teacher—how you start the school year strong in September, but then it's very easy to find yourself wearing down over the coming weeks and months as a teacher's interactions with her students can take a devastating emotional toll.

It was fascinating to hear her describe this phenomenon and how teachers aren't taught what to do about it. I don't know what it's like to be a teacher, but as I looked around the group while Diane was talking, I could see everybody was as compelled as I was by her energy and insight and joy and honesty and fierceness.

That word FIERCENESS. Is that actually a word? Diane would know.

FIERCENESS is important here because she wasn't complaining, she was explaining what she had learned about how to deal with these very real emotional challenges and how she wanted every teacher everywhere to discover what she's learned. Which, of course, is why you're holding this book in your hands.

It's all here—coffee and tornadoes and doormats and AI and several decades of Diane's wisdom on how to be a teacher in such a way that you find yourself saying 'THIS IS WHAT I SIGNED UP FOR.'"

—Rob Bell, *New York Times* Best-Selling Author, International Speaker, and Spiritual Teacher

FOREWORD

When Diane joined the English Department, I was comfortable in my identity as a weather-worn, jaded English teacher. And here she came, bouncing in. Who was this young, endlessly cheery teacher? I hope she can keep it up, I thought.

And she did. Every day. Diane was and is one of the most relentlessly joyful people I have ever met. To this day, if I'm feeling low, I seek out some "Diane time" to make me feel better about myself.

Diane was also, I soon came to learn, very serious about being as effective an English teacher as she possibly could. She always participated during in-service workshops, and regularly took the lead presenting new initiatives and techniques in department meetings. During the pandemic, she volunteered a workshop on Nearpod, a tool she had found useful in ensuring participation while teaching online.

I've learned not to judge what is going on when walking by a classroom with an open door. However, if I did happen to walk by Diane's room, her students were always engaged, be it listening to her, giving speeches or working in groups. I saw her students nervously practicing for presentations in the hallways, practicing because they knew Mrs. Manser wouldn't hesitate to hold up the sign that said "louder" or "slow down" from the back of the room. It mattered to them that they do a good job. So I admit, I judged. She was killing it.

But one day, I saw what I realize now was a little bit of a crack. I didn't think much of it at the time. We were in the hallway of my current wing in June, the students gone for summer. The lights were low because not many people were left in the building, and we chatted for a minute under a skylight by the printer in the hallway. I didn't get to talk with Diane much because we were in different parts of the building, so it was nice to have an opportunity to catch up before leaving for summer break. Diane had gotten her schedule for the following year, and she shared that she had willingly given up her freshmen honors sections because the workload had gotten to be too much. She had been struggling to keep up with the prep and grading; it was taking too much time from life with her family. As she spoke, there seemed to be a hint of disappointment on her face—like she was justifying her decision to me. And it was a shame, I thought, because she worked so hard to push the top freshmen and prepare them well for the teachers who had them in years to come. However, I understood completely.

A couple of years ago, I got to know Diane better. She had been struggling in other areas, and we talked about it quite a bit. It turned out the biggest struggle was coming to the realization that trying to fight back with a relentlessly positive nature was no longer enough. Little did I know that this dynamic had also been playing out in her classroom. The hint of disappointment I had seen a couple of years ago apparently had a deeper root.

At the end of the 2021 school year, in a more brightly lit hallway on a different floor, she excitedly shared with me an idea she had for a book. She wanted to write about the emotional reactions students trigger in their teachers. Cool idea, I thought, but it sounded like the exasperations of a teacher at the end of the year. We were all becoming increasingly frustrated with what is now a well-documented epidemic of student disengagement, and it was June after all. She would write some journal entries over the summer, I figured, play with her children, and come back in the fall ready for a new year as usual.

And then, in the fall of 2023 she asked me if I would take a look at the manuscript for her book. What?! "Remember that discussion we had? I did it! I wrote the book!" she told me. I was honored to be asked and agreed immediately.

Diane Manser, joyful teacher of teachers, has written a book that allows us a glimpse into her classroom and into herself. In this book she shares the struggles, doubts, and obstacles she has encountered teaching high school freshman English. While it's not entirely surprising that it hasn't been all sunshine and roses, it is a little surprising that for someone like Diane it has at times been so far from that. While she was doing her best to keep spreading sunshine and tending roses day after day and year after year, cloudy days and rainless droughts were taking their toll. She was suffering more and more, all while trying to keep a smile on her face. Teaching can test the joy in all of us.

Teaching can also be lonely if we all shut our classroom doors and keep the challenges to ourselves. Diane has been brave enough to open up her door and let us in, and I believe you will connect with parts of her story and feel a little less alone. I believe you will also find hope, and maybe even some new strategies for managing the inevitable challenges.

Diane is absolutely right. What we are endeavoring to do in this vocation is emotional, and we all need more joy. And no one brings that like Diane.

—Mrs. Kimberly English-Murphy,
Gifted Support Teacher

"For what it's worth: it's never too late or, in my case, too early to be whoever you want to be. There's no time limit, stop whenever you want. You can change or stay the same, there are no rules to this thing. We can make the best or the worst of it. I hope you make the best of it. And I hope you see things that startle you. I hope you feel things you never felt before. I hope you meet people with a different point of view. I hope you live a life you're proud of. If you find that you're not, I hope you have the strength to start all over again."[1]

—Benjamin Button,
"The Curious Case of Benjamin Button"

INTRODUCTION

THE START OF IT ALL

Though I've officially been a teacher for almost two decades, my "teaching career" started more than three decades ago in the basement of my childhood home, where I created a classroom filled with eager-looking stuffed animal students.

I would spend hours making up tests and answer keys, creating coloring pages and posters, and filling prize bins with stickers and trinkets. I'd teach for an entire afternoon in front of the green chalkboard my dad bought for me at a garage sale, wearing a play dress and my mom's old jewelry and heels.

These precious memories nestled into my subconscious, and I think a part of me trusted that my real classroom would play out similarly. Playing teacher was fun, simple, and uplifting—with no surprise stress.

As I grew older, I stopped playing teacher, but I loved my actual teachers, and I loved being a student. Many current teachers enter the profession because of similar poignant memories. Perhaps they always loved school and teachers and being an integral part of their schools'

> MANY TEACHERS WILL TELL YOU THEY DIDN'T EXPECT THE PROFESSION TO BE AS CONSISTENTLY CHALLENGING AS IT IS, IN THE WAY THAT IT IS.

activities, or they loved being around their peers and socializing, or they needed some extra attention and care when growing up and found it through a special teacher.

Most teachers can tell you exactly why they became a teacher and what they thought they would accomplish in being a teacher. They can also tell you what they *thought* the profession was going to be like for them, and what the profession is *actually* like for them.

Many teachers will tell you they didn't expect the profession to be as consistently challenging as it is, in the way that it is.

I am one of those teachers.

The challenge wasn't a matter of working hard. I could do that. I just wasn't expecting to work as hard as I was and, strangely, feel like I was getting more and more behind despite that hard work. I also wasn't expecting the heavy emotional stress that came to me from a variety of places, particularly from the people I was working the hardest for: my students.

I was the teacher who couldn't wait to get started. In the final round interview for the job I still have, I responded to intricate questions while anxiously sitting in my school's guidance suite with its large, circular windows inviting the hot summer sun on my back. I wore my professional dark green business suit I had just bought at Macy's with my long, curly hair pulled back from my face with a taupe headband. In the last question, I took a deep breath while leaning just a bit more forward and shared that, "I may be young and have a lot to learn, but I have endless enthusiasm, and I am so very excited that I am 'this close' to finally getting *to be* a teacher."

There wasn't more I could say. I had made it all the way to the final round. For years, I had dreamt of being a teacher and having my own classroom. I stated my intention to work hard and to honor the job with every ounce of my sincerity. I meant every word. I still do.

The problem wasn't my "endless enthusiasm"—though that contributed to some disappointments. The problem

> THE PROBLEM WAS THAT I HADN'T PREPARED MYSELF FOR THE PAINFUL SIDE OF TEACHING, SIMPLY BECAUSE I DIDN'T KNOW TO PREPARE FOR IT.

IN THE PROCESS OF FIGURING OUT HOW TO TEACH AND WHAT TO TEACH, I NEGLECTED TO UNDERSTAND AND SELF-EXAMINE WHAT IT WOULD FEEL LIKE TO TEACH...

was that I hadn't prepared myself for the painful side of teaching, simply because I didn't know to prepare for it.

In the process of figuring out *how to teach* and *what to teach*, I neglected to understand and self-examine what it would *feel like* to teach, especially when things do not go well. Similar to a foggy windshield on an overcast day, I did not clearly see what was in front of me until I was right up on it.

I hadn't prepared myself to understand what it would feel like to think I was in charge, but to be insecure and self-doubting. I hadn't prepared myself to know what it would feel like to work long, late hours already exhausted to only then be criticized or disrespected.

I hadn't prepared myself to be a living Sisyphus.

What I did expect—and which I also do experience— is being a consistently positive influence to students who need it and serving as a guide for young people into the depth and intrigue of literature-to-life discussions that grow introspection and character.

But every positive, rewarding experience cannot fully erase the figurative blemishes I carry from the painful experiences.

FIGURING IT OUT

My name is Diane Manser, and I didn't at first set out to write a book about the emotional impacts of teaching. This all started with a personal, cathartic journal, stemming from the pain points of teaching high school English for nearly two decades, from which I've experienced work overload and emotional fatigue, causing me to question my worth, my capability, and my desire to continue teaching.

Perfectly timed, just as I desperately doubted whether I could *truly* do any more school years the way in which I had been doing them, I experienced a breakthrough with the help of a therapist that gave me self-understanding, guidance toward empowerment, and much-needed hope. I did the inner work and reflection, and I applied this learning to my teaching life and my personal life. This work is continuous, despite all I've learned, because teaching—just like life—is never a finished product.

TEACHING—JUST LIKE LIFE—IS NEVER A FINISHED PRODUCT.

The more I wrote, the more I knew there would be at least one teacher out there who would feel validated—maybe even helped—by my words. I also recognized there was a whole group of teachers entering the profession who could have a steadier start than I did, if they could learn from my experiences.

As my chapters were morphing into a full-book outline, I learned of an opportunity to sit across from Rob Bell, one of my most admired spiritual teachers, to talk about an idea or problem. I couldn't believe my luck that this mentor I had appreciated and learned from for years would be an hour from my home. I took the chance and shared to Rob and a beautiful group of "strangers turned friends" that teachers, especially those entering the profession, must know themselves deeply and be secure in their self-awareness and introspection before they start teaching, so they are not blindsided by the emotional pains and fatigue that teaching will throw at them.

I asserted that everyone needs to see teaching not just as a content-driven profession, but also as an emotional profession.

This special group of new friends embraced me, validated me, and encouraged me to finish this book and put it out there. More things aligned, such as a friend from the Rob Bell event connecting me with a supportive editor, loving people encouraging me when I shared my self-doubt, and generous and helpful friends giving me their time and advice when reading drafts of this book while also guiding me into the world of social media for the first time.

Whereas some people's Facebook profiles boast "established in 2006," I joined in October of 2023. "It's never too late to do something new," I reassured my nerves. I joked that I had an email, and I texted—sometimes with delay—but this world was fast and intimidating. But I knew if I was going to reach even one person who could feel validated by my honesty about teaching, then I needed to get out there with everyone else, even if I felt uncomfortable.

In just the first week of joining Facebook, I reconnected with old friends, started a teachers' group called "Teaching is Emotional"™ *and* got kicked out of another teachers' group for ignorantly sharing about my FB group while responding to a post. Just in case you aren't aware, you can't promote your group in someone else's group. There are rules against that. Whoops!

In the first three days of "doing" Instagram, I tagged every teacher and every teachers' group I knew about, so they would see my posts. I thought that's how it worked. Tag, Tag, Tag! No, it's not. Thank you to my dearest friend, Lauren, for informing me if I continued tagging everyone on every post, I'd surely annoy everyone I knew. I didn't realize tagging people on one, two, three posts a day was like ringing someone's doorbell ten times a day, and, well, ya just don't do that. I quickly learned the world of social media is both boundaryless and bound by rules.

On my own with no one near me, I opened the social media door that had a TikTok sign. It was like a hoppin' club in there with bodies dancing and videos booming—and no bouncer because I had yet to acquire any type of algorithm. For sure, I had innocently entered the big leagues. I closed that door (but didn't lock it) and retreated to the jazz room of Facebook with the intentions of staying in my lane, and the coffeehouse of Instagram with the intentions of keeping my doorbell-ringing fingers to myself.

I have learned a lot, trying to get this journal-turned-book into your hands, with one such realization being that others might benefit from my journey. If I had a person out there, stranger or otherwise, tell me as I went through my first years of teaching that they also cry despite being years into this profession, or that they also feel overwhelmed despite having taught the same content many times over, or that they also feel insecure despite seeming so confident, I would have been grateful and relieved by the honesty and support.

WHO THIS IS FOR

You are holding this book in your hands because something in this—the title, the back cover, the table of contents—spoke to you. Maybe you also feel the pains from a job that should be so good to you, since you are so good to it. But it hasn't been as good to you as you thought it would be, and it is time that it is.

I wrote this book primarily about teachers and for teachers. Or for anyone who wants to understand how teaching is an emotional profession that will unearth the deep stuff within us that may be dormant or surprising, leaving us feeling confused and tired.

I wrote this book, also, for non-teachers who recognize their lives and jobs are emotional experiences, even if they are positioned to be results-oriented. Yes, my story is based in teaching, but my story is about *life*—all life and the universal stories we share because life is *emotional.*

> I WROTE THIS BOOK THINKING ABOUT THE TEACHERS WHO LOVE TEACHING AND WHO KNOW THEY ARE MEANT TO BE TEACHING, BUT WHO ARE SURPRISED BY THE DISSONANCE BETWEEN THEIR EXPECTATIONS AND THE REALITIES OF TEACHING.

I wrote this book for education professors and new teacher orientation leaders, so they can continue honest conversations with those they are guiding about the realities of teaching.

I wrote this book thinking about the teachers who love teaching and who know they are meant to be teaching, but who are surprised by the dissonance between their expectations and the realities of teaching.

I wrote this book to prepare the emerging and new teachers who are excited to start, and I wrote it for the teachers who feel the pains of teaching, but don't know what to do with those pains.

The truth of teaching is that it's fulfilling and defeating, rewarding and painful. I would tell anyone who wants to become a teacher to absolutely without a doubt become a teacher. Do not listen to anyone tell you otherwise. It has been my privilege to be a teacher, and it remains a privilege that I get to be a teacher. I honor what I do, and I wouldn't go back in time to choose something else.

> THE TRUTH OF TEACHING IS THAT IT'S FULFILLING AND DEFEATING, REWARDING AND PAINFUL.

Even so, the job is intensely emotional, and we must prepare ourselves for the full truth of teaching before we begin, so we can continue to do the work we are meant to do. And like anything else that is worthy of consideration, this shift in perspective requires a great deal of honesty and courage.

MY HOPE

This book will share that the challenges of teaching are from both the lesson planning and keeping up with records, as these are monumental, and also from the emotional impacts of teaching. The shocking realization about what it's like to be a teacher typically happens *after* one starts teaching. But the understanding and preparation about what it's really like to be a teacher must happen *before* one becomes a teacher.

I didn't know this when I found my calling playing teacher to my favorite stuffed animals and when I sought that calling in an undergraduate program. Those stuffed animals didn't bring their emotional trauma or anger to class. They were willing participants in all things learning and always tried their best.

As loved as they were, those open-eyed, silent cloth faces didn't prepare me for what it would mean to be a teacher. Likewise, I didn't know I needed to be emotionally prepared when I spent hours working on just one lesson to teach my undergraduate cohort, who good-naturedly and generously engaged in my teaching with the goal of making me a strong lesson-planned teacher before my first day.

I didn't know I needed to learn how to be emotionally strong when I naïvely said in my final round interview "I have a lot to learn..."

The intent of this book, then, is to offer how I came to understand my own personal triggers through the profession of teaching, and how I learned solutions that helped me navigate the pain points.

It is my life in teaching that has guided this book. Living through—and reflecting on—my experiences has helped me to recognize that every teacher, whether new or veteran, needs open conversation about the emotional fatigue of teaching and what we can do about it.

From this, I hope teacher training will continue supporting the importance of strong lesson planning and assessments, while it broadens to embrace teaching as an emotionally challenging profession. This will give teachers all the necessary training, so they can have their mental and emotional states considered before they enter and while in the profession.

Let's be courageous together and bring our shared experiences of teacher pain to the surface, so we can see them, name them, and put them in their proper place.

Only then can we determine our next successful steps of empowerment, joy, and, of course, hope.

Thank you so much for allowing me the opportunity to share my story with you.

THE CALENDAR FEEL OF THAT FIRST YEAR

A few years ago, I made the executive decision that I would make no judgments about any part of my life during the month of March. There would be no judgments about my body, my deepening wrinkles, my clothes, my kids, my husband, my house, my parents, my friends, my classroom, my students, my administrators, my coworkers. Nothing. No judgment.

It's like living in a perpetual Planet Fitness NO JUDGMENT ZONE.

I have been careful not to tell my children about this philosophy, fearing they'll take way too many liberties. I joke with friends and colleagues that March Madness may be coming for them, but March Planet Fitness is coming for me. I started the philosophy as a survivor's mechanism to lighten the feeling of March and to stop me from creating an endless "to do" list during one of the most tiring months of the school year, when it feels like time is moving slowly and teachers and students are itching for Spring.

For teachers, even in the best school years, March comes upon us like a slow storm approaching in the nearing distance. Its thick, gray clouds block the sun, and it hovers immovable with every week feeling like someone slipped in an extra Thursday. All we can do is take a deep breath, put our heads down, and plow through.

On the other side of March is April, naturally. It even sounds prettier. *April*. And that's when we realize March wasn't quite the problem at all. It's May. May is a trickster month, a teaser, and we wake each Monday morning in May after a full weekend of outdoor activities, uncertain how we will maintain our energy to do school right.

Suddenly, quicker than we realize, we are past the first week of June and saying things we never thought we'd hear ourselves say, like "This school year flew by," and "I can't believe it's been another year," and, one of my personal favorites, "This was both a long and short year."

Just going through one school week can feel like a mud run for which you haven't trained with Friday afternoon being the finish line your wobbly legs and wearied body crosses. How many Friday nights (before kids) I spent asleep on the couch with my school clothes still on and the TV flickering, just so immensely grateful it was Friday, knowing I could sleep in (before kids) on that blessed Saturday and regroup my neglected life.

I know all this, and I feel all this, because that is how my first year of teaching went, and it still pretty much feels the same all these years later. Only now with children of my own.

A WISH TO WARN

I started teaching in 2006, before cell phones in classrooms, social media, and ever-demanding state testing. My teaching career started when special education programs were developing and when kids (and their parents) weren't afraid from the tender age of 11 that they might not get into a good college. As many of us can do, I think back to those earlier years, and I see a different version of myself inside a simpler, less complicated classroom. I see me there, like in a teacher's snow globe, frozen in time, realizing that I had no idea what lay ahead.

I'd like to warn her, this earlier self. I'd like to shout and get her attention. "Be careful," I'd caution. "It's not you," I'd sympathize. "There are going to be tough days, and you're not ready for them," I'd warn.

Time has passed and the fatigue from teaching only half a career so far has left me bewildered. I'd admit that it wasn't supposed to be this exhausting, that it was supposed to be so much better, and that I'd better figure out what I could do to make teaching what I had always hoped it would be.

But there is no way for me to go back in time and shout "Heads Up!" to my younger, naïve self. What I can do is share my story to validate current teachers and to help prepare newer teachers. I can reflect on the journey and do my best to tell others what it's really like. I can offer my learning of what I did to make teaching as consistently close to the job I dreamed of when I was young.

THE UNDISCOVERED PROBLEM

From my perspective, the truth of teaching is an untold story that is kept too private, and, if told, is told too late. With the advent of social media, more and more teachers are boldly sharing their pains and disappointments from teaching, but we have to find each other to connect, and most likely the ones connecting are the ones already in the profession—doing the work and experiencing the pains.

Teachers take pride in their hard work and are often high achievers. To share and expose that we aren't excelling, but are actually struggling, opens us up to so much vulnerability and possible judgment that it is arguably more comfortable not to share, especially with our newest teachers. Veteran teachers and education professors find themselves in a predicament between preparing teachers for what to expect while also nurturing their enthusiasm, so as not to scare young teachers away or plant seeds of negativity.

But the truth is teachers are struggling emotionally. This is causing fatigue, self-doubt, burnout, and a high turnover rate. We can no longer rationalize it, reduce it, or excuse it away.

In my almost two decades of teaching, I have witnessed and experienced countless examples that signal an important, and undiscussed, reality: teaching should be considered an emotional profession from start to finish.

I have witnessed substitutes teach numerous courses and handle complex problems while they painstakingly wait for full-time teaching contracts, only to resign those full-time positions after a few years in the classroom. I have witnessed teachers with desirable, unique positions resign when they have a child, or resign when their spouse does exceptionally well in corporate America. I have witnessed dozens of teachers exhaustingly calculate the remaining years of their career into months and days until their retirement day. I have witnessed fully capable and put-together men and women 15+ years into the profession get so worked up that they slam something, throw something, curse, or cry.

I have witnessed teachers share vulnerably and honestly about how hard the day is for them, and then apologize for feeling that way. I have witnessed new teachers start eagerly and full of energy, confused about why the experienced teachers are so darn cranky, only for them to also lose that eager spirit a few years in. I have witnessed teachers leaving their classroom positions for opportunities anywhere outside of their classroom, but still in education, unwilling to truthfully answer why they left the classroom. I have witnessed teachers get degrees and certifications that will take them out of the classroom. I have witnessed teachers choose early retirement because they are stressed and tired. I have witnessed teachers say "I give up" and I have witnessed teachers actually give up.

The list could go on, but I feel anyone reading, especially teachers out there, could check off a few of these examples from your own experiences. It wasn't until I became a teacher and began to experience my own disappointments and pains, while observing and listening to the same in others, that I began to wonder why there wasn't a warning sticker on my job acceptance contract. What a gift it would be if I could go back in time and clarify to that young, 22-year-old Diane in the taupe headband and green power suit about the actual journey she was about to go on, just like so many thousands of others.

THE GREAT ESCAPE

Today, there is the Great Teacher Resignation, as I am calling it, as well as fewer and fewer college students choosing education as a profession. According to a 2022 comprehensive study conducted by Ed Fuller[2], Ph.D. from the Department of Education Policy Studies at Penn State University, my home state of Pennsylvania issued the lowest number ever of new teaching certificates during the 2021-2022 school year, and emergency certifications exceeded the number of formal teaching certificates.

Data from the Pennsylvania Department of Education shared by journalist Chanel Hill[3] from *The Philadelphia Tribune* in March 2023 confirms that thousands of new teachers will be needed by 2025, but fewer college students are entering the education field and more teachers are leaving the profession each year. Hill continues that the Pennsylvania Department of Education issued licenses to 20,000 new teachers a decade ago, but only certified 6,000 during the 2022 calendar year. For The School District of Philadelphia alone, they "opened the [2022-2023] school year with more than 200 teacher vacancies, and [in February 2023] the Philadelphia Board of Education approved more than 100 teacher resignations and retirements."

In February 2024, *CBS* reporters Dan Snyder and Casey Kuhn[4] announced that Pennsylvania lawmakers and educators determined ways to "fix the teacher shortage" as Pennsylvania came close to losing almost "10,000 teachers" in 2023 with "fewer teachers there to fill those losses." State Senator Vincent Hughes is quoted claiming Pennsylvania needs "'more teachers [given there is] no more important job in our life than a teacher'" (qtd. in Snyder and Kuhn).

While this information is regarding the state of Pennsylvania, this is not exclusively a state of Pennsylvania problem. Teacher shortages and the great teacher exit is a national issue. Whereas before, there were higher attrition rates in Title I schools, charter schools, or urban school districts, teachers are now leaving all areas. Senator Hughes, in Snyder and Kuhn's article, confirms with "'This is not just an urban issue. This is not a Democratic issue. Many rural school districts…have a significant problem of not having enough teachers.'"

Correspondingly, it is well known that one of the highest attrition ranges for teachers is between one to five teaching years, but now we are seeing higher than usual averages of teachers with 15 or more years of experience stating that they will leave teaching earlier than originally planned.

Teachers are suffering and have been suffering. Before, it was easier to brush off, but now we are in a teacher crisis, and the evidence of the suffering can be seen in the quantifiable, diminishing numbers.

There are plenty of reasons why this is happening. Some are political and some are financial. In *CNN*'s September

2023 article "…How schools are dealing with the ongoing teacher shortage" by correspondent Gabe Cohen[5], he shares data showing that teacher turnover is on the rise, and that "education experts blame a range of issues for the teacher exodus, including the profession's low salaries, growing workload, worsening student behavior, and growing politicization of school curricula and teaching."

Conduct any Google search on the issues within public education, and you will read controversies ranging from woke curricula, AI generators, crowded classrooms, resource limitations, staffing shortages, fighting and bullying, changing student morale, and clever ways to recruit and maintain teachers without affecting tax-bases.

Perhaps the most enticing way higher-ups are "solving" the teacher number crisis is waiving credit hours and student-teaching expectations for our undergraduate students studying to become teachers and incentivizing emerging teachers with monetary compensation while student teaching. Yes, this will get new teachers into classrooms sooner and may even fill vacancies, but those young teachers will be so surprised by what they encounter, they may not stay.

It becomes a predictable, and predictably, painful cycle.

Beyond this, we also have to remember that the current students entering college, who are not choosing education as their major, are the same students who just spent their 18 years in possibly difficult classroom and school settings. Each year, I have students tell me, "I could never be a teacher. How do you deal with this every day?"

"For every tough student," I implore them, "I get the gift of teaching five or more great students." Despite my truth, they look at me incredulously and say, "No way. I'd never." Honestly, there are some moments when I can't blame them for feeling this way, though I'd never tell them that.

From my perspective, the biggest reason for the great teacher recession and exit is because teachers entering the profession—and those already in the profession—are wholly unprepared for the emotional provocations and stresses that are frequently presented to them one after another from multiple places. Without a doubt, teachers will absolutely, 100%, be face-to-face with their own

> ...TEACHERS ENTERING THE PROFESSION—AND THOSE ALREADY IN THE PROFESSION—ARE WHOLLY UNPREPARED FOR THE EMOTIONAL PROVOCATIONS AND STRESSES THAT ARE FREQUENTLY PRESENTED TO THEM ONE AFTER ANOTHER FROM MULTIPLE PLACES.

> *THEREFORE, IT'S NOT SO MUCH THAT SCHOOL DISTRICTS HAVE A STAFFING PROBLEM. WHAT WE HAVE IS A TEACHER EMOTIONAL SUPPORT PROBLEM.*

personal triggers from their classrooms, and we must prepare ourselves for this.

Hard-working, achievement-oriented, accomplished adults will be shaken unexpectedly from criticism, devaluing, and resistance. Well-liked, funny, interesting people will suddenly be disrespected and personally hated with no means to defend themselves. Without any preparation or proper emotional training, teachers do not know what to do with the sudden feelings of ineffectiveness, insecurity, and vulnerability they receive from a day's work.

Therefore, it's not so much that school districts have a staffing problem. What we have is a teacher emotional support problem.

APPROACH WITH CAUTION

I remember sitting in an undergraduate class with a professor everyone liked. He was attempting to tell us that teaching wasn't going to be easy, and that we had better prepare ourselves. I didn't know what he meant.

He had spent 30 years as an English teacher in a suburban middle school and was now teaching undergraduates how to teach. This professor was kind and warm-hearted and gracious with his time. So, when he went into this mini-lecture/warning, we all just stared quietly at him. What did he mean, exactly? What was he saying, really? We didn't even know what follow-up questions to ask. His vagueness was enough for us to blow off the warning, but his warning was in such contrast to his personality, in my opinion, that it stuck with me.

I wouldn't know for another two years precisely what he was talking about, and many times since then, I'd wished he'd been clearer. Contrary to this professor, I had a clear negative warning during student-teaching with my host teacher's colleague, who told me in the hallway outside the classroom that I "should leave today and never come back." He warned me that teaching is awful, that I would hate it, and that the kids don't care and don't want to learn. He told me to take my degrees and do a different job.

I couldn't believe it. Where was my host teacher? Why wasn't she hearing this to set this colleague straight and to straighten me back up? I was so excited to be in that classroom teaching those students and learning how to do better. The furthest thing from my mind was to evaluate what else I could do with my degrees. Unbelievable.

This man was an abrasive grouch who even looked angry and miserable. I didn't identify with him, so my natural thoughts were that he was angry and looking to hate his life. There was no way I'd have anywhere near the same problems he did because I was a totally different person, full of joy, enthusiasm, happiness, and grit. He didn't seem to possess those traits. Sizing him up, I knew I'd never be that guy, so I just ignored what he said.

All these years later, I can still say he was wrong. But not 100% wrong. These two were foils of each other. The one probably didn't want to scare us, so he gave just a gentle, unclear heeding. The other probably wanted to scare me to justify his own misery. There is a middle ground to what both of these professionals shared that is not being talked about in education, and it is our newest teachers who are taking the hardest hits.

THE REALITY IS BOTH/AND

The majority of teachers will tell you they entered the profession wanting to help kids and to serve something much bigger than themselves. While teachers receive appealing benefits for their service, the primary reason someone becomes a teacher is because they genuinely want to give something valuable of themselves to young people, and they believe what they offer will matter deeply.

Teachers, especially at the secondary level, expect the profession to be content-driven. I am teaching students some*thing*, and that some*thing* is interesting. The plan is that students hold on to that some*thing*, so they can use it tomorrow and continue to build. The long-term hope is that the some*thing* will guide students to a meaningful place in the world. Their teacher training makes them content experts, who can inspire and *teach* content to young people who don't know the content—yet.

Teachers, especially at the elementary level, expect to warmly and enthusiastically nurture willing, young learners to make big leaps in their abilities and to understand what it means to be a person in the classroom, the school, and the world. The teachers' training builds them as creative engineers, who can masterfully make any learning consequential and fun.

But as many teachers get further into the profession, they begin to say crushing things like: "This is not what I expected" and "I didn't sign up for *this*."

Because teaching is more of an emotional profession than it is a content profession, newer teachers did not expect the road in front of them to have potholes, detours, and blockages. Teachers studying to enter the profession did not realize they needed to be just as prepared in their introspective understanding as in their lesson planning.

After years of compounding frustration, exhaustion, and feelings of inadequacy, many of our best teachers have unfortunately felt their best option, despite all the good they do, is to put teaching in their rearview mirror.

Other professions, such as specialty doctors and therapists, know their jobs are emotional because of who they treat and what they encounter. Teachers, not so much. Teachers haven't been trained to view or discuss their profession as an emotional profession, even though so much of the everyday job gradients into the emotional and into the fatiguing.

When teachers learn *how* to teach, they are absorbed in the urgent matters that comprise being a classroom teacher: designing lesson plans that incorporate state and national standards; creating assessments and providing feedback that are purposeful; accommodating the needs of special education students; differentiating instructional methods that effectively reach all learners; understanding how to teach students learning English as their second language; incorporating effective classroom management strategies; and sending consistent parent communication that provides transparency to their child's day.

While learning to teach, the focus is on the physical components of the job, and because there are so many of these, it leaves little time for teachers to learn how teaching will impact them emotionally and what they can do about

> *WHILE LEARNING TO TEACH, THE FOCUS IS ON THE PHYSICAL COMPONENTS OF THE JOB, AND BECAUSE THERE ARE SO MANY OF THESE, IT LEAVES LITTLE TIME FOR TEACHERS TO LEARN HOW TEACHING WILL IMPACT THEM EMOTIONALLY AND WHAT THEY CAN DO ABOUT IT.*

it. How teachers are trained for the job needs to shift from being only about the physical components to also including courses and understanding about the emotional impacts.

This is because teaching is a both/and profession, meaning it holds two seemingly contradictory feelings at the same time, with both feelings being true. Like many of you, I experience the both/and concept of teaching every day, sometimes even during the same class period.

Teaching is both rewarding and worth all the hard work, and also exhausting and defeating. One class period can make me feel purposeful, smart, and valued while students in the next class period can make me feel low, self-conscious, and embarrassed. Teaching is exhilarating and overwhelming. It can make me feel like I am doing something much bigger and more purposeful than myself, and it can also make me feel so frustrated that I begin to count the hours until the end of the school day, school year, or teaching career.

When students I had the year before make special trips to my classroom to tell me I was their favorite teacher and that they miss my energy and warmth, I get this feel-good reminder that tells me I am doing exactly what I am supposed to do in this life. I feel joy and pride. When students entering their senior year tell me they still use the writing packet resource I gave to them in their ninth-grade year, I feel gratitude and purpose.

Yet, within the same day of hearing those words, I can be disrespected by other students, making me feel insecure. This can even happen from students I've tried to make a relationship with or from students I am working extra hard for. I can experience stonewalling, eye-rolling, and complete lack of cooperation within the same day of feeling like I am the sole reason for a student's success.

It's far too easy to invalidate these experiences with "They are just kids," or "Consider the source," or "Focus on the good." These painful experiences matter. They are distracting and can be personal, and they are not what we consider when we sit and spend hours crafting our lesson plans.

There are parts of my day that fill me with joy and pride because I get to be an important part of a young person's life, and there are parts of my day that make me question why I even bother.

I've even attended a retirement seminar as a result of my complicated relationship with teaching. The older woman sitting next to me asked me why I was there. I told her flatly, "To learn about retirement options." She sized me up, notably the lack of gray in my hair, leaned towards my left shoulder, and whispered with a chuckle while patting my knee, "You've got a long way to go, honey."

I replied, "I know." Then, I asked if she had ever thought about retirement when she was only through half her career. She laughed a big laugh and asserted, "Oh, yes! Everyday!"

I wasn't alone in my thinking, and neither are you.

I am one of the lucky ones because I work in a beautiful school building alongside intelligent, talented, hard-working teachers. Some of my colleagues are my closest friends in life. I have a brightly-lit, temperature-appropriate classroom with updated resources. The sun literally shines through my classroom windows, and I have a view of grass and trees. I have an administration team that works to support teachers and students as best as they are able. Their jobs are complicated and require a delicate balance. Honestly, they could write their own books. I work in a school where people show up, *every day*, giving all they can of themselves, sometimes to the point of exhaustion. I get to work in a place where the teachers and administrators are trying to make the tough situations better.

> *TEACHING IS A BOTH/AND PROFESSION WITH COMPLICATED PROBLEMS THAT HAVE NO EASY SOLUTIONS.*

Despite all this going in my favor, teaching has *still* been hard.

Teaching is a both/and profession with complicated problems that have no easy solutions. Teachers can be glamorized by Hollywood as heroes who will change the trajectory of a troubled life if the teacher sacrifices his or her whole life to be the hero. People generally consider teaching a rewarding profession above anything else and are usually quick to give the reminder of getting summers off to the teachers who share their struggles.

Because we are trained to see teaching as rewarding, fulfilling, and sacrificing, we are not trained to see it as a profession that will also be overwhelming and emotionally triggering. What we must do is remember the reality, because the reality of teaching is that it is both/and.

Precisely, this is why our teaching jobs are so complicated and tricky. In one single school day, we can be adored and appreciated by some and disliked and criticized by others. The criticisms and unreasonableness hit us deeper than the praise and cooperation, and that is where we tend to focus our thoughts, attitude, and energy. It's hard not to take those criticisms and judgments deep into our personal selves.

It's important we validate the shadows within our day, while choosing not to live in the shadows. We got into teaching because we love teaching, and we have something of value to offer young people. We love giving. We *also* see the reality and we feel the hurt and exhaustion. You are not alone in any of this.

INTERNAL TEACHER CONFLICT

We feel that internal teacher conflict when we question the profession and say things like "I didn't sign up for *this*," and when we question ourselves and say things like "What is wrong with *me*?" We question the gratitude we are supposed to have when we say, "At least I have a job," and "How could I dislike a profession that allows me to teach that awesome student sitting right over there?"

Once we begin to *feel* the effects of teaching, we are already overwhelmed and tired—perhaps even frustrated and defeated. We begin to question ourselves, feeling inadequate: Wasn't I supposed to love this job? Wasn't I so excited to start this job? What am I doing *wrong*?

But you are doing nothing wrong and are most likely doing everything you know to keep up with all the systems and demands of your day. I argue this happens because we collectively evaluate teaching in an incomplete way. We evaluate it in terms of results and what we are producing. We need to also evaluate how teaching makes us feel and what is within our power to help us manage those feelings.

Before the first day of school, whether a teacher is new or veteran, there is a strong attempt to have as much prepared as possible. The classroom is clean and set up, the opening lessons are ready, the resources are primed, the outfit is chosen, and the plan is in place. It's similar to the 10 minutes before a party at your house. You might feel a little rushed and frazzled, but, in all, things are ready to go, and you are just waiting for family and friends to arrive. Minor, seemingly insignificant details are considered to set one up for the strongest possible first impression. The perception follows that the more physically prepared teachers are, the better things will go in that classroom. Learning will take place, retention will occur, students will conduct themselves appropriately, and all will be smooth and meaningful.

What is not considered in all this anticipation is whether the teacher is *emotionally* prepared for the school year and the unsettling that will come from managing many different people, their values, their needs, and their expectations. Teachers who have late-August nightmares aren't alone. They wake with a pounding heart having dreamt that something was physically amiss in their classroom. They don't have enough desks, don't have the right rosters, have forgotten the Pledge of Allegiance, haven't copied something, haven't hit "Publish" on the class webpage, or are wandering lost in the building through empty school hallways.

We know these things won't happen. If they do, we can still fix them before the school year starts. The dreams are a warning, and they signify something much deeper and more emotional that has no easy button and hasn't been mastered yet.

These observations and realizations have come from my own failures and struggles, my own successes and growths, and my own evaluation of what I thought teaching would be and what it actually is.

Acknowledging and understanding the personal emotions that come from teaching—then giving teachers emotional strength training—is a crucial component to teacher training that has been accidentally overlooked but will help ease teachers' internal conflicts about the profession. It is imperative that teachers get coaching in intrapersonal understanding within their undergraduate course training, new teacher induction programs, and professional development sessions to equalize their emotional strength with their lesson-planning abilities.

It is not that these conversations are completely absent. I do not believe professors, principals, and administrators are unwilling to talk about the emotional toll on teachers or listen to teachers' stress. But these professionals also have a responsibility to train teachers how to teach, and they also have a full schedule dealing with urgent matters.

A teacher's career doesn't have to be short-lived. It doesn't have to involve an internal conflict. It doesn't have to include counting down days, resigning coveted positions, crying, giving up, or not sleeping. It doesn't have to be like this. It can be so much better. So much healthier. So much simpler.

First, we need to look within and examine ourselves for the reasons why we feel a certain emotional weight. Only after that can we determine what to do with it all.

Without a doubt in my mind, teaching will lead every person encountering it on an emotional journey. Be honest and real. Ask a teacher out there already doing the work if they have ever felt hurt, bothered, irritated, or in emotional pain from their teaching day. Observe their body language. Pay attention to the sounds they make. Listen to their words. A teacher's job doesn't have to be so painful. It doesn't have to be. It can be—and should be—enlightening and empowering.

> ### THERE IS ALWAYS A SOLUTION. AND THERE IS ALWAYS, ALWAYS HOPE

My life in teaching is not perfect and I am a full work in progress, but I have learned a lot that has helped me hold the joy and the love I have for this job, which is the hope I have for all of you.

So, again: we will first look at the problems. Then, we will look forward to the solutions.

There is always a solution. And there is always, always hope.

Especially when we are brave enough to talk about it.

ILLUSION OF CONTROL

PURPOSE OF CONTROL

When I think back to my childhood classroom filled with stuffed animals and the smell of crayons and chalk, I am conscious of something so obvious, so powerful, and, yet, so overlooked. I was in control. How could I not have been? I was teaching the stuffed animals that I had carefully chosen out of my toy bin. Everything I designed went exactly to plan with no unexpected surprises or disappointments. Everything was predictable.

Control in itself has a negative connotation. People don't want to be controlled, and they don't like when they are around someone who is controlling. I am not referring to people who are inflexible, unwilling to listen, and abusive. I am referring to people who seek control because they want things to go well and because they want success for themselves and others.

When we spend our time, money, energy, resources, and thought putting something together, fixing something that was broken, creating something, or cooking something, we want it to go well and to work. Otherwise, it was a waste of time, and that is most infuriating. If we need that thing to work the next time around, we adjust our methods for a better outcome. This is when people seek control.

Control is one of the deepest needs we all have, not just teachers. No one likes to feel powerless. No one likes to feel out of control, especially with something they care about. The need to be in control is at its core fear-based, with fear being an unconscious reaction that exists to protect us. When we experience something that we do not have control over, we become fearful of the many possible outcomes, so we work consciously and subconsciously to control what we can to land in the best possible outcome. No one wants to be powerless and ineffective; in fact, we fear it.

This feeling of fear is not a conscious decision. It happens to us subconsciously, resulting from not being in control or even from the *possibility* of not being in control. This fear-feeling can show itself in many ways, such as: a pounding heart, tightening of one's chest or

> *THE NEED TO BE IN CONTROL IS AT ITS CORE FEAR-BASED, WITH FEAR BEING AN UNCONSCIOUS REACTION THAT EXISTS TO PROTECT US.*

shoulders, crying, insecurity, depression, fatigue, anger, anxiety, rejection, or quitting. This is all the result of feeling powerless.

No matter how fear from lack of control shows up in our lives, we don't like how it feels, and we don't like our response. For the introspective ones among us, we work to avoid these awful feelings by evaluating and reworking what is out of control to achieve the most successful outcome possible.

Teachers do this all the time. Teachers evaluate and consider what went well and what didn't. They even make these evaluations and adjustments in the middle of teaching a lesson, if necessary. Teachers have the most skin in the game. It's their classroom, their job, and they want the outcomes to reflect their hard work.

Teachers want better outcomes in the classroom more than anyone else in that classroom because, if they are having a problem, that problem will come back to them the very next day and the day after that and the day after that if they don't work to fix it or try to improve it.

Additionally, teachers want to feel effective and purposeful while teaching. Hard-working teachers spend hours reworking already skillfully designed lessons, units, and assessments to find the right combination that will keep students engaged, cooperative, learning, and retaining information. They work and rework to position themselves in the highest levels of success in all the categories.

As it happens, teachers may have different stories with the same main idea: they do not have control the way they think they should have control. The teacher certainly has full control over how he or she responds to any situation, but being in full control of what occurs in his or her classroom is an illusion.

JUST A PERCEPTION

Teachers are sent the message that if they improve their physical teaching—their lessons, delivery, and assessment—then the problems in front of them will cease to exist. Kids will be interested and want to learn and problem behaviors will go away.

This creates a perception that teachers can control all parts of their classroom, simply because they are willing to work on the things that aren't going well. It's an assumption that teachers hold the only set of keys to fixing what is not going well in their classroom, and that they have the cryptological ability to crack a challenging code.

Most of what teachers experience during their day is out of their control. School demographics, administration personality and support, discipline protocols, parent expectations and involvement, resources, curriculum designs, the grade level(s) taught, student needs, and student behaviors are, overall, out of the teacher's control.

Additionally, schools are perceived as community centers that can offer endless resources to fix any and all problems in an individual. This is not true, and to assume that a school day will fix a deep-running problem in an individual is unreasonable. Schools offer a plethora of resources that can improve the social, emotional, and cognitive lives of students, but they are a limited entity, and should not be looked upon as a one-stop shop that will fully fix all problems. The hours in school are a part of a student's day; whatever happens there to help manage a problem should be enforced and supported in the additional hours that exist outside of the school day.

Understanding the limitations of control in the classroom doesn't make the difficult situations better, but it does help to alleviate the stress and the pressure that come when the teacher's identity and ability is wrapped up in classroom outcomes. For those who are not teachers in the classroom, it is important to understand that teachers may be "in charge," but they have limited control, even if it's easier to believe that they should be in complete control of every outcome of their classroom.

The teacher "being in charge" and "being in control" are dichotomies and this creates a false perception. Like

> *...IT IS IMPORTANT TO UNDERSTAND THAT TEACHERS MAY BE "IN CHARGE," BUT THEY HAVE LIMITED CONTROL...*

all false perceptions, it results in a distorted view of reality. Teachers holding the power of control is an illusion—a trap—that many of us fall into, especially if we are good at what we do and if we are willing to put a lot of time and effort into trying to make those bad situations better. It's wild to think we can control another person's behavior or responses, despite how much we'd like to.

As a short example to this idea, a colleague once told me about the hours and hours he poured into a student to help him pass a credit-based course for graduation. In the end, the student didn't show up to the final exam, and he failed. When he took the same course the next year, the student said he was tired that day and wasn't ever planning to come in. What a waste of the teacher's time and how frustrating. Certainly, that wasn't in the teacher's control.

When the teacher is perceived as the all-fixer and all-doer responsible for our children's educations *and* behaviors, we leave out the most important subgroup from the conversation: the students. Because, in teaching, the teacher cannot accomplish her job, which is to *teach*, without the cooperation and willingness from her students to *learn*. Expecting the classroom to be a shared space, in which all must do their part to have it function effectively, is a much more productive conversation than expecting teachers to control all classroom outcomes, simply because they are the teacher in charge, perceived to be the one in control.

In reality, we recognize part of our job is classroom management and we acquire strategies that positively influence our classrooms and students, given we are in charge but not in control. Through our positive influence combined with taking the time to establish procedures and build community, we manage. When my methods of classroom management are not enough and I have students act up or engage in disruptive, immature behaviors, I remind these students, and everyone in the classroom, that I am first and foremost a teacher, not a disciplinarian or behavior manager. "I was hired and

THE TEACHER CANNOT ACCOMPLISH HER JOB, WHICH IS TO TEACH, WITHOUT THE COOPERATION AND WILLINGNESS FROM HER STUDENTS TO LEARN.

trained to teach you," I assert. "And while managing this space is part of my job, it is not my job to determine how to control you or manage you and your off behaviors." I finalize, "That is your job as the student or the job of the disciplinarian. My job is to teach." Sometimes a simple reminder like this helps to refocus the roles and the expectations. Unfortunately, sometimes it is not enough.

BREAK THE PATTERN

Being unable to control students' behaviors or responses can make a teacher feel frustrated and ineffective. The students' output is perceived to be the product of the teaching methods and all the teacher's work. If that is not going well, then it can feel like all was for nought. Teachers will start to second-guess themselves: "I must not be very good at this," or "Does what I do even matter?" or "Maybe these students have no respect for me," or "I am probably wasting my time." These feelings of inadequacy and self-doubt are harmful and can permeate the mindset and attitude of even the strongest and most capable teachers.

I have fallen into the trap of thinking I had more control than what I did many times over. In each example, fighting the illusion of control left me exhausted and frustrated, sometimes even shamed and embarrassed. I have fallen into the control-trap because of my own mistakes, and I have fallen into the control-trap because of what was handed to me.

In my early teaching experiences, a few rough situations gave me a form of PTSD that played tricks on me, making me approach innocent circumstances with uncertainty and fear of judgment and rejection. They also gave me a false sense of control. If I could be 100% in all areas of teaching, I assumed I'd never have behavior problems, criticism, or issues. Unfortunately, trying to be perfect in all areas of teaching, thinking that would solve problems, set me up for a lot of hard work, impossible expectations, and fatigue.

Naïvely and admittedly, I created my lesson plans with high engagement strategies, assuming the students in front of me would be excited or, at the very least, cooperative. I set my students up for an unfair expectation, thinking they'd be just as eager and interested as I was. That high expectation gave me a high drop of disappointment. As mentioned earlier, teaching is both/and. Some students are very eager. Some students are cooperative. Some students are neither. It doesn't transfer to me being an ineffective teacher, but it does transfer to me not being in full control.

What ended up happening, to my exasperation, is that, year after year, I was faced with more of the same challenges, despite all the hard work and the improvements I was making as a teacher. Some students and some classes were so challenging I couldn't teach what I had spent my time planning, and I became bothered and defeated.

So, what did I do? I did what a lot of us do, which was all I knew to do at that time. I worked and reworked lesson plans and classroom management. I improved my teaching abilities, assuming this change would fix the problems. Improving lesson plans and unit designs or changing the physical space in my classroom, such as seating arrangements, did create positive improvement, but it didn't solve the problems entirely. Yet I kept affirming to myself that I was in control and the problems would get to nil because I was willing to meticulously craft my lessons and unit designs.

I repeated this cycle hundreds of times trying to protect myself, and I've seen others spin in this cycle, too, trying to protect themselves, perhaps not even realizing they are doing it. Within all of this, I came to see the job as hard. I was tired. And I had lost myself somewhere in the chaos of it all. I didn't understand my emotional fatigue and pain was because of a pattern I was in based on how teaching is perceived to be.

As each school year ended, I had hope that the next would be better. "These groups were just challenging," I'd reason to myself, or "Some of those kids were hard for other teachers, too, and I won't have kids like that next year." I *knew* the next school year would be better because I had improved my teaching and had redesigned curriculum. Each end brought the expectation of certainty that I wouldn't have *those* problems again.

This pattern happens to a lot of newer teachers. The first years are tough, and we learn a lot. We think that if we just apply what we've learned the first year to the second year, our problems will be solved. Between years four and seven, we start to realize that we keep coming upon the same problems despite all our personal improvement as teachers. Our units are better, our assessments are better, our purposes are clearer. We've made huge strides from when we started. But we are still experiencing emotional stress and triggers, and our improvement as teachers isn't harmonizing with how we *feel* about teaching.

This is when our teachers with less than 10 years of experience begin leaving the profession for opportunities that make them feel better, more in control, and less stressed. Similar to me, these teachers didn't realize they needed to prepare emotionally just as they needed to prepare lesson plans. Helping teachers to learn about their emotional selves will break the pattern of teachers entering the profession, working really hard, and then leaving the profession defeated.

This dichotomy that teachers are in charge but not in control needs to be recognized and discussed to help break the pattern of teachers feeling defeated from the control-trap, and then leaving the profession. If we could accept that teachers have limited control in their classrooms, then teachers, parents, administrators, and students could have honest and meaningful conversations that would share responsibility and accountability for what happens in classrooms. It would signal teamwork instead of finger-pointing and blaming, which seems to be the game most well-played. It would move the teacher away from thinking, "What is wrong with *me*?" Additionally, opening this conversation, especially to younger and newer teachers, would provide awareness that there are some components in the teacher's control and there are some out of the teacher's control.

I look back to when I was in this teacher pattern, repressing my feelings and not admitting that I was struggling. As I'd walk down hallways, giving high fives and smiling at students and colleagues, I'd often hear someone say, "She's always so happy. I love her!" It's not that I was unhappy. For anyone who knows me, I love being a sunshine and delight in people's lives. I love giving high fives, hugs, compliments, and praise. But I was also struggling and confused by teaching, and I didn't know how to tell others that I was struggling. It all seemed to be a "me problem."

What I came to learn is that the change I needed wasn't so much in my lesson plan re-working. It was in understanding myself to consider *why* I was behaving the way I was, *why* certain parts of my day consumed me, and *why* I felt the way I did.

Once I started accepting that I have limited control in my classroom—not limited responsibility—it lightened the expectations I held over myself, and it enabled me to recognize that I am simply part of a whole system that is *meant to be cooperative*, but is seen as single-sided. Overall, we don't see the education system as cooperative because the responsibility for classroom success tends to fall on the teacher, with most conversations and professional development circling how the teacher can do better or more, as if the teacher has full control.

Understanding and accepting that I would be entering a profession in which I'd have limited control, with the perception being that I had way more control than what I actually did, would have benefited me before I started teaching and would have saved me countless hours of emotional distress as I oscillated between feeling like a great teacher and a failing teacher, depending upon the class or students in front of me. It would have saved me from second-guessing myself, and it would have saved me from feeling like I was inadequate and not good enough.

Teachers can control their attitude and their responses. They can control the manner in which they teach a lesson, even if they don't have control over what they teach.

> *WE SEE THINGS FOR WHAT THEY ARE, AND WE EXAMINE THEM FROM A BROADER LENS.*

Teachers can control the feedback they give and how they make others feel. Teachers may not, though, be able to control some situations despite valiant intentions.

There are some things in our classroom and within our jobs as teachers that are out of our control. We can break this thought pattern of assuming teachers are in control simply because they are in charge. It doesn't mean teachers stop managing tough situations or stop bettering them. It doesn't mean teachers give up, get lazy, or relinquish responsibilities.

It means that we see things for what they are, and we examine them from a broader lens. It means we give ourselves grace, and we remind ourselves that we are fully capable and fully adequate—just not fully in control.

I have learned this lesson the hard way, starting on my very first day of teaching, and it has taken me years to identify the illusion of control and how that confuses teachers and those who work with teachers. Now that I know it, I still have some of the same experiences, but I view them differently, and I navigate my teaching life in a much healthier way that I will share with you next, as it has come from my pains and mistakes in teaching and subsequent learning.

THE COFFEE RULE

MY FIRST DAY

While I certainly got the message loud and clear in a most painful way how much I lacked control—and lacked being in charge—as a teacher when I first started teaching, it remains enigmatic to me all these years later how an adult professional cannot maintain control of child students, and how that lack of control can be so emotionally affecting.

My innocence about teaching peaked in the seconds before the bell rang for my first ever class on my first day of real teaching.

It was the day after Labor Day in 2006. The sun was still summer hot and I had my typical beach tan that made my skin glow. I started my teaching career in a modular classroom—a trailer, if you will. These modulars were considered by others to be crappy classrooms because they were a bit beat up upon arrival and were held up by cinderblocks. They were also located just outside of the school building. Some said being moved into those classrooms from the building was a demotion. But for me, being a first-time teacher, I couldn't have been happier to have my own classroom space that I could decorate, welcome students into, and call my own. I laughed to friends that this half trailer space was *my* crappy classroom, and I *loved* it.

I arrived extra early that first day, full of excitement and nerves, wearing a grass-green short-sleeved dress with a white sweater. My hair was curled and pulled back in a loose bun, and I felt an excitement that was like none I had ever experienced. I was *here*! I did it. I was a teacher! This was *my* classroom, *my* desk, *my* students, *my* plants on the windowsill, *my* cliché posters on the walls, *my* curtains hanging from the window. That trailer looked as beautiful as I could make it, and I genuinely couldn't wait for it all to start.

I wrote a welcome message on the board in various colors, and my introductory packet of information, which included classroom expectations, was copied and ready-to-go. Books I'd give out later were neatly piled in front of the classroom, and each pencil in my Shakespeare pencil holder was perfectly sharpened and ready for use.

I had so much nervous energy I couldn't even check my email or do any lesson planning in the time that lingered between my arrival and that bell sound. I just wanted to meet my students and get started and finally introduce myself as "Ms. Lucas, your English teacher!"

The bell rang. Standing outside my door (which was literally standing outside because I was in a trailer classroom), my 22-year-old-self greeted each of my 12th grade students to their classroom, to their English class, and to their first day of senior year!

But, as I smiled and shook hands to enthusiastically and warmly greet my incoming students to their first period class, greeting after greeting was unmet. Not by all, but by enough that an ache of anxiety came over me. I took notice. Some students would stop, shake my hand, say hello and tell me things like, "I can't believe I'm a senior," or "I'm so glad this is my last year," or "Hi, thanks, my name is…"

But there were others who walked into the classroom without any return hello or even eye contact. Some even grunted or rolled their eyes at me as they walked in, giving me the feeling that I was a bit too much for them or that they already didn't like me or the class.

Out of the gate, I never expected that some students wouldn't even return a simple hello or would walk past me as if I weren't standing there talking to them personally.

> I LEARNED VERY QUICKLY THAT I WASN'T TEACHING MYSELF AS A STUDENT.

I wasn't expecting it because I never would have ignored a person or brushed past them if they were talking to me directly. In fact, I am usually the one who initiates the hello and the conversation. And, most certainly, I never would have done this to one of my teachers. I learned very quickly that I wasn't teaching myself as a student.

I stood outside by myself, awkwardly, for a few moments with no other students coming up the path, assuming all the students I would have in that class period were already in the classroom. I was just about to walk into the room and enthusiastically greet the entire class (choosing to take this stance even though some of the students in that room had ignored me) when a student looking very unapproachable and very angry opened the school building door and turned right, which led to the path directly to my door. He was also holding a rather large coffee.

My first thoughts when I saw this intimidating student were: *Oh God*. He's coming in here. With a coffee. What am I supposed to do with this kid?

I was young. I was new. I hadn't had a lot of experiences handling troubled youth, and I certainly didn't have a lot of experiences *teaching* troubled youth. Prior to this first day, I had taught stuffed animals. I had taught my college cohort members. I had taught high school students during my student teaching semester, who—before my arrival—were already trained for half a school year under an experienced teacher of 20 years.

My main concerns before starting my teaching career were ensuring that I understood the grade-level content to stay on track with my colleagues, that I had prepared thoughtful lessons, and that I was following assessment procedures. Anything preventing success in these areas made me fearful and insecure, for I worried what my colleagues and administrators would think of me if I were not able to keep up with the demands of the job or if I were unable to do the job well. In all, I wanted to build a strong reputation, and I wanted to gain the respect of those I was working with and for.

Up until that point, no one had shared with me their specific stories of when things had gone wrong and what they had done. No one had prepared me to understand that teaching is imperfect and that some things just won't go very well, even if the teacher is prepared and trying so hard to make it go well. No one had said to me, "Hey, if you happen to come across some tough situations, here are a few things you can do, and this is definitely what you don't do."

So, when I saw this student coming toward me with a coffee, I did what I knew to do and what I always do when something feels tense: I was kind and inviting, and I attempted to say something that would lessen the tension.

I cheerfully said while sticking out my hand for a handshake, "Good morning! You found me! Did you ever think your first class of your senior year would be in a trailer?!"

He didn't look at me. He didn't shake my hand. He tried to move past me into the room. I couldn't let him do that. He had a large coffee in his hand. I couldn't let him get into that room. At the time, there was a school rule of no food or drinks outside the cafeteria. I knew this student wouldn't easily comply with me telling him he had to get rid of his coffee. His unreturned greeting and his countenance were enough for me to know that this was a tough kid, and I was not at all ready to manage tough students.

Being a new teacher in a new job, I paid careful attention to all the school rules. I didn't want to break them, and I didn't want my students to break them. Building a strong reputation meant—in part—upholding the school rules and systems and not allowing a student to blatantly break a school rule.

Here is where I made my first big mistake, and it is not a mistake I would make today. I tell you this shamelessly because I want to be honest about my teaching career with the good and the bad. I want to share the emotional consequences and how I have learned to manage these emotional consequences. I value my teaching journey and how far I have come and how much I have learned, even if I had to learn some lessons the hard way.

In the quick instant when I saw the student with the coffee walking toward me, I had a choice to make. I could choose to let him have the coffee with the intention of circling back to the school rule at a later point. Or I could choose to hold fast to the school rule and tell him to get rid of the coffee.

I valued holding fast to the school rules, and I valued developing a solid reputation. I was also nervous that if others saw him with coffee, then they, too, would have coffee the next day, and I would have a larger issue. Above and beyond these reasonings, I also valued students listening to me and following what I said. I thought I was "in charge" and "in control," and I thought students listening to me equaled respect. I valued these things over the intricate balance this student needed because, in the first five minutes of my teaching career, I didn't understand the depth of a student like this.

> I THOUGHT I WAS "IN CHARGE" AND "IN CONTROL," AND I THOUGHT STUDENTS LISTENING TO ME EQUALED RESPECT.

WHAT I DID

Before I let him walk into the classroom, I said, "I see you have a coffee. There is a school rule about no food or drinks in classrooms, so I need you to throw it away."

He stopped and looked right through me with anger in his eyes. He retorted and defiantly stated, "What?! A school rule? Since when? You want me to throw this away? I'm not throwing my coffee away! I just bought it."

I replied, "I'm sure you did just buy it. But I need you to throw it away. There is a trashcan right when you walk in."

His response: "Fuck you! And fuck this school and their stupid fucking rules."

He then pushed right past me before I could even get the surprised expression off my face or say anything else. Before the door slammed, I heard him yell into the classroom, "Yo, this teacher just told me to throw my coffee away. Can you believe that shit? I'm not doing that!"

I stood outside by myself with my classroom door closed and a full class of students waiting for me. My hands were shaking, my heart was pounding, and my stomach was in a knot with my face turning redder and hotter every second.

Oh God. What do I do now? How do I make this better? How do I go into that room? What is that kid going to do once I go in that room?

I didn't know what to do in that moment. What I did know was that it was the first day of school and I had to walk into the room and start the school year. So, that is what I did.

I walked in cheerfully, which was all I could think to do. Be cheerful. Pretend it didn't happen. Don't let the other students see you frazzled. Act like you can handle stuff like this. Act. Pretend.

My eyes went immediately to the student with the coffee, and I was met with his incredulous stare as he sipped and sipped with no intentions of getting rid of that coffee.

As I greeted the class and told them I was so happy they were there with me that first morning, I made my second mistake.

I took this student to task with twenty-six other students watching the show. I met his eye contact and declared, while bringing the trashcan over to him, "I need you to get rid of your coffee, like I said, because there are no food or drinks outside the cafeteria, and we are outside the cafeteria."

He laughed a "whatever" type of laugh, challenged me to "just try" and take it from him, and defied he'd "never throw it away."

I was sunk. Done. Game over. Loser.

My heart pounded even harder, and my hands shook. I put this entire situation on display, and I had no second move, back-up plan, one-liner, or solution to his defiance after trying to force him into submission.

I caved to his disrespect, and I felt the embarrassment wash over me. Putting the trashcan down, I shakily introduced myself while some kids chuckled and others put their heads down. What an absolute disaster, and how awfully embarrassing.

For the first time, I felt the walls of the lose-lose corner, and I realized way too late that I lacked a huge part of my game that I had overlooked in my steadfast planning and preparation. I never considered what to do with blatant noncompliance. Nor did I ever consider what it would *feel* like when a student chose to be rude and disrespectful or how I would handle the turmoil of my own emotions in the aftermath.

I wish I could share some heroic ending, and how I recovered from this sucky situation by flipping a cape over that green dress and showing those students I was a powerhouse teacher.

Nope. Not even close. That's not at all how this story goes.

Instead of finding a cape, I wanted to find a hole. I shakily delivered my prepared first day of school notes about—of all things—classroom expectations, all the while trying to avoid looking at that student who was still staring at me sipping his coffee, and while trying to ignore the students who still had their heads down. The words on my handout seemed to mock me:

You thought you were ready for this? You don't even know what you're doing.

As if this couldn't get worse, in that same class period on that same dreaded first day, I asked for a student volunteer to read a short passage for the class, so we could hear it with an intelligent, relatable tone. A student volunteered. I was so thankful and relieved! Finally a win!!

Then, within an instant, he mocked, "Yeah, right! I'm not reading out loud for you."

"Why would you volunteer, then?" I implored him. His response: he thought it would be funny for me to think someone would actually volunteer to read aloud.

When I asked for another volunteer, no one stepped up. I looked at the clock. Roughly 30 minutes had passed on my first day of "real teaching" that I was so excited and "so ready" to start. I still had 55 minutes to go in that class period.

CONTROL-TRAP

I didn't understand this at the time, but my choice to address this student about the coffee as pretty much the first thing I said to him was a mistake. I could read his disposition. He didn't look cooperative whatsoever. He looked mean and intimidating. It's possible the coffee was the only thing making him show up to school that morning. Telling him to get rid of it as directly as I did, without any prior relationship-building, was a rookie teacher error.

Instead of letting him go with the intention of circling back later for a *reasonable conversation*, I tried to out-match his power. I fell into the quicksand of the control-trap. I naïvely thought he would listen to me, simply because I was his teacher. I assumed I had control. I assumed I was in charge.

I know I am not alone in this choice because there are stories out there and videos on the internet of teachers and students escalating otherwise petty problems. Why do we do this to ourselves and to our students? Because both parties want to be in charge, and both parties do not recognize control is an illusion.

Teachers live in a system in which we assume we are in charge and in control because the system is set up with these perceived expectations. This perception is not the full reality. The teacher has an expectation that being the teacher means students will be respectful. When the teacher is disrespected, it flares up an expectation the teacher had of herself. The teacher thinks students will listen because she said to listen. When students don't do this, and the teacher hasn't prepared for that possibility, the teacher won't know what to do, and will most likely *react*, just like I did by grabbing that trashcan. I didn't want to be shown up and I landed myself in the control-trap of thinking I was both in control and in charge.

I also had extra layers of worry that contributed to my vehemence about his coffee. I didn't want a student breaking a school rule because I was, first and foremost, concerned with setting myself up to have a strong, reliable reputation. I also didn't want other students to think this was allowed. I had only started working at my school the week before during the in-service days. I didn't want students to think I could be pushed around. I didn't want colleagues to think I was incapable. I didn't want administrators to think I couldn't do my job.

The irony is not lost on me. By challenging this student, I contributed to those exact situations. Everything I was concerned about did happen, and it happened because I collided with a defiant student, and I egregiously mishandled the situation.

In those opening moments of my teaching career, I could have had the *same exact situation* with another student who brought coffee to my classroom. I would have said, "Hey, I see you have a coffee. There is a school rule about no food or drinks in classrooms, so I need you to throw it away." This student may have replied, "Oh? There is? I didn't know that. Ummm...okay...I guess I can get rid of it."

And that would have been that.

But it wasn't that simple, and I had to deal with the consequences.

THE AFTERMATH

After that class ended, I had another come in, and another after that. I didn't have any additional instances of heads down, side-talking, or coffees. In fact, I had the opposite. These classes went much better and smoother, and I felt myself relax into the teaching experience I was expecting with my opening lesson plan and get-to-know you being met with cooperative, engaged students, who greeted me at the door, shook my hand, and seemed eager to get the school year started.

I felt comfortable and capable in those other classes, which made me realize something deep inside I had to work on—much of my confidence in teaching was not based within me and what I was offering but was rather based in who was in front of me and the energy they were giving. I was allowing my self-confidence to be determined by circumstances outside my control.

As my first school day ended, I didn't get a chance to breathe or think until later in the afternoon. What a day. I remember thinking I can't believe I will come back and do this again tomorrow. There should be a day off for teachers after the first day of school.

> *I WAS ALLOWING MY SELF-CONFIDENCE TO BE DETERMINED BY CIRCUMSTANCES OUTSIDE MY CONTROL.*

I didn't tell anyone about my first period class or about the situation with the student. Not initially, anyway. I was way too nervous and way too embarrassed. The teacher, who was in the classroom next to mine, is smart and strong and put together. She also happens to be one of my dearest friends now. She would have been enormously supportive and helpful to me if I had shared with her what had happened, but I was too uncertain to tell her, fearing judgment and embarrassment. What if she never had this kind of situation because she has only ever been a great teacher? What if she called me on my huge mistake of escalating a situation instead of de-escalating it?

The teacher group at lunch talked about how great their classes were and how students from the previous year came to visit. They shared about their summer fun. I couldn't tell them. I'd be totally alone in what happened, and I had only just met them. I could hardly eat my lunch as my chest felt tight and my stomach was on fire. All I could see was that student's angry face and all that went through my head were thoughts about what the next day would be like.

I didn't have anyone around who I felt had gone through a first day like mine or had ever experienced a first day like mine. Here I was, wearing a figurative school uniform that screamed "WORK IN PROGRESS!" while my colleagues all seemed totally together, capable, and in control.

I didn't know at that time that it takes nearly five years for any teacher *to start* to pin down this thing they are in called teaching. I didn't recognize all those year three and year eight teachers I sat next to at lunch had gone through similar situations at some point, but had learned their own lessons, had acquired strategies, and had developed a thick skin. Teaching, like all important things in our lives, takes practice, patience, and reflection to improve.

And the greatest factor that makes one improve in teaching is time. Becoming a "seasoned teacher" literally signals that time has been provided for one to improve the art.

For the rest of that day and on the drive home, I replayed those opening minutes of an otherwise very good school day. I couldn't shake that first period class,

> ...IT TAKES NEARLY FIVE YEARS FOR ANY TEACHER TO START TO PIN DOWN THIS THING THEY ARE IN CALLED TEACHING.

> *TEACHING, LIKE ALL IMPORTANT THINGS IN OUR LIVES, TAKES PRACTICE, PATIENCE, AND REFLECTION TO IMPROVE.*

even though the rest of my day had been positive and fun. The rest of my day made me so excited that I got to be a teacher. But I couldn't shake the gnawing of that opening class. As I drove, I questioned myself, "What happened in there?" and "Why did I challenge a kid like that and think I would win?"

My stomach hurt recognizing I had never been treated so disrespectfully, nor had I ever challenged someone so aggressively. No one, prior to that first day of teaching, had ever pronounced an emphatic "F-you" to my face before. I was a recent college volleyball captain and student leader. I was coaching the volleyball team for the school where I had just felt like an idiot. I was young, but I had experienced hard conversations and had previously stepped up during uncomfortable situations.

Where was that person, and why didn't she step up like she had before? What on earth happened?

That first class didn't resemble my expectations *at all*. I ruminated over it, and I felt self-conscious and weak. Worst of all, I feared what the students in that class must have thought about me. "Certainly," I thought, "they think I'm stupid and incapable." I couldn't understand why I had picked up the trashcan and challenged him. I also couldn't understand (at that time) why I wasn't able to simply accept that I had made a rookie mistake and that I'd figure out a plan for the next day.

So, I did the only thing I knew to do. I stayed quiet about the embarrassment, put my head down, and focused on my lesson plans: the only thing in my control. I figured if I could make my lessons so sharp and cover every moment of a class period, then I'd never have issues with students.

My drive home was almost complete when I realized it was all on me to step back into that room the next morning, try to regain control and expectations, *and* teach stuff. Even though the rest of my teaching day had gone very well, thinking about that first period class made my stomach spin in revolt. I didn't sleep very well that night.

The next day, I showed up to school, of course. No one was going to do that for me. I showed up, but I had a lot less enthusiasm and a lot more worry.

Before the first bell, I stood outside, like I had the previous day. I decided I would try to talk to the student one-on-one to recover the situation from the day before.

Here he came up the path. With coffee. I was ready for this. I could do this.

"Hi. Good morning," I said. "Can I talk to you for a second about what happened yesterday before you go into the classroom?"

"UHHHH, yeahhhhh…Nope!" he coldly and rudely stated, as he briskly walked past me into the classroom, with the door slamming shut.

I stood there, feeling rejected and embarrassed, by a 17-year-old, who seemed to have the upper hand, though I was the adult teacher "in charge." I had attempted a dialogue, and it was refused. I thought, at best, I could explain why I had made the choices I made, and I thought we could come to an understanding. I thought I could talk to this student the way I had talked to others when I was in conflict, and that we could rationally resolve it together. I didn't expect such stubbornness and refusing, and I didn't expect to feel so inferior because of his behaviors.

I don't remember all these years later what I taught on that second day of school or how it went. But I know I did what I had done for many years: put on a brave, friendly demeanor, push the feelings down, and get the job done.

Eventually, after a few dreaded days of the student in that class sipping coffee, acting rudely to me, and overall being uncooperative, I finally told a trusted colleague about what was going on. He is the kind of friend who will feel all the feelings for you and with you. I've been so blessed to have such an empathetic and loving person in my life. He was angry for me and reassured me that all teachers have oppositional students at some point in their careers. He even shared with me a few examples from his own career. What a relief. I wasn't alone. I wasn't dumb. I wasn't incapable. He guided me through the process of talking to administration about the discipline issue. He guided me through contacting home, and he guided me through meeting with the guidance counselor for mediation.

The situation in that class period never recovered to where this student skipped joyfully into my classroom or where others in the class were suddenly thankful to be taking senior English. In fact, the class was hard the entire semester and had daily challenges. But what happened on that first day never happened again and things didn't get any worse.

When I stood outside my classroom door on my first day of teaching, I thought I was in control, and I thought I was in charge. I was lesson-plan ready, but I had no strategies in my back pocket to manage noncompliance and difficulty. Overall, even if I were more prepared to manage noncompliance, I don't think I would have expected it to come at me as strongly as it did.

After that incident with the coffee student, I started working really hard—I mean really hard—to be prepared and to fill every minute of class time with engagement and work, so no student could ever act that way again. How could they, when I would be so prepared? I fell into the control-trap, and I was exhausting myself trying to stay in control, not recognizing how limited my control was.

I was filling every moment of my time in and out of school trying to keep up with my content, lesson plans, grading, and emails. I was reading books in the curriculum I had never read before and was organizing materials at 9 p.m. trying to figure out how to teach it meaningfully with engagement for my 7:30 a.m. class the next day. I was researching strategies and activities to enhance student engagement and interest. I was staying up late and setting early alarms to grade and give meaningful feedback on essays and tests, so my grades didn't fall behind and so students would treat the current work with urgency and care.

I was working tirelessly on the physical components of my classroom, squeezing in deadline after deadline, that I gave myself no opportunity or time to even consider my emotional state, in which I felt metaphorically barely above water.

WHAT I WOULD DO TODAY

If I could go back in time and redo my first morning of teaching, there would absolutely be no trashcan grabbing. I still have lessons to learn, and I am still a work in progress, always eager to gather advice and strategies from others to make the hard situations better. But I know one thing with certainty: I never challenge students who show me they need another approach than simply listening to authority. In teaching, we may assume that our proven techniques will work for all students, but we have to accept that each student is different, and some may require a different approach. Being resistant to modifying our approaches to different students may cause us, in the end, our greatest frustrations.

If I could go back in time, I would start my first day of teaching exactly the same way. I loved my grass-green dress and that white sweater. I loved my lesson plan. I loved my modular trailer classroom with the one tiny window. Keep the enthusiasm, Diane. Keep the eagerness and excitement. Ditch the need to be in control, in power, and in charge because of fear of school rules and what people may think. Don't fall into that control-trap quicksand. That didn't get me anything but a hard time and a student challenge, and I could always address those other things when the time was right.

Here is how I would redo meeting the coffee student on my first day of school.

I hear the bell ring, and I walk outside my classroom with my head high and my body feeling proud. I tell myself, "You are here! You are ready! You will handle anything that comes your way with kindness and compassion."

I greet the students the same way I did before. It's their choice not to immediately gush over my enthusiasm and energy. They may come around, in time. They may learn to trust that my enthusiasm to be with them is not just an act.

I see the student coming my way, looking mean and angry. Holding a large coffee. I panic. I stop my panic by taking a deep, five-second breath, and reminding myself that things have a way of working out. I remind myself: there is *always* a solution.

I do not challenge him. I do not remind him about the school rule. I greet him warmly and tell him I am glad he is in my classroom, because I know building relationships is a crucial component of classroom management.

I walk into my classroom, and I teach, and I enjoy that class, and I do the best I can to change the energy in that room because my energy and my choices as the classroom teacher have the most effect on the overall energy of that room. Even if some of the students don't come along with me, or my positive energy doesn't matter to them, it matters to me to be the person I want to be.

I ignore the coffee.

Because I am playing this out as if I am still a new teacher, in the first moment I have free, I tell a trusted colleague about the conflict, and I ask what to do (now I know the school systems and discipline protocols). I learn that coffee is prohibited, and that this student cannot have coffee. I tell the administrator who handles discipline about the issue, in case the student isn't compliant when I address the coffee the next day, and I work out how I am going to talk to the student.

The next day, I approach the student in a non-threatening way, such as outside the classroom or perhaps during a transition when other students are distracted. Maybe I bend to get on his level, or I kneel next to him, or I turn a bit sideways, so my body is not straight at his as if in a challenge.

I say calmly and with little to no emotion, "How are you today? I'm glad to have you in class. I hope you are

> *I REMIND MYSELF: THERE IS ALWAYS A SOLUTION.*

off to a good start. I need to talk to you about something that I learned recently, and it's important to me that you try to understand. Can we talk?"

In this manner, the student always says, "Yes, we can talk."

I continue with, "I don't know if you are aware, but there is a school rule of no coffee. I see you like coffee and you like to drink it in this first period class. I like coffee, too, and I also care about following the school rules. I want to support the administration and the school systems. So, I need to share with you that I can't have you drink your coffee in here. It would be against the school rules, and it will make me uneasy to allow a student to go against a school rule."

Where things go from this point is uncertain and unpredictable. This is just one reason why our teaching jobs are so hard. One student may not need this approach at all. We could simply say, "You can't have coffee in here," and that's the end of it.

But this student wasn't typical for whatever reasons. I am unsure what made him act and look so angry. I am unsure why he was oppositional. I just know I didn't handle it well, and I needed to learn fast how to handle these situations better because he was not going to be a one-time incident in my full teaching career.

In my experience, when I approach situations in this delicate, non-threatening way, there is not a negative, strong reaction against me. The student may disagree and say it's a stupid rule and that it's stupid I uphold it, but they aren't aggressive.

I always end by thanking the student for understanding my perspective and my need to uphold the school rules, and then I share that I'm looking forward to the next day's class period.

I never negate a school rule or an administrator for having a school rule. I never pit one party against another party as that will show division and cracks in the foundation, which can allow a student to argue, "Why do you care if I do this in your classroom if you don't even believe in it?" I try as best as I can to be careful with my language and to assert that *we as a school system* believe in these ideas, and I am here as one part of supporting that system. My hope is that the administration I work for feels the same about me when I need support and I need the "we as a school system" idea.

If the student comes into my room with coffee *after* this conversation, it's an immediate referral for insubordination to the administrator with contact home. If the student comes in with no coffee, I make it a point to acknowledge this choice and to thank him for his cooperation. I also find another situation in the class period in which I can uplift this student, so our only interaction is not about coffee and school rules.

This may seem like pandering, and sometimes when I share my methods, I hear teachers scoff. This method is not for everyone. It's a big picture perspective. I make the conscious choice to get my ego out of the way. I could power-struggle the student every day and see who can be more aggressive and who can be the boss. I learned on day one in the opening minutes of my teaching career that challenging a student who won't back down is a bad idea that will land someone like me in a losing record. Student—1. Teacher—0. I don't want to lose that student for an entire semester because of coffee. I don't want that student to make my class period harder and uncomfortable because of a power struggle over coffee.

Before this student was within a foot of me, I knew he wasn't going to comply with my request simply because I said it. I confronted him because I didn't know what else to do, and I wanted him to listen to me. I didn't want to be shown up, which, ironically, is exactly what happened.

In the approach I take now, the student listens to me, but it's all a lot calmer and far less stressful. Who knows how things would have gone if I had done this approach all those years ago. It's possible that entire class period would have been a different experience.

This method does not work all the time. Sometimes students receive this approach and laugh at me or mock me.

Maybe they aren't used to an adult treating them with respect and a "let's talk" method. Sometimes I have students—to continue with this same example—not show up with coffee the next day, but then oppose me or the school rules in some other way. This is most frustrating because then I am always chasing their opposition and their need to power over me and my class. Without some other intervention to improve the conflict, such as parent support, guidance counselor support, or administration support, a student like that can make for a very long, frustrating school year, and I will enter those classes pretty much every day steeling myself for the next example of opposition.

I don't have control over everything. I have little control. Accepting that concept is the precise reason why I am now able to focus on my preparedness and my responses.

I have learned a lot since my first day of school. Of course I have. How could I not, when I've been in a career for years and years, becoming seasoned? I learned that reworking lesson plans shows tremendous effort, enables my classroom to run efficiently and with quality, and makes me proud of my work value. It doesn't solve all the problems.

I have also learned that we must be both physically and emotionally prepared for teaching, or else we will fall into unhealthy patterns that can steal our time, energy,

> ...WE MUST BE BOTH PHYSICALLY AND EMOTIONALLY PREPARED FOR TEACHING, OR ELSE WE WILL FALL INTO UNHEALTHY PATTERNS THAT CAN STEAL OUR TIME, ENERGY, AND PEACE OF MIND.

and peace of mind. Before I started teaching, there was a lot I needed to understand about myself that I hadn't realized were a part of me. Insecurity, inferiority, people-pleasing, seeking approval. This is a good short list.

I got through that first day of school and that first semester, and many other firsts. I learned a lot of necessary lessons, particularly about people-management, resiliency, and introspective awareness. I am here sharing that some hard days and moments may come to you in teaching. They don't encompass the entire day or an entire school year, and there are many things we can do to prepare ourselves for them, in particular learning about ourselves and those we teach.

AWARENESS 4

(NOT) TAKING IT PERSONALLY

Early on, when I heard people say, "Don't take it personally," I had no idea how to untangle that. How could I not take some of the stuff happening in my classroom personally? The student was doing this *to me*. Of course it was personal, and I would take students' behaviors toward me personally. Even if I learn later that students who are tough for me are also tough for other teachers, it is only a consolation prize. It doesn't make me feel less inferior or make the situation easier. It only makes me wonder how we as a school system allow the same student to be tough for multiple teachers year after year.

It takes thoughtful effort to separate yourself from the student choices within your classroom, so you do not take the bad stuff that happens personally. It takes thoughtful effort to leave the tough situations *at school*, so they don't stay with you as you leave school and go home.

I have an observation as to why all of this can be difficult.

When a student comes back to me—as I'm lucky to experience often—and they want to thank me for being one of their best teachers, or they need someone to talk to and they choose me, or they go out of their way to share with me some good news, it's personal. There is something in me that makes them want to thank me. There is something in me that makes them trust me to talk to me. It's personal.

When a lesson goes well and the students love it and appreciate the experience, or someone observing that lesson praises it or applauds it, they credit you—the teacher—for the good lesson, the preparation, the delivery, and the connection with the students. It's personal.

So, when things don't go well, like when a student says "F-you," or when students talk over you or through you, or think they can walk all over you, it feels personal. All the positives feel personal. Why, then, wouldn't the negatives feel personal?

This may be *my* most important lesson in teaching. When I tangle myself in student behaviors, I feel defeated

> ALL THE POSITIVES FEEL PERSONAL. WHY, THEN, WOULDN'T THE NEGATIVES FEEL PERSONAL?

and emotionally fatigued. I will think about the situation during off-times when I'm not even dealing with the situation, such as when I'm making dinner or getting ready in the morning. All that extra energy being given to a frustrating point in my life has its way of eroding me and bringing me down to where I am in low-battery mode. To this day, I still take some things personally, but I have better ways of reducing this feeling and managing this feeling than I did years ago. I share a lot of my coping strategies later in this book.

I learned from a professional development speaker who was coaching teachers about trauma-informed teaching that "All behavior is a form of communication." There is a reason—some reason—why students act the way they do in our classrooms or toward us. In a November 2023 article "Human Communication: Connection and Disconnection" by Dr. Padraic Gibson[6] published in *PsychologyToday*, Gibson attributes this behavioral theory to psychologists Paul Watzlawick, Jane Beavin Bavelas, and Don D. Jackson in "their most seminal work *The Pragmatics of Human Communication*," in which they explain the theory of human communication. Gibson asserts that this behavior theory "gives us a map to better navigate the nuances of our daily exchanges," since we are always communicating through our behavior, and because

> *IN THE CLASSROOM SETTING, SOME REASONS WHY STUDENTS BEHAVE THE WAY THEY DO MAY HAVE TO DO WITH US AS THE TEACHER OR OUR CONTENT, OR IT MAY HAVE NOTHING TO DO WITH US AT ALL.*

"every behavior communicates something, even inaction or silence."

In the classroom setting, some reasons why students behave the way they do may have to do with us as the teacher or our content, or they may have nothing to do with us at all. Moreover, some reasons why a student acts a certain way could contradict why another student acts a certain way. This can make managing a classroom of differing behaviors and their causes very difficult.

I will have students tell me they don't like me or my class because I am "too happy" or "have too much energy," especially early in the morning. Sometimes these students are downright rude to me or haughty, all because I am nice and love my life and my job. I will have students tell me they love me because I am "so happy," and I will have students tell me they are thankful to have me, especially early in the morning, because I "wake them up," and I give them "something to look forward to." I will have students tell me I, alone, am a huge reason why they even come to school, because they can't wait to see me and be in my classroom. And, I will have students act coldly to me until the friend or person they care about in the class approves of me.

Students will tell me they appreciate how I challenge them and give them "real work to do," and that I teach them things they will "actually use in their lives," while I have other students complain to me that I give "too much work" or that I expect too much.

When I hear these contradictory opinions, I remind myself that I am not in control of how someone else chooses to view me or how they show up in my classroom space, given I am professional and respectful in how I treat my students and my classroom. Learning that all behavior is a form of communication has helped me to separate myself from the other person's opinions or behavior and to see it as a form of communication. I can focus on *what happened* in that student's life that has made him or her act a certain way, instead of focusing on why they are doing this to *me*. This helps me to separate myself and untangle myself, so I don't take things personally.

I never once thought before I became a teacher that a student would resist me or my class because I was too happy. I never once thought that I'd have students hold my positive personality against me. My personality is my personality and it's this way no matter where I am or who I am with. I have no control over their reaction to me because they are coming to me with their own needs, experiences, and pains. My school, like each of our schools, has students who are human, navigating their own paths, who have their own motivations and needs. They are not fully grown up yet. In fact, I often remind myself that I work with people who only *look like* young men and women; they are not yet men and women. I tell myself the students in front of me are young and will change 1,000 times before things are said and done.

When I learn about trauma-based teaching, for example, it gives me a layer of explanation to the claim "Don't take it personally." Some students go through hard lives. Some students have experienced more pain in their short fifteen years than I will in my entire lifetime. Some students have parents who are mean to them or send the message they don't want them. Some students have no parents at all. Some students have been dealt a crappy, cruel hand in life. This is why we can't take it personally.

SEEING STUDENTS

Students who are angry or who need to show their power have their reasons for wanting to be angry and in power. I may not understand these reasons. I may not even be given a reason, or I find out much later there was a possible reason for their anger. There is no way for me to fully understand the complexity of the students who come to my classroom semester after semester. Just because I don't know why they are angry or disagreeable doesn't mean it doesn't affect me.

Their emotional complexity that has not been managed gets handed right to the classroom teacher to deal with. If we don't have this awareness and we don't have strategies that work for us, then we will continue to walk into a classroom that confuses us and makes us feel bad about ourselves, when a lot of what we experience really has nothing to do with us.

Because I enjoy reading and listening to spiritual teachers, I have learned that every experience and every interaction we have is for the benefit of our personal growth. It's not always easy to see situations in this way, but I try to remind myself of this perspective as often as I can. It helps me to untangle myself from taking something personally. The interaction, whether good or bad, is in front of me for my personal growth, and it helps me to consider how I want to be and how I want to grow.

Early in one school semester, I had a student resist me and the class. I learned later it was because her previous class had friends in it, and this class did not. She'd avoid eye contact and would look away anytime I tried to engage her in the lesson. She'd roll her eyes when it came to groups and would sit apart from others, aside from one peer. Overall, she looked miserable, was not pleasant to be around, and made others—myself included—uncomfortable. I asked her at the end of class one day, just a week after meeting her, how she was doing and how she felt about the start of the school semester. She replied with, "I hate my classes, and I don't want to be here."

My first thought was she didn't like me or my class, and that I was the issue, especially since we had just changed semesters and she had new teachers. I reminded myself, "Don't take things personally" and "Every interaction is for your own personal growth."

I told her I could understand how hard it is to be in school when you don't like it. I told her I hoped things would turn around for her, so that she could enjoy more of her week in school. I shared with her that my door is always open and that I was glad she was in my class. I reminded her of an intelligent point she made earlier in the week about something we read, and how that had helped to move the conversation forward in a meaningful way.

I did not lecture her about attitudes or mindsets. I didn't get the impression she'd want to hear it, and I figured I could always slip that in at a later time.

She looked at me, I think for the first time, and said, "Thanks." The bell rang, and she left the class.

After a few days, things stayed the same, and I was continuing to get the same poor attitude and resistance. I went up to her again and said, "Listen, I understand you may not like this class or the people in this class. I understand you may miss your previous classes. But you do not have permission to treat me poorly, roll your eyes at me, resist other students, or make this class uncomfortable. I am requesting you work harder at managing yourself and not affecting others."

Some students are hard and they push our buttons, making us feel inferior or defensive. I've been there. I have to battle these negative feelings, too. I have to work myself through them and remind myself that I am part of a system, that it doesn't serve me to take things personally, that behavior is communication, and that every interaction is an opportunity for me to grow.

In this incident, I chose to extend compassion, patience, and kindness. Then, I chose to talk to this student directly and express that I expected more. I could have ignored her. I could have matched her negativity and misery. I could have made her feel my annoyance. I think those choices would have gotten me a semester with a student battling me and showing power, which is never what I want and never in my best interest.

As it turned out—which is not always the case, unfortunately—this student was great for me and started to shine, especially with my willingness to acknowledge her good work and praise her efforts. She'd have her days of being grumpy or needing some positive attention, but overall, she was great, and she came back to me often throughout her high school years to talk with me in study hall. Before graduating, she wrote me a heartfelt note about how I was her favorite teacher freshman year and that she needed me that year "more than I knew." I don't know the exact reason for these words, but I am proud of how I showed up because I chose a higher path that grew me as a person versus a lower path that matched her attitude.

When a student pushes our buttons, they may be doing it on purpose or they may not. That part matters when it comes to figuring out what to do, such as in establishing boundaries or discipline. In teaching, the emotional focus tends to be on the students. My intention is to add teachers to this focus because teachers matter, too. Teachers are human, too. It matters that teachers are emotionally strong when they start teaching and that

> ...TEACHERS MATTER, TOO. TEACHERS ARE HUMAN, TOO. IT MATTERS THAT TEACHERS ARE EMOTIONALLY STRONG WHEN THEY START TEACHING...

they are supported to stay emotionally strong within their careers.

It is important to understand why we have the buttons and why they get so hot when pushed. Understanding our students *and* ourselves is paramount to our success as teachers, and I assert this is just as important as knowing how to teach curriculum. When we understand ourselves better, we can move to understand our students because we have separated their behavior from our responses. Ideally, everyone involved in education— professors, administrators, professional development speakers—is part of the system that supports teachers' emotional health.

Some of my students have anger issues that they haven't even recognized in themselves, yet. That has nothing to do with me, but it affects me, nonetheless, and when it does affect me, it is something I must work through. When we are bothered by a student's words or behavior, there is something *in us* that is bothered. It helps to first separate these two things—student behaviors and our reactions—and then consider why they have been so affecting.

Understanding our students, though, doesn't mean they get to act or do whatever they want to us or in our classrooms. Trying to balance what makes our students act the way they do, while holding them accountable, and while also managing our own emotional reasons for why their behaviors affect us, is complicated business.

Understanding myself through student behaviors and trying to stay consistent with the person I want to be, despite what is in front of me, has been very difficult at times, but it has also given me the most advantage. Just because I choose to be the person I want to be, doesn't mean it's not challenging to enter a class that has an uncomfortable personality and try to burst through that thick barrier. In doing this, I may pull more students with me, or that class period may end just as it started, even after a full school year of effort and hard work.

It doesn't mean I like it, brush it off, or think it's fair. In fact, I highly dislike the part of my job where I have to figure out how to win over a tough student or class, and I especially dislike when a student or group treats me how they want to treat me and my efforts to fix this are useless. It can make me feel like I am in a system of abuse that I must endure until that school year ends. Tough students and tough classes can make me feel inferior, weak, and like I am not good enough. When I got to my most defeating point is when I sought a therapist. Since then, I cycle through self-talks, share with friends and colleagues, and revisit the books and podcasts that help me to reset.

All I can do is prepare myself for the possibilities that things may not go the way I hope they will, and then I

> *MANY THINGS ARE OUT OF MY CONTROL, BUT MY PREPARATION AND MY RESPONSES ARE IN MY CONTROL.*

determine my best response, either for the external situation I'm dealing with or a look within myself. Prepare and respond. That's all I can do. Prepare and respond. Many things are out of my control, but my preparation and my responses are in my control.

Being more open to "behavior is communication" helps me to understand there is a reason that lies outside of me for why a student may act the way he or she does. It helps me to see that none of this has to do with me, even though it still does emotionally affect me. I am just part of a system they are in. It isn't grounds for me to be walked all over or abused as their teacher, but it gives me the perspective that I have been given a tough situation, and I can choose to separate myself to try and make that tough situation just a little better. This helps me to stay out of the control-trap and to maintain my peace of mind.

TORNADOES

To help with this, I visualize students who have tough energy—who are angry or who are consistently uncooperative—as tornadoes, which is my way of giving a quiet acceptance to what is, so I don't fight and sink myself into the control-trap. Their behavior is communication. I'll ask myself, "What are they communicating to me, and how can I help this?" It's easier for me to calm the winds of a tornado when the tornado is isolated and not twisting other students into a larger tornado. With an isolated tornado, I can feel compassion and sympathy. Who wants to be a churning, seething mess? Sometimes approaching a tornado with compassion is enough to still the winds, and I know my kindness and confidence-building can be enough to do this.

But sometimes the tornado isn't isolated or it's raging, and then it's a lot harder to calm. Simple compassion may erupt the tornado even more. I will see these tornadoes as ripping wind speed, angry, and chaotically sucking up mass amounts of debris in their wake. I realize it's best for me to keep the tornado in front of me to protect myself because teachers and our emotional states also matter. If the tornado is behind me, I don't know when I'll get sucked up. If the tornado is next to me, I have some control, but I could still at any moment get caught up in its winds. But if the tornado is in front of me, then I can see its movements and see its path. That gives me the best opportunities to prepare and respond. What is this behavior communicating to me? How can I make this work in my classroom space, while maintaining my own peace of mind? How can I be sure I don't get caught up in this tornado and that I keep it in front of me?

When the student with the coffee responded to me with such vehemence, he was already angry, like a tornado. That anger had nothing to do with me. I didn't have control over why he was angry, and I didn't have control over him driving to a coffee shop to buy the coffee. I also didn't have control over the other teachers he passed in the hallways who didn't tell him to get rid of it before he walked into my room. Overall, I had no control over this situation before it happened, yet it was in my space, nonetheless.

I only had control over my preparedness and my response. At that time, I was not prepared to know some students are angry and some students will take that anger out on me. I was not prepared with how to handle these types of students. I didn't see some situations as tornadoes that I should keep in front of me. Telling that student in the first minute of meeting him to get rid of his coffee was me placing the tornado next to me. Grabbing the trashcan and challenging the student was me placing the tornado behind me. Greeting the student with the intention of circling back to the school rule later was me placing the tornado in front of me.

As much as I've learned through therapy, books, and podcasts about separating the feelings I have about myself from my external environment and others' opinions, it remains a most difficult lesson for me. I thrive when things go well, when people like me, and when people value what I do. I struggle when there is dissonance, disagreement, and conflict. In one class period, I can have both, and the emotions that tie to both can compete simultaneously.

After experiencing a lot of what has gone well and what has not, I am now much better, though not perfect, in working through when I take things personally, with a reminder that much of what I experience has little to do with me. Sometimes it may take me a few days to reset, or I need to talk with a few people about my feelings until I can regain my composure and feel more settled. I remind myself that I have the ability to focus on my preparedness and my responses to keep myself steady and in control over me.

CONSIDER THE DEEP

Teachers are human, just like everyone else, and they are in an emotional profession. Certainly, I didn't want that first day of school experience. I wanted to shine and to love my first day and to gush over how great it was. Some parts of my day did afford me this, and that one part did not. My first day of teaching, though, did give me the gift of learning very important lessons. We all want the best outcomes for ourselves when we care and work hard at something. These are the vulnerable and hard conversations we need to have to express honestly what it's like in the classroom and how we can shift the present situation to something better.

When the intention is to have the most positive, effective day possible, but there are negative influences, it's hard for the teacher to feel like they are winning.

Instead, what needs to happen, which will continue to be discussed, is deep introspective work. This will bring us clarity and solutions that are far outside lesson plans, assessments, and state standards. When teachers are emotionally affected by their classrooms, they need to pause, take a breath, and examine why they feel so affected in that moment by that thing. The real work isn't necessarily in redoing lesson plans, but rather in untangling the psychology within us.

The student with the coffee made me feel inferior, like a doormat, and like people were disapproving of me. Why? Because I sometimes wrestle with these feelings in my life. There are times I approach situations showing confidence while simultaneously feeling fear that I'm not good enough. Just as teaching can be both/ and, we can also be both/and. We can be confident, and we can be uncertain. We can be willing to stand alone for what we know is right, and we can be people-pleasing. We are human, so we are complicated. I am no different.

> *WE ALL WANT THE BEST OUTCOMES FOR OURSELVES WHEN WE CARE AND WORK HARD AT SOMETHING*

I already wrestled with feelings of self-doubt and people-pleasing before I even met this student. I don't encounter these insecurities all the time, as I live with confidence, joy, and positivity, but those insecurities are there, and when provoked, they will surface.

This student—he exacerbated the "fear of being judged" and "the fear of rejection" feelings I already had deep within.

Without understanding these feelings, I reacted because I didn't know explicitly, at that time, I had these feelings and that I would react so strongly when these feelings were triggered. It wasn't until years later, through my own learning and the help of a therapist, that I got closer to the heart of these feelings within me and was able to learn from them. When we do this type of work, we come to understand ourselves and the situation in front of us. After, we can move away from control as an illusion, away from taking things personally, and away from reactive behaviors. We can move toward welcoming real control—control over ourselves and our responses.

If I were asked in a course within my undergraduate college education program or within my new teacher training to consider a time when I was emotionally bothered by a situation and had a reaction, I would have been curious as to how my personal life and my teacher life tie together. When I thought about teaching at that time, it felt objective and separate from my personal life.

I didn't understand that teaching will expose one's personal "triggers," even if we think it will not. I didn't understand how much of one's personal self is contained in teaching.

Teaching will affect us emotionally because we are emotional human beings in an emotional profession working with, for, and alongside other emotional human beings.

That is why it is important for us to be aware of our students and of ourselves.

Preferably, I'd be aware of myself and my emotional triggers before I started teaching or I would have the guidance to learn about this early in my teaching career. One could argue this kind of introspective work is not appropriate for undergraduate teacher training programs or new teacher induction programs because teachers are supposed to teach content and move students through skill growth. I argue emotional training *is* appropriate because teaching is more than lesson planning and analyzing

> ...TEACHING WILL EXPOSE ONE'S PERSONAL "TRIGGERS," EVEN IF WE THINK IT WILL NOT.

assessments. Teaching is emotional and to keep teachers emotionally healthy in an emotional profession means we must teach, train, and support their emotions and self-understanding.

This training could ask people to reflect on a time when they were emotionally triggered or bothered by something. The next step would be to share that this same type of feeling will come to them in teaching, even though the contexts will be different. As examples, if we get mad when someone cuts us off in traffic, or we feel defensive when a sibling tells us we aren't doing enough for a parent, there will be some circumstance in school—from a student, colleague, or administrator—that will cause us to have similar feelings. *Something* in our school lives will trigger the same feelings we have in our personal lives.

Then, there would be strategies and options taught that could help a teacher learn more about themselves, this personal trigger, and how to manage it *without* reacting.

Let's prepare beforehand. Let's understand that what bothers us in real life will also bother us in our teaching lives. The people will be different, and the circumstances will be different, but the feelings will be the same. Let's plan, let's learn, and let's get emotionally strong.

If I were asked in my undergraduate program about a time when I was emotionally bothered by something in my life, I'd have a few examples I could signal to from high school and college. If I were walked through a process to evaluate these and to consider them deeply, I'd come to learn that two of my "shadows" are that I seek approval from others to avoid rejection and that I over-work to combat being judged or feeling not good enough. This has played out in my personal life and my classroom life over and over again. I am much better at managing these feelings now because I know about them and know about their roots. I also know how to work through them, which I'll share more about later.

Here are two examples.

The one from high school involved two friends with whom the relationship changed for various reasons, and I eventually learned I was being misrepresented to another friend. These friends were part of a larger friend group, and I found myself sitting newly uncertain in the larger friend group, unsure where the allegiance was and unable to accurately defend my character. I remember feeling defenseless and powerless, two feelings I strongly dislike.

This flared up my need *for people to like me* or my *need for approval*. This need stems from a fear of rejection. I wanted my character to be seen as it should be and not in some false way. I didn't even know I had these insecurities when I was in high school. I never identified them objectively. They seemed, at that time, to be the result of high school drama and conflict. But they were actually much more. I don't like when people don't like me. I don't like when my character is misrepresented. I still have these feelings today, but I understand them better, and I work through them much healthier because of the learning I have gained about myself.

As a newer teacher, I found myself falling into confusing patterns of needing my students to like me as a teacher and like my class, while also holding a high course standard. These things didn't always mix, and I'd experience the discomfort of being disliked or misrepresented as a teacher. I didn't understand myself well enough to objectively state that there is a part of me that feels secure as a teacher when students like me and are in good favor with me, and there is a part of me that feels insecure when the opposite is happening. When this occurred, even if it was from 15-year-olds, it would flare up my need to be liked and for people to see my well-intentioned character.

The other example I'd think of involved playing volleyball in college for a coach I highly respect. He held a high standard and was not one to quickly praise, though he was always supportive and believed in his players. He has remained a support to me all these years later, and I still get to watch him coach while I cheer my alma mater. He expected us to *work* and he held us accountable to that work. I wanted to get his approval and his praise. I wanted to impress him. I wanted to be *good enough*. I remember having an exceptional game against a competitive team. At one point, he stood up, made eye contact with me, and lightly applauded in my direction. I had done it and it felt *great*! I called my mom after the game and excitedly told her not about my stats or about the athletic plays I made, but rather that Coach Kachinko stood and applauded toward me. Having his respect was of utmost importance to me, so I worked to earn his respect and his approval. There would be times when he was dissatisfied with the team as a whole or with me in my playing. I didn't understand myself well enough at the time to know that having someone I highly respect dissatisfied with me meant I would work even harder to regain the person's approval and satisfaction, even if that hard work came at a personal sacrifice. Because, overall, I steer myself toward being good enough.

As a newer teacher, I found myself working for the approval of those around me, some of whom were an authority and some of whom were my students, parents, or colleagues, so I could feel good enough in my own estimation and in theirs. At the time, I worked to garner the approval of all those around me, thinking I could do this if I worked long hours, put school as my number one priority, and figured out what everyone wanted and expected of me. I was seeking approval from every person in nearly all ways. So, when people were dissatisfied with me or criticized me, especially those I have great respect for, it flared up *my need for approval*, and then I would work even harder to try and regain their approval. This all stems from my fear of being inaccurately judged and not being good enough, and I work through this in much better ways today.

These are just two aspects of the introspective work I needed to have figured out before I started teaching. I didn't do the inner work because I didn't know I needed to do the inner work. Self-awareness would be what I'd place as an equal priority to learning *how to teach*, if I

> AS A NEWER TEACHER, I FOUND MYSELF WORKING FOR THE APPROVAL OF THOSE AROUND ME, SOME OF WHOM WERE AN AUTHORITY AND SOME OF WHOM WERE MY STUDENTS, PARENTS, OR COLLEAGUES, SO I COULD FEEL GOOD ENOUGH IN MY OWN ESTIMATION AND IN THEIRS.

> *EMOTIONALLY STRONG TEACHERS, WHO FEEL SEEN AND SUPPORTED, I ASSERT, ARE TEACHERS WHO WILL STAY IN THEIR TEACHING JOB.*

could turn the clock back and start over. Viewing teaching as an emotional profession as well as a content profession means we are more likely to consider ourselves within the full framework of teaching.

For each of us, we should examine what provokes us. Consider the shadows. These are the most important parts to pay attention to because the provocations will elicit a reaction, an emotional pain, or a behavior we will regret. It's not easy to do inner-work, and it may make you feel bad, or defensive, or blaming to some other person or circumstance. It is *very* courageous to examine our inner-selves, to be honest, and to be open to adjustments. When we do this, we learn about ourselves and why we react the way we do. This helps us to become aware, which leads us to be better versions of ourselves and emotionally strong teachers.

Emotionally strong teachers, who feel seen and supported, I assert, are teachers who will stay in their teaching job—the job they wanted to have. Imagine a classroom, or a whole school building, or an entire school district full of emotionally strong teachers! Imagine all they could accomplish. Imagine all they could do. Imagine all they could persevere through.

They could do anything.

SCRAMBLING

Emotionally strong teachers *can* do anything. Including doing something teachers have never had to deal with or consider in the history of teaching: how to teach with smartphones in classrooms, how to maintain academic integrity with the rise of Advanced Intelligence (AI), and how to maintain control over one's emotions within these ever-changing environments.

The first time I saw an iPad was in my trailer classroom in late January 2010. It had literally just hit stores and the next day was in my classroom. The student proudly pulled what looked like a thin, gray textbook from his bag, and the room went silent, staring at this foreign device sitting on his desk. I was astounded and sincerely asked him: "What do you do with it?"

Even the students were baffled. I can still remember kids surrounding his desk like this was some strange artifact that had landed on Earth from outer space. We were all mystified, and it was fun to gawk and innocently laugh as a class.

The laughing stopped three years later. It didn't take long for the classroom world to change because of electronics. In just three short years after first seeing that iPad, teachers were scrambling in classrooms, fighting for students' attention, disciplining phone use, and taking phones and iPods for principals to give back.

We were trying to understand what world had descended on us and how we could reclaim our classrooms. Some of us fought really hard. Some of us gave up. Some of us were told to create higher-engaging lessons that students couldn't resist paying attention to, even if they had a phone near them. The behavior was reduced to when students wrote notes to friends in class five years earlier, but for anyone who has recently taught in the classroom, you know phones and all they offer are in no way synonymous to passing notes.

We were out of control, and phones were the cause.

It's not that electronics don't have their value in the education setting. Many of my lessons have been enhanced because of technology and learning programs, and, of course, when schools were shut down due to COVID, we were reliant upon technology systems to help us deliver as much education as we possibly could to remote learners.

However, using electronics to engage and enhance a lesson is very different from the individualized ways students use electronics to disengage.

> THREE SHORT SCHOOL YEARS WAS ALL IT TOOK FOR THE CLASSROOM WORLD TO BECOME SOMETHING IT HAD NEVER BEEN BEFORE.

I cringe thinking back to that era when teachers would race to main offices to drop phones off in principals' offices before the end of the school day. Sometimes phones were locked up in principals' offices over weekends. That solution is illegal, and now just a joke from the past. Three years. Three short school years was all it took for the classroom world to become something it had never been before, and we were all ill-prepared for how far it would take us. Today, it's not unusual for guidance counselors to ask students to remove their headphones when the counselor is attempting to explain the student's future options, or for news reports to express that students in survival situations (i.e., school shooting tragedies) were videoing footage, consequently slowing themselves down, instead of running for their lives.

"Phones are here to stay," I remember an administrator telling us in a faculty meeting years ago. "We need to figure out how to teach with students having them." Research, data collection, and whistleblowers have proven over recent years that our biggest tech companies make their platforms addictive and tempting. In the Spring of 2023, the U.S. Surgeon General[7] released an extensive and courageous report stating that extensive social media for young people may lead to higher risk of poor mental health. Young people's mental and emotional health being negatively affected because of social media and phones is not a separate issue from their behavior, attitude, and output in school. These tie directly together, and teachers hear about this every day from meanness in group chats, fight meet ups, rumor spreading, and overall stress from phones.

Phones and AI are here to stay, sure, but they have made our teaching jobs even more complicated than they were years ago, in physical ways and in emotional ways. Notably, when people talk about managing these devices in classrooms, they mostly task teachers with this, leaving students out of the conversation with when, where, and how they can use phones and AI programs in their educational setting. I don't think many teachers have figured out managing phones any more than they

> PHONES AND AI ARE HERE TO STAY, SURE, BUT THEY HAVE MADE OUR TEACHING JOBS EVEN MORE COMPLICATED THAN THEY WERE YEARS AGO...

have figured out the newest onslaught of AI programs that instantly write essays, translate languages, and generate math answers.

Every teacher is astonished and scared at the ease and speed in which generative AI like ChatGPT and Google Gemini can produce the work students are asked to complete, such as spitting out an excellent, well-organized, professional essay within seconds. It's an impressive tool and it's bewilderingly good. It's also wildly frightening. It exacerbates teachers' fears of being useless and increases their intensity to hold students accountable for their work in a world that is challenging integrity and pride. It also makes teachers scramble, just like we did with phones, to stay ahead of tech that is much faster than we are.

Hands down, the single most distracting thing in the classroom for any secondary-level teacher is misused electronics, including games on computers, apps on phones, and music in ears. For those who are not in the classroom, you probably aren't aware of how habitually students scroll phones, play games, and disengage with headphones, if there are not clear expectations or discipline measures in the school, nor do I think you know how difficult it is to manage these devices. Unless you are teaching in the classroom on a daily basis, you are unaware of the challenges electronics present, and how there's no simple solution without clear guidelines backed by the school's administration team. Students misusing cell phones and tech in class is the single most devastating distraction to effective teaching, learning, and classroom community.

I've gone through my own pains in trying to manage these devices, and have, again, learned lessons the hard way, just as I did the student with the coffee. These are the same situations, in a way, with students not seeing what they are doing as wrong and reacting with intensity, and with me wanting students to comply because I've asked for their cooperation.

One instance included a student with whom I could not get to put his phone away, and it was, unfortunately, giving others in the class permission to use their phones and to misbehave. I was experiencing another day with him in this manner, and as I walked toward him, he shouted, "Get *the fuck* away from me! Don't touch my fucking phone. It's my phone. You can't just take it."

Sometimes it's not this intense, but the student can be just as angry. Even with my school having an

STUDENTS MISUSING CELL PHONES AND TECH IN CLASS IS THE SINGLE MOST DEVASTATING DISTRACTION TO EFFECTIVE TEACHING, LEARNING, AND CLASSROOM COMMUNITY.

electronics policy, and with me choosing to always give students warnings and reminders, some students can get resentful toward me when I take that next step and send through an administration discipline referral for their electronics violation, after the individual conversations with the student are ineffective. Some students can act indignantly, not taking responsibility or accountability. They can become smug in my class after getting into trouble because of their electronics use. They will refuse to answer questions, will refuse to say hello to me, and will disengage in all classroom happenings, except for graded assignments. It takes effort not to take this personally and it takes effort to rebuild the climate and the relationships in that classroom. It also makes me question if holding the line was worth it.

Some see managing phones or tech in classrooms as simple. When people reduce it to being simple, they are not factoring in how classrooms and students have changed over the years. Some students aren't compliant just because they are asked to be compliant. Some students see teachers as extensions of their authority at home, and some see teachers as authorities that can be ignored, questioned, or doubted. Teachers take a huge gamble with what reactions they will get in managing electronics, possibly providing a bigger problem for the teacher and the atmosphere of the class than if the teacher had just ignored the electronics. Sometimes it can feel like replacing one problem with another.

For example, asking students to put their phone away or to remove their headphones may be met with resistance or defiance. It may also be met with cooperation, but only for a short time, causing the teacher to give multiple reminders in a single class period for the student to disengage with electronics and engage with the lesson. Compound this with multiple classes a day and this occurring every day. Eventually, teachers feel defeated and fatigued. They begin to question "Why bother?" and they can feel purposeless. They may even say things like, "I didn't sign up for this."

Similarly, trying to check if an assignment was generated using AI is not always that simple. AI detectors and other tools are emerging, but they are not perfect. AI continues getting "smarter," too. Teachers can spend their time giving feedback on essays that weren't even produced by their students or can spend the greater portion of their planning period trying to prove that the assignment collected was not originated by the student. Mostly for English teachers, it's comparison of previous writing samples, the vocabulary used, the sentence structure provided, and the professionalism of the writing. How does one prove this, though, when a student denies using AI to generate an essay and when the detector tool has a disclaimer that it may not be accurate?

Students have this beautiful, advanced technology at their disposal provided by school districts or by parents, and it has caused many teachers to go back to pencil and paper packets, handwriting assignments, and poster making. These are all valuable, of course, and I love a meaningful packet and poster, but it's peculiar how we are squeezing ourselves out of tech because of the overrun of tech and what we have allowed.

ALLOWING

For an English teacher, like me, the study of literature is built on conversation, sharing, analyzing, and evaluating. Philosophical discussions stemming from literature are very difficult to have by yourself or with only three or four students. I've tried. It's not fun, and it can feel lonely and pointless. Or, trying to teach students how to improve their writing when they don't show interest is exhausting. For other teachers, it may be recreating tests or assignments to prohibit cheating. These are the

...WE ARE SQUEEZING OURSELVES OUT OF TECH BECAUSE OF THE OVERRUN OF TECH...

circumstances in classrooms that cause emotional fatigue and erode a teacher's motivation and morale.

I cannot claim that I had 100% participation in my classes before electronics ran rampant. I can state with no revisionist history, though, that I had more students expecting to come to school *to do school*. We are in mixed worlds now and have been for a decade. It's confusing for teachers, and it's confusing for students. The singular thing—the phone—that gives students entertainment, escape from boredom, safety and comfort, and connection is now with them as they enter the classrooms they like and the ones they don't like. This mental distraction didn't exist before. So, when I open a deep dive into literature, or introduce a writing skill, or provide an extension activity, I know my students will make a choice: join or separate.

Yes, that choice was always there, but now there is something way more enticing that had already been pulling students' attention from the moment I said, "Please put all electronics away." Students may physically put them away, but they aren't mentally away.

Likewise, when students are working on a writing piece, they have a choice: write the prompt themselves or use an online generator. There have always been ways to cheat. But none has ever been so good, so effective, and so crisp as AI.

The fallback argument regarding student phone and headphone use is that teachers are unengaging, boring, and ineffective. The argument is that, if teachers supplied more engaging lessons or higher stakes assessments, then students would recognize the natural consequences of missing out on something cool, or would do poorly and get a bad grade, which would curb their choice to be distracted. This is true to some extent, but not true enough to fix the problem, especially for all students, and especially when school systems are set up to continuously soften natural consequences.

If teachers hold the line of natural consequences from students being distracted by phones, they are risking students—maybe even many—failing their classes. This sets off an entire complex system of work on the teacher's shoulders. The teacher has to document why the student is failing. The teacher has to make contact home by any means necessary. The teacher has to call the student into study hall numerous times to give ample opportunity to improve the grade, and then document the attempts. Sometimes these efforts fail, and then the teacher has to provide modifications to work or exempt work to help the student catch up.

Every time I have experienced this situation, the responsibility falls on the teacher to inform, plan, and strategize. Accountability must shift to include the student, if we want to uphold teacher emotional support and decrease teacher overwhelm regarding problems they didn't even create.

Despite these frustrations, the purpose of teachers teaching is so our students learn and use their brains and challenge themselves and acquire new skills. Distraction from electronics impedes all of this, or sometimes blocks it completely.

In the complex world that is teaching, we must evaluate what we want to allow and what we don't want to allow. Students, just like everyone else, need boundaries. Young people, developmentally, thrive with boundaries and expectations. It's imperative we remember why we are in school, why we are doing this work, and what we want students to gain from being in school. Just as we utilize the backward design method for our unit and lesson planning, we can apply the backward design to our classroom expectations and subsequent boundaries. How do we want students to conduct themselves in our classroom space? How do we want classes to behave and engage? Determine that visual and those specifics. Then, work backward to get to that place through consistently communicating expectations and upholding those expectations through boundaries.

This conversation should be ongoing in schools amongst all in the building to magnetize teachers,

> *IN THE COMPLEX WORLD THAT IS TEACHING, WE MUST EVALUATE WHAT WE WANT TO ALLOW AND WHAT WE DON'T WANT TO ALLOW.*

administrators, and students back to the point of it all, so we don't allow distractions and temptations to dissolve all the good that is to happen in classrooms and for students' growth, maturation, and learning.

For me, cell phones and headphones have played the biggest role in eroding my classroom culture, togetherness, and skill-retention. And we have *allowed* them. We have allowed the distraction. I can recall in my not-so-distant teaching past when the beginning of class was greetings, story sharing, and updates with most students listening and laughing while getting to know each other. There was a building of community from a simple "Tell me about your weekend," or "How is that job going?" or "What happened at your game last week?"

Now, when I attempt those same conversations, students don't even hear me. Literally. They have headphones in and can't hear me. Or they are doing something on their phone or their game, and they can't attend to both situations. They aren't impolite. Well, maybe sometimes. To a greater extent, they are distracted, and the conversation goes flat. Or no one else is listening, so the conversation doesn't circulate.

The saddest thing I have found in recent years from the misuse of phones in classrooms is not so much that students don't talk to me in the larger capacity of the classroom, but that they don't talk to each other. If there is time remaining at the end of the class period, a teacher can observe a quiet classroom with heads bent down and students swallowed by their phone—messaging, gaming, watching, scrolling. I've had many class periods end in complete silence, and as much as I try to exuberantly give my fist bumps at the door while wishing each student to have the best day or while wishing good luck at a game, there can be an uncomfortable quietness that leaves my space before the next group comes to fill it.

This does not describe every student. This does not describe every class. Some students and classes require no reminders about electronics. Skills are taught and lessons are given without the overarching stress of electronics management or distraction. I'll find myself thinking, "This class is so easy to teach!" and "These students are a dream!" Free time in the room is filled with talking, laughing, enjoyment, and sharing. And, of course, there are times when I hear students manage each other with "Hey! Put that away. I'm trying to talk to you!"

As much as I want this to be the whole of my experience, it is not, and I know it's not the whole of the experience for my fellow teachers, which is why we need to talk about it.

These devices, for so many of our young people, have become their safety nets, helping them to avoid awkward and uncomfortable situations because they have been trained to do this, just as we all have. Phones are a socially acceptable addiction, and our students will choose feeling comfortable to avoid feeling awkward over pretty much anything else. When students say to me that their phones and headphones make them feel less awkward, they are really saying that they do not have the self-confidence yet to be in the world just as they are; instead, they need a covering, a protection, in order to face the world around them. Some students are so painfully shy that these devices are their safety net, and without them, they wouldn't know how to navigate their world.

Does this illustrate the way every student behaves with their phone? No, definitely not, and I don't want to misrepresent the many students who can manage their phone use. If phones weren't a problem, though, they wouldn't be making headline news and be segments aired on top broadcasting programs. Additionally, we wouldn't have so many teachers vocal about their frustration and fatigue over phones, nor would we have sad-but-true videos playing on social media with teachers repeating to an unresponsive classroom audience, "Put your phones away. Put your phones away. Put your phones away." It's important to remember that even if the majority of students may not be misusing phones, any substandard classroom behavior will permeate and its consequences will grow.

Cell phones have replaced much of what we used to carry: cameras, watches, calendars, notepads. It should stop there. We shouldn't allow phones to also replace the community of our schools or the purpose of our schools.

We have to continually ask ourselves: Is this what we want to allow? Do we want our older students having their teachers strategize how to get them to pass without expecting them to be in the conversation, holding accountability? Do we want to allow distraction over learning? I don't think so. I don't think anyone wants any of these things. It's important, then, that we continually ask ourselves what we are allowing and why we are allowing it.

RESETTING

After years of trying to manage phones, getting yelled at by students, calling home, sending through discipline reports that didn't change behavior, and feeling walked on by kids, that dark feeling of "Why even bother?" had come into *my* teaching world. I was emotionally fatigued

> *CELL PHONES HAVE REPLACED MUCH OF WHAT WE USED TO CARRY: CAMERAS, WATCHES, CALENDARS, NOTEPADS. IT SHOULD STOP THERE. WE SHOULDN'T ALLOW PHONES TO ALSO REPLACE THE COMMUNITY OF OUR SCHOOLS OR THE PURPOSE OF OUR SCHOOLS.*

and drained by "teaching," simply because I wasn't able to do what I wanted to do: *teach*.

I went school years feeling defeated by phones in my classroom space as I tried to teach to groups of students not even listening. I went school years feeling fatigued by the constant losing battle. I went school years frustrated by something I was allowing.

Every time I entered class enthusiastically and gave an exuberant greeting and was met with students who couldn't even glance up from their phones, a part of my love for teaching died. Every time I posed an interesting question for discussion or journal writing, and I watched students turn to their phones instead of engaging in the conversation, a part of my love for teaching died. Every time a student argued with me about their phone, a part of my love for teaching died. Every time I tried to teach a writing skill and I'd see students' eyes glued to a computer game, a part of my love for teaching died.

> *I WAS EMOTIONALLY FATIGUED AND DRAINED BY "TEACHING," SIMPLY BECAUSE I WASN'T ABLE TO DO WHAT I WANTED TO DO: TEACH.*

How many scuffs and chips could my teaching life take before it was completely gone? Why would I want to live like that? That is not the teaching world I had worked to create. I didn't sign up for that. Why would I want to work hard to feel defeated before even beginning my day? I am joyful and positive, and I want to engage fully in the life that is in front of me. There is little room for that dark feeling in my world.

All of this over allowing phones.

It wasn't that the students in front of me didn't care, though that is how it seemed. It was because we had allowed them access to such a strong pacifier that they weren't able to unfix their eyes or their brains. We allowed it. So, it was time we disallowed it.

This is when I became part of the "resetting." For starters, I faced the truth of what was happening in my teaching life. I was part of a system that was *allowing* my classroom to be devalued by phones, headphones, and computer games. These devices are a societal problem, and that societal problem infiltrated my school building and my classroom.

No longer did I want to be part of a system that devalued my lessons and my attempts at teaching skills. No longer did I want to be part of a system that devalued students' classroom purposes or teachers' purposes or the school building's purpose. I decided I wanted—no, *needed*—something more if I was going to pull myself out of the eroding feelings I was experiencing because of the electronics battle.

I also faced the truth of how electronics were making me feel as a classroom teacher. They were making me feel devalued, under-appreciated, frustrated, and rejected. No one wants to feel this way from their job.

At first, I lamented my frustration in department meetings or to friends. Then, I sent an email to my same grade level colleagues and the administrator in charge of that grade level expressing the futility I felt each day being ignored while trying to teach, and I asked for a meeting to discuss the problem and determine solutions. Response after response was returned to me from colleagues expressing similar feelings of frustration and defeat, again showing me that in our teaching world, we are never alone in how we feel from our classroom experiences.

Some colleagues expressed hesitancy if students, especially older students, would be able to change their behaviors, or if teachers and administrators would be able to keep up with consistently managing the problem throughout a long school year. "Reasonable points," I agreed. But this was too important for me to just let go, as students misusing their electronics in class became the single thing that eroded my classroom and my love for teaching.

What I have going for me in my teaching career, which I sadly recognize is not the experience for all teachers, is that I have an administration team that is willing to reset expectations when the resetting is necessary. So, when I sent that email to my grade level colleagues and the principal who works with that grade level, I learned electronics, in particular phones, was already going to be a topic of review by my head principal and my administration team in the summer before the next school year began.

The meeting I held in my classroom with roughly 50 teachers and my grade level principal was a crucial start as it generated energy and a coming-together of conversation that continued in the summer when my head principal, as already intended, organized a group of teachers to examine the problem closely to create a building-wide resetting of expectations, which included a full action plan and accountability, beginning immediately the following school year.

In our work as educators, the team approach is best. When everyone is on the same page—working toward the same goals, understanding each other's needs, and willing to make adjustments—we can do our jobs most effectively. It sends the message that *we as a school system* believe so strongly in this idea that we have a policy behind it, or a rule behind it, or a regulation behind it. *We as a school system*, united and working together, sends a most powerful message.

To date, this "electronics policy" resetting has created the largest positive shift in my classroom in all ways from community building to lesson engagement to skill retention. Having clearer boundaries around electronics that come from me as the classroom teacher as well as from the administration team, has reset the purpose *of school* in my classroom.

Equally important, it has assuaged those harmful, negative, eroding feelings I was having when I spent way too much time teaching to a sea of distracted students. To look at my students now and to see them looking back at me is enough for me to reverse my "I didn't sign up for this" to "This is what I signed up for." Now when I pose questions, or I ask students to read, or I offer a thoughtful journal prompt, I am not immediately conflicting with phones and computer games. The change in school expectations around phones has helped to lower what was otherwise high teacher frustration and fatigue.

As a collective entity, we should not allow something to devalue the intention of our schools and teachers. We didn't sign up for that. We must be braver than that and expect more from ourselves and our students. Teachers are in the middle of the chain. We can't do our jobs effectively without administrative support and student cooperation. I am lucky that my administration team is willing to reset expectations when that resetting is necessary. I know not all teachers are this fortunate. I urge that all parties must be on the same team, believing in the same ideals and part of the same solution if we are going to keep teachers emotionally healthy and out of the murky waters of emotional fatigue.

THE HIGHEST VALUE

What in your teaching day, in your classroom, or in your building requires some "resetting of expectations?" I like showing up to my job feeling purposeful and effective, and I don't like feeling so emotionally drained that I can't do my job effectively. If resetting is what we need to bring our classrooms back from going off the rails, then that is what we need to do because we shouldn't allow ourselves to be devalued when we are of the highest value.

I have considered my role in what I allow in my classroom in other ways, too. Instead of relying solely on computers, I provide handouts, journal books, and other

> *TEACHERS ARE IN THE MIDDLE OF THE CHAIN. WE CAN'T DO OUR JOBS EFFECTIVELY WITHOUT ADMINISTRATIVE SUPPORT AND STUDENT COOPERATION.*

activities that require pencils to paper. When I have the same students not adhering to important deadlines or not responding in class, I move to solutions. I'll ask these students *why* they are not caring about the deadlines or *why* they won't respond in class. We make a plan, or I tell them that their extensions are used, and now they have to step up. I use the "Wheel of Names" as a random cold-call option, or I tell a student directly, "Question 3 is on the board, and I know you'll have something good to say. That's the question you will answer in two minutes. Be sure you're ready." I hold the student to an answer, even if I have to guide them through an answer.

At some point, we must hold ourselves—teachers, students, and administrators—accountable for what we allow in our classrooms. We must see ourselves as the high value we are, and not let interferences diminish our value.

Consider a school that has taken away all the dedicated, reliable, creative, compassionate, and intelligent teachers and students. Consider what is left behind. What does that school look like? What does that school feel like? How would anyone emotionally thrive in a school like that?

I am a teacher, and, therefore, I am valuable, and the good I try to do in my classroom is valuable. I am one part of the group that upholds the highest value in my school system. That is how I treat myself, and that is how I look at myself. I know I am replaceable because I am not ignorant of that concept. Being replaced won't matter to me until I am replaced. Until then, I am one of the highest valued commodities in the school in which I work.

But teachers can't do their high-value jobs alone. Teachers are in the middle of the system, spider-webbing to connect all the other pieces. Communicating our needs and expectations with our students, families, and administrators is vital. How else will they know what we need? How else will they know if we are experiencing our highest levels of emotional fatigue?

If we choose to place the highest value on ourselves and the work we do in our classrooms, then resolving problems will go in our favor more than it will not, even if it sometimes doesn't go in our favor.

The decision to have phones in the classroom was beyond my control, yet it nearly undid my teaching career. Phones brought me to a low place—a place of fatigue, powerlessness, and frustration. I don't like to live like that. I needed to make a change, and I am lucky that the change I needed was supported.

How can we start talking about these problems, so people who can help us make changes will listen? For starters, begin by talking to anyone. Students, parents, grade level partners, department members, and administrators. Communicate your value. Communicate your needs. Try to elicit support and try your best to come to an agreement. Don't give up.

Let your students' parents know your lessons are falling flat and your students aren't attending to the work at a high level. Talk compassionately with your students and let them know that they are part of an important process of teaching and learning. Tell them your expectations and needs.

If you are in public education, remind your students and their parents that they get an opportunity to complete an education for free, which is statistically the one thing that makes the biggest difference in their adult financial lives. Remind your students about the sacrifice some in our world go through for education, and that they should appreciate its value. Do anything you can. But don't give up.

Don't devalue yourself or your work because kids want to be on their phones and have noise in their ears all day. Of course they do. That's easy. We don't want our schools to be places where students feel "easy" all the time. We want them to feel challenge and pride. Ray Bradbury warned us of this, for all you *Fahrenheit 451* readers. Don't devalue yourself for any circumstance that is bringing you down.

You know the time you spend on your lessons and the time you spend managing your students and their needs. You know it. Don't do all that work and dedicate all that time to allow it to be devalued and dismissed. I have learned and decided that I don't allow others to devalue the work that I do. I don't accept that. You don't accept that either. You don't allow someone else to devalue your value.

Cell phones may not be the cause of your classroom teaching being "devalued." It may be something else or someone else. If there is something in your teaching day that comes up over and over again as a problem, be curious about it, face it, name it, and try to work toward a solution.

Be willing to reset expectations, and I hope if you are willing to do this, those around you are willing to as well. If we want to maintain emotionally strong and positive teachers, then we have to be willing to accept

> ...DON'T ALLOW SOMEONE ELSE TO DEVALUE YOUR VALUE.

that there are urgent and important matters that come up in schools and these matters may be ever-evolving. We cannot only examine the urgent matters because the important matters, if left unaddressed, can cause the most destruction.

No one will value your classroom, your lessons, and your time more than you because you know how much you have given to it all. Don't let anyone else come in and devalue it. You deserve a lot better than that. We all deserve a lot better than that.

Value yourself and all that you are giving to every part of your day. You are part of *the highest value*, and you deserve to be treated as such. Settle for nothing less.

JUST ONE PERSON

GRACIOUSLY AND SENSIBLY

There isn't, in my opinion, a profession in which just one person is judged as acutely as teachers are judged. Well, maybe there are professions that are judged more—famous celebrities and athletes. But a common profession? I think teachers top the chart.

Everything teachers do is right on the surface, ready to be praised, applauded, shared, scrutinized, and judged. Others' jobs have some behind the scenes aspects. Not teachers. It's like working in a fishbowl. Teachers are not only judged on their teaching abilities and style, but also on a lot of items that fall into personal categories that really should be separate from their professional abilities. What I have learned, which I have to remind myself about from time to time, is that teaching is a delicate profession, surrounded by pressure, and we must navigate through this delicacy and pressure with grace and sensibility.

We are just one person, but those we teach can expect us to be many people all rolled into one. That is a lot of pressure, and we simply can't be everything to everyone, even if the job expects that of us. The overwhelm and the

> *TEACHING IS A DELICATE PROFESSION, SURROUNDED BY PRESSURE, AND WE MUST NAVIGATE THROUGH THIS DELICACY AND PRESSURE WITH GRACE AND SENSIBILITY.*

pressure can tilt us to an imbalance, and even trying to rebalance ourselves can be one more thing for us to do.

In the end, we are just one person trying to manage *many* differing variables of our day, and the pressure to do it right can be enormous. To "survive" teaching, we must figure out how to *graciously* and how to *sensibly* move through the judgments, criticisms, and evaluations we receive. It's important to learn how we will respond to others' opinions or judgments and what we can do with those feelings because we are in a job that is scrutinized. These are important considerations to have before we start teaching, and they are important considerations to have if we are resistant to feedback, or if we get defensive when given feedback. Learning how to sensibly move through the judgment of teaching is a skill, just as developing lesson plans is a skill. If we don't develop this skill and awareness, we may experience emotional fatigue and feelings of low motivation.

JUDGMENTS AND EVALUATIONS

Early in my career, the sheer volume of judgment and evaluation was all new to me. I didn't have prior experience being the person in charge, getting judged and evaluated by dozens at the same time between students, parents, and administrators, especially as each subgroup brought different expectations and approaches to their judgment. When we are young and new to a career, this is something we must learn how to deal with and how to manage. I did have prior experience being evaluated as I was a student, after all, and an athlete. I appreciate evaluation because it gives me a chance to improve and grow, but judgment is very different from evaluation, and I was not used to so much judgment, particularly from students and parents. The exposure of being judged, especially unfairly, made me feel more pressure, and I wasn't aware of the stress it caused until I saw the system holistically and saw myself as one part of it.

For example, I'd make the mistake of getting into back-and-forth email conversations with parents, with the parent trying to prove her perspective and me trying to prove mine. I hated it when I'd check email on Saturday afternoons or Sunday nights, knowing an email of criticism or defense would be waiting for me, dishing me another layer to an argument, subsequently affecting my mood and mindset. I don't know why I logged in, knowing what could be waiting for me. It was like I couldn't resist the anticipation and would want to get it over with, even though all it did was affect my mindset for the rest of the day. Early in my career, I wasn't sensibly moving through judgment from parents because I wanted their approval, and I wanted them to see how hard I was working to create a good classroom for their child. I wanted to hold the line on the standard of work, and I wanted to challenge students, so they would grow. Sometimes the person on the other end wouldn't see my perspective and back and forth we went.

I am now more sensible with my approach to parents and their needs. As a parent myself, I have a deeper understanding of the fear parents have for their children's success and safety in the world. Not that I wasn't sensitive to this before, but now I know it from experience.

The most important choice I have made when I have issues in my classroom is that I never go back and forth in email. Never. If I know there is an issue, or if I get a long email from a parent, I always set up a time to talk on the phone, and I'll only respond to long emails that I have received the message and look forward to a time to talk. Sometimes the phone call can be abrasive at first or defensive, but I have found that within time, perspectives are shared, reason is determined, and a plan is in place. When this shift happens, I remind myself that much of the concern doesn't have to do with me—there could be a dozen things going on with a student in their household and in their personal life that affect school and my class.

Seeing it this way reminds me that I am just one person and I cannot fix all the problems. This realization doesn't happen as easily over email, because there is no voice and no immediate opportunity for conversation exchange. There are times when the phone call ends fine, but the disagreement is still there. Either way, at least I know where I stand and who I am working with. It's much cleaner, healthier, and clearer with a phone call.

Only one time in my current 18-year-career did I have to end the phone call because it was disrespectful. In that situation, I placed the issue in the guidance counselor's and administrator's hands and shared that future correspondence would have to be a team approach. Again, I am so lucky that I have people who are willing to step up and support, as that makes the harder parts of our jobs much more manageable.

Teaching is full of complicated situations that we figure out as we go along because we have to, and I have found the most success when I remind myself that I am just one person in an intricate system, and that I must move through this system with grace and sensibility.

Teachers are intertwined in the network of judgment and evaluations not only from students and parents, but also from their own evaluators, whom are typically their principals.

At first, early in my career, I viewed end-of-year evaluations to how I experienced courses and grades as a student. If I worked hard and did what was expected of me—and even more—I'd get an A grade. That is not how end-of-year evaluations work, and I believe this is a conversation we should be teaching our newer teachers, who will work very hard and devote themselves to a complicated job and land on the other side of a school year with an average evaluation. To start, it must be expressed that the evaluation process is rigid and does not consider the personality or emotional contributions of a teacher and how that impacts the school or classroom, despite teachers being in an emotional profession. Moreover, throughout our careers, we concurrently have remarkable competencies and areas of growth, and these are difficult to appropriately mark on a rating scale.

In my school, the supervisors evaluating me are also the same principals I need when there is a student problem, and they are the same people we rely on for professional guidance if there is a major issue in our lives. It would be better if principals in the building, who are leading, directing, and supporting teachers and students, could be separate from the role of evaluator and observer for classroom teachers, especially when those observations are connected to end-of-year evaluations. The intention is to work together, so making principals take on the role of both teacher supporter *and* teacher evaluator does cause confusion and sometimes division. That is unnecessary when there could be separate evaluators, allowing building principals to focus on support, relationship building, and problem-solving.

I have had some school years where my evaluation is great, and I'm like "Yes!" And I've had some school years where my evaluation is average and there are improvement comments. It makes me feel good when I get a good evaluation. I value my work, and it's important to me that others value my work and my efforts. We typically get this validation through end-of-year evaluations. There was one school year, though, when I struggled with my end-of-year evaluation, and it's not because it was bad. It's because it was average.

Long ago, I had a full school year of difficult classes and difficult student situations. It was an exhausting year. I declare that I could teach 20 more years and still signal that school year as being the hardest one for me. This particular school year consisted of students in and out of mental health treatment centers, students dealing with drug addiction, students with emotional needs, students misbehaving and attention seeking, students learning English, and students with learning needs. I had other students who did charity work on the weekends, who played instruments in the marching band, who were on sports team, who asked me to write letters of reference for a summer enrichment program, who vacationed in other countries, and who considered which Advanced Placement English course would be best for them. It was a confusing, tiring teaching experience, and I carried that school year on my back. Additionally, I was taking extra education courses, was coaching a volleyball team, was a top-participant on a volunteer school committee that was trying to build connectivity and morale in the building, and was a new mom.

My end-of-year evaluation that year was nothing remarkable. Good. Fine. Average. With improvement comments sprinkled in. Experiencing that challenging year, I personally needed a build-me-up, or at least a conversation about the good I brought to the building, to make me excited to come back the following year. I needed my evaluator to give me a high five, a "thank you," and maybe even a medal (just joking about the medal). I handled delicate, sometimes messy, student situations and did a fantastic job balancing it all and keeping my positivity and enthusiasm. I didn't complain and I didn't give up. In fact, I worked harder trying to make sure my classes still maintained a standard and that I nurtured the difficult student situations while also pushing the students who were ready for next-level work.

My supervisor knew this because I'd often hear, "I don't know how you're staying so happy with some of those situations you have." So, it was acknowledged in hallways or in meetings, but not on the end-of-year evaluation.

That evaluation, which was average and fine, felt impersonal, dismissive, and unmotivating. It took out any wind I had left in my sails. I regrouped over the summer to be excited again for the next school year, and I realized something very important.

There are human beings on both sides of the evaluation process. I accepted that this person didn't evaluate *me*. They objectively evaluated a classroom. That classroom, especially in that particular year, wasn't *me* as a person or as a teacher. I tried my best and I think I did an outstanding job, but there were many other school years in which I was a better "teacher," formally speaking. Additionally, this supervisor was no less appreciative of me because I got an average evaluation. This person marked it as it was. I was the one who put the other meaning to it. I made it bigger because I was emotionally tied to my classroom, its results, and my efforts.

I was the one who saw the average evaluation as "You—Diane Manser—are average and that is how you are viewed." This is not true at all. I now move much more sensibly through evaluations and feedback. I see a person on the other side, and I also know I am so much more than what that evaluation shows. But, certainly and admittedly, I like when I receive a great evaluation.

Moving through evaluation processes graciously and sensibly allows us to recognize that it is one part of a whole, imperfect process. An end-of-year evaluation could be based on one 40-minute lesson, adding stress to teachers, and sometimes walkthrough evaluations or email follow-ups about an observation may be the last thing a teacher needs if they are undergoing other stress.

How we handle evaluations and feedback is part of our teaching jobs, and it's important we keep all of this in perspective and figure out how to be gracious with evaluations, so we don't have a negative reaction last for too long, or so we don't quit over an evaluation, or so we don't stop doing the good we do because of an evaluation.

> I WAS THE ONE WHO SAW THE AVERAGE EVALUATION AS "YOU—DIANE MANSER—ARE AVERAGE AND THAT IS HOW YOU ARE VIEWED."

Evaluations are part of teaching, even if we don't like it. There are years when I don't like it. Giving myself a proper evaluation, especially when it may not match an external evaluation, whether from students, parents, or administrators, is something I continue to work on.

I am fortunate that my administration gives me time and offers me understanding. I know it is not like this everywhere. I have had many conversations with a principal in my school about the state of teaching and "principaling," which have given me a trusted authority when I need support and which have also given me a different perspective when needed. In one meeting, I got unexpectedly worked up talking about how hard some students are that I had to choke back tears. I felt embarrassed and needed a few deep breaths to gather myself. This principal didn't make me feel embarrassed. He gave me space and understanding.

I have another principal who held individual meetings with every person on the faculty to reclaim relationships and to reconnect with the *people* in the building. There were five prepared, meaningful questions about life (not about school) and a conversation ensued in which the understanding and the relationship between teacher and principal deepened. This was *a lot* of time and *a lot* of effort, but it was important, and, in my opinion, it widened community and understanding. When I see this principal for my end-of-year evaluation, I know this person will see *me* in that evaluation, and whether average or great, I will feel part of a whole system.

How we are viewed as teachers is sometimes out of our control. Not every principal is willing to invest in his or her leadership skills and growth. Not every parent is going to be reasonable when there is a disagreement. Not every student is going to see our intention as the teacher, even if we try to explain ourselves. We are just one person trying to do the best we can to give value and to feel valued with many factors out of our control. It's important we try to navigate all of this sensibly, so we don't get weighed down by emotional fatigue. Sometimes the only thing we can do is step in for ourselves and build ourselves up.

This lesson is hard for me. Knowing some students don't like me or that some parents judge me makes me uneasy, flaring up my own feelings of inadequacy and inferiority, and I can fall into the comfort of people pleasing. I haven't found the magic formula to take this feeling completely away, but I keep improving every time I am met with this lesson by delivering a personal pep talk.

I'll remind myself of the way—or ways—that I am doing the job really well and how I am a positive, valuable

> WE ARE JUST ONE PERSON TRYING TO DO THE BEST WE CAN TO GIVE VALUE AND TO FEEL VALUED WITH MANY FACTORS OUT OF OUR CONTROL.

influence on my students. I know you can do this, too. It's vital we do this for ourselves, or do it for others, or find the people who will build us back up when we need it. Teaching is an emotional job, and it's a job that is judged, adding on even more emotional weight. We mustn't stop reminding ourselves of the good we are doing.

I'll think about how I am one of the most positive lights in my students' lives and that I shine that everyday. I'll recall when I am at my teaching best and how good that feels, such as when my students are eager to be in my room and tell me how much they love being in my class, or when many students want to speak about something we are reading and the insightful thoughts circulate and get deeper. It'll make me smile just seeing so many arms in the air. I'll own when I am *the one person* in a student's day, who can make their day better and make them feel better about something that is bothering them. I'll remember how good it feels when I joke with students and when we laugh over funny things that happen or when I teach my students how to write—like really write—and I notice those lessons in their writing submissions, and I think to myself, "Yes! I taught them that and they are doing it!" I'll reread past emails from parents or students that were kind and appreciative.

By doing this, it helps me to see the truth of what I offer. I may experience a student who doesn't like me, or a parent who criticizes me, or an average evaluation, but I also have many ways that I can build myself up and refocus reality.

EMOTIONAL FATIGUE

I have listened to and have talked with many teachers to gather experiences outside of my own to learn about the emotional complexity of our jobs and what it feels like to be just one person in teaching. My purpose in sharing these stories and examples in this chapter and the few ahead is not to preclude an emerging teacher from entering the profession. These stories are given to validate those already teaching and to prepare newer teachers, so we can remember our grace and sensibility and the purpose of being emotionally strong teachers from start to finish.

You will be just one person and may have a class that is incredibly overwhelming, and you teach that class every day for a whole year. You will be just one person and may have a student who decides he does not like you and he may look at you with antagonism, even though you didn't do anything to deserve that dislike. You will be just one person and may become confident and experienced teaching a class or grade level, and then, without any input from you, be changed to a different grade level or course the following school year.

You may start your career working multiple long-term substitute jobs, until there is finally a teacher's contract with your name on it. Moving from school to school, always being the new teacher yet having years of experience, is tough and emotionally draining. Do you get close to your colleagues, knowing you will be gone in a few months? Do you volunteer to coach that team or run that club, knowing you may not be there the following year?

Teaching is a microcosm of life, and it encompasses the emotions of life from joy to fulfillment to disappointment to grief. This is all part of teaching, and some teacher roads are not straight lines. Not at all.

One of my friends told me of his classroom neighbor who resigned his fifth-grade position after a particularly awful class and school year. He had been teaching for 11 years. I was curious why he would leave when the following year could have been better, and my friend told me that, "He just wasn't going to keep being a teacher when he couldn't actually teach and when year after year was more work." I don't know this person, but I understood what he meant from my own teaching life and as I continued to see resignation and early retirement emails from my own district.

I happened to meet a third-grade teacher on the beach one summer, and we began talking about our school experiences, both good and bad. She told me she "loved her job, but..." (I knew there was a "but") there were times in the past school year when she needed to step into the hallway to do deep breathing exercises because the class she had that school year was so tough, and she often felt overwhelmed. Singularly, her greatest source of stress came from one student, she told me, who "hit her in the head twice and bit her arm once." I know behavior is communication, and I do not know the needs of this child; nonetheless, teachers getting hit by students at any age is upsetting and distressing. I asked her how she went through the rest of her day after being hit or bitten. She told me, "It's not easy. It can shake you up. It can make you mad. It's a choice to

> TEACHING IS A MICROCOSM OF LIFE, AND IT ENCOMPASSES THE EMOTIONS OF LIFE FROM JOY TO FULFILLMENT TO DISAPPOINTMENT TO GRIEF.

push all that away and to continue loving the student. It's a choice to move on with the rest of the class and teach." She shared, though, that there were lots of times when she'd cry at night or would wish the school year over. Honest, raw, and helpful as I thought about my own moments that made me cry or that made me wish the school year over.

Furthermore, this new teacher friend told me she could barely get through one 10-minute exercise without kids in this same class acting up, getting up, shouting, yelling at each other, or asking for help without raising their hand. It sounded exhausting and impossible. My eyes got larger and larger with every example she gave. I asked her, "Do you ever feel it is perceived we should be able to fix these problems in our classrooms? That we should be able to somehow maintain complete control?" She leaned forward, lightly hit my arm, and exclaimed, "YES!" Then she continued to tell me that her principal marked her as "Needs Improvement" in classroom management on her end-of-year evaluation. There we stood on the beach with the orange and pink setting sun in the distance and the cool sand under our feet. But I was too distracted with worry about the year in front as I talked with her to even notice the beach scenery. I felt bad for this teacher and for the students who didn't act out. What kind of education were they getting every day, despite the teacher's efforts? How long would this teacher last in the next school year before having to deep breathe in the hallway?

I asked her if a class like that is typical for her. She said no, but it's happened before and will happen again. She joked that she "took a lot of sick days." We all know they weren't actual sick days, but rather mental health days. Teachers are fortunate to get paid time off as many professionals do not. I also want to recognize that teachers often use their paid sick time because they are emotionally fatigued, not actually sick. It makes me curious about the state of teachers' minds when they need to take time away from their jobs, just so they can come back and do their jobs.

Attending a community event, I learned from an elementary teacher in another district about the struggles some elementary students and teachers have faced, especially since COVID. When it comes to post-COVID education, we must be honest that the stresses we have experienced since the shutdowns are exponential, but the stresses were building before COVID took away all our predictability. In my opinion, COVID intensified an already brewing storm.

Because of COVID or because of all things happening before COVID, we have more children identified with emotional needs, cognitive needs, and

> *...COVID TOOK AWAY ALL OUR PREDICTABILITY.*

neurodevelopmental disorders. Doctors' offices and mental health facilities are taxed, and teachers are called on to be major consultants in a child's health care. Classroom numbers are higher, and paraprofessionals and aides are fewer. Classrooms for our youngest children can be a mix of children new to holding pencils, writing letters, sitting still during instruction, sharing, and being away from mom and dad. In every way, the teacher is called on to nurture and care for these special cases within the full classroom, which contributes to teacher fatigue and burn out.

With that said, taking away the few precious minutes a teacher has free in her day to pile something else on is just inconsiderate and out of touch. When this happens to teachers, it also gives the implication that the teacher's planning period isn't valued and that the teacher will figure out how to get it all done. When, precisely? If teachers lose their planning time over and over, when are they to write a thoughtful email response to parents or complete an important report for a student, or plan for conferences, or organize that new unit, or grade those assignments? During their 25-minute lunch period? Or at home after they've already worked a full day? This is the death by a thousand papercuts analogy that I urge district leaders to consider, because teachers are in the middle of the system, and they are overall unable to make any healthy change in their work lives without the support of the whole system.

Seeing the same 20+ students all day every day certainly has advantages, such as with our elementary school teachers, but it also has disadvantages. Elementary teachers are *on* all day long, and their days are saturated, sometimes with young students who don't know how to be in a classroom setting. From the minute they arrive to the minute they leave, they are on. No pause button. They may rush to get their own children where they need to be, only to come into school to soothe a child who is upset, or reassure a parent who is nervous, to then run through their day and return right back to picking up their children. All of this while they can't use the bathroom without getting coverage, and while they often have meetings during any prep time that may be afforded to them.

When we are just one person dealing with so much emotional intensity, we can lose ourselves in the complexity, confusing our overall purpose with everything else happening around us. We may question ourselves, as did I, with things like, "Do I give that essay when it seems my students are going through so much?"

or "Do I agree to volunteer for that committee when I'm already feeling overwhelmed?" or "Does anyone out there even see how crazy all of this is?"

Life for a secondary teacher is different than life for an elementary teacher, obviously, but there are commonalities. Both groups of teachers, according to a 2021 *Education Week* article by assistant editor Alyson Klein[8], make over "1,500 decisions a day, equating to three decisions per minute." Susan Wetrich, who teaches prekindergarten, is interviewed stating, "'Decision making is absolutely nonstop throughout the day…[and] I find myself] gaming out the day's potential trouble spots in the shower or on the drive to school.'" Wetrich, who used to be a Head Start Administrator and college instructor, continues by sharing that she experiences "'more decisions on her plate now [as a teacher] than in any other role or career.'"

It's not just the decisions regarding grouping this student here instead of there, it is also decisions "'When dealing with students from a variety of different racial, cultural, and economic backgrounds…[and] teachers

FROM THE MINUTE [ELEMENTARY TEACHERS] ARRIVE TO THE MINUTE THEY LEAVE, THEY ARE ON. NO PAUSE BUTTON.

having to think carefully about whether their own unconscious biases are impacting some of the split-second decisions they make on things like discipline, grades, or even who to call on to answer a question during a classroom discussion,'" according to a former school district special education administrator.

As the school day goes on, the decisions and the sharpness get "'foggier and less disciplined'" when teachers are battling "'fatigue,'" according to Neema Avashia, who teaches ethnic studies in the Boston Public Schools.

Decision fatigue—emotional fatigue—affects all of us, which is why teachers come home and sometimes just *can't* deal with one more decision. Simple questions like "What's for dinner?" or "Can you help me with this?" or "What do you want to do this weekend?" can spiral a teacher who's halfway through the school year, causing them to snap: "Stop asking me questions!" or "Figure it out yourself!"

Is this all of us? No, of course, not. But it's me, sometimes. I will pull into the driveway, take a deep breath,

WHEN WE ARE JUST ONE PERSON DEALING WITH SO MUCH EMOTIONAL INTENSITY, WE CAN LOSE OURSELVES IN THE COMPLEXITY...

*DECISION FATIGUE—EMOTIONAL FATIGUE—
AFFECTS ALL OF US...*

and tell myself that I am going to treat the next 10 minutes as if they are the most important 10 minutes of my day. I do this so I don't walk into the house smelling of fatigue. I want to shake it off and be the mom I want to be, even if I have to will myself to push through a tiring evening. Then, there are other times when I just can't play that strategy, and I walk into the house wishing I could take a nap or not talk to anyone. This is when trying to hold it together usually ends with me snapping or getting irritated.

My emotional fatigue was the most devastating when I was upholding high classroom standards, thinking that would save me from any criticisms or behavior issues, while also leaving the school day at 3:00 p.m. not having finished my work, so I could pick up my young children from childcare. I miss my kids being little. But I was also so bone-tired when they were little.

I would leave school at a code-red 15% energy level, knowing the mom I wanted to be for my children, just hoping I'd have it in me to show up and be that mom. I resented school sometimes because I had to expend so much energy to do it right, and then I'd have inadequate energy to give my own family or even myself. I remember rushing from school to childcare, sometimes hearing from the childcare about an incident that day, to race home to play and be a good mom. Then, it was making dinner, cleaning up, and getting ready for the next day to do it all again. After I put the kids to bed, I would do at least two hours of work to make up what I hadn't finished from, ironically, leaving on time because I was trying so hard to hold a high standard with school, knowing I could avoid many issues if I had it altogether in every aspect. Those afternoon and evening hours seemed to slip away like water through a wide sieve, and I just couldn't seem to catch up in any way. At the time, my husband worked two jobs—sometimes three—to help us financially. We were both doing what we could to keep all the plates spinning as evenly as possible.

There are single parents who are also teachers doing this every day. I can imagine being a teacher *and* being a single parent must be one of the most emotionally fatiguing jobs ever.

Through a lot of trial and error, I have figured out better ways of how to satisfy my need to be a *great* teacher with the *reality* of my overall life than just working, working, working, which is not sustainable. It doesn't matter that it's considered our job to teach and manage all these things and deliver day after day. The teacher's day could never end, if we allowed that. My goal in writing all of this is to share the message that teaching is an emotional profession and can be an emotionally fatiguing profession, if we don't see it the way it needs to be seen and protect ourselves. It deserves to be looked at as such because much of what we do has an emotional outcome.

I elaborate more in later chapters, but I had to go through the unhappier period of emotional fatigue to understand that teaching will do this to us if we aren't aware of the possibility. After realizing this, I worked to shift my emotional fatigue to empowerment. I am one person, just like all teachers. One person trying to be a *good* teacher and a *great* mom. When I feel the emotional fatigue presenting itself, I visualize my life as a teacher and my life as a mom, wife, and homeowner as competing tug-of-war athletes. You know the ribbon—it's usually red—that is tied to the middle of the tug-of-war rope that indicates when a team has won the game? Well, I imagine my life, sometimes, as a tug-of-war, and I try to keep that red ribbon tied on the rope as close to center as possible, with nothing powering over anything else. Some call this balance. Sometimes it's a battle, just like tug-of-war can be a battle.

I do this by saying no when I need to say no. I'm getting better at saying no, and it feels good to see that life goes on after I've said no. I don't always say no, but

I evaluate if I am able to do something extra, and I consider the reason why I would say yes. This has been an important skill development for me, given my natural inclination to want to please and have approval. I'll now evaluate committees, or student events at school, or coaching my kids' activities, or attending meetings for my kids' school, or hanging out with friends. I always want to say yes, and I do a better job now than I did years ago of first evaluating *why* I would say yes.

I ask my supervisor and my department chairperson for similar classes each year, so I can reuse materials and work to create a few new units or lessons each year.

I bring home take-out at least once a week, and I always try to have bagged salads in the fridge, so I don't eat only take-out that night. I get my clothes and jewelry ready before I go to bed, and I have lunches and bags packed by the door, so the mornings aren't stressful and chaotic. I get my kids ready for bed and then I sometimes go to bed because I know my emotional downfalls happen the most often when I'm tired.

I grade most things, but I don't grade all things. I give students time to write and time to create, so I can circulate and evaluate. I give students opportunities to lead, so I can listen.

I provide hard copy materials, just as I did years ago, not as a rejection to technology, but as a way of using

SOME CALL THIS BALANCE. SOMETIMES IT'S A BATTLE...

technology when it will serve me best and giving it a break when it can cause distraction.

It's all a trial and error, but I am much healthier now than years ago. I hope one day when my kids are older, I can circle back to those committees and student events and can do a lot more friend hangouts, because those have remained important to me, even if I am not currently in high-attendance.

This is when being a teacher can be difficult, because we believe in supporting and being integral parts of many aspects within our building, and we also know we can't do it all at school and at home. It's a tug-of-war sometimes, and it's best to try and keep that ribbon in the middle of the rope. No one's job is supposed to be 24-hour business. That is what teaching has become, and it is up to us to figure out where we want to see our own ribbon.

Balancing our emotional teaching lives may not always require such conscious effort, and then there are times in our careers when we have to work to balance ourselves. This can be hardest when we know painful student stories and when we experience our own painful stories.

KIDS' PAINS

When I have asked teachers who began their careers decades ago what they think the biggest change has been in education, almost all of them tell me, "The increased workload." As a follow-up question, I clarify: "Do you mean just in the actual work, like in assessing and planning?" They all return with an emphatic "No." I asked one individual, who has been teaching various history courses for 38 years in a district neighboring mine, to further explain. He resolved that, "Yes, just the sheer workload is more and there is more for teachers to do now, but the students are also different now. They are more needy, less independent, and more emotional, and teachers are asked to take care of it all."

I don't know precisely what has contributed to more students being emotionally fragile or more dependent, but the combination of many factors has placed teachers in a unique place of both social worker and teacher, which is a role that has fatigued many teachers and has been an unexpected part of the job.

Kids come to school with a lot of pain, distrust, and hurt. Kids act up because they are hurting. Hurt people hurt people, as the saying goes. For some of our students, the years that comprise their secondary education are some of the most painful years they will ever have in

> ## NO ONE'S JOB IS SUPPOSED TO BE 24-HOUR BUSINESS.

their lives. When our students struggle emotionally, it will show itself in the classroom. I try to keep this in mind when I have students who are withdrawn, nervous, and harder to reach. I try to place myself in their day to feel what it must be like, and also to remember that we are in a human service profession.

Deb Gordan[9], healthcare contributor for *Forbes* magazine, reports in her September 2022 article "The Kids Are Not All Right: New Report Shows Pediatric Mental Health Hospitalizations Rose 61%" that there have been "dramatic increases in utilization of acute mental health care. Hospitalizations among kids under age 19 increased 61% from 2016 to 2021, jumping from 20 admissions per 1,000 patients each year to 48 per 1,000 patients." She continues that the "biggest jump in hospitalizations was among teens ages 12 to 15, rising 84% among girls in this age group and 83% among boys."

Stats can be impersonal. For anyone teaching in today's classrooms, you know the students who fit these stats and you know how emotional it can be to teach students who are going through immense distress. When people are in constant emotional pain, such as depression, anxiety, anger, resentment, jealousy, loneliness, hate, or insecurity, they are not at their best and their nervous systems are in constant fight or flight mode. Their nervous systems are completely exhausted and so are they.

Some students are lonely, and they don't have a friend. The pain is deep, and they crush under the weight. Some students are anxious to the point where they can't get themselves into the school building, and any change in semester or schedule sets them teetering. Some students are insecure, and they insulate themselves, fearing eye contact with their peers or their teacher. Some students get sick, and they don't come back to school.

We know what it looks like for students to require serious help outside of the school environment, and it is scary for them and their families. It's also upsetting for the teachers closest to these students. We know what it means to be a mandatory reporter and to advocate for a student, while also not knowing what will happen to the student after we make the report.

KIDS COME TO SCHOOL WITH A LOT OF PAIN, DISTRUST, AND HURT.

Filing a mandatory report doesn't get easier the more one does it; in fact, from my experience, it gets cumulatively harder. We have our students for a short time, but sometimes their stories and their pain stay with us years and years later. My mind can drift to a student I had in my opening years—nearly twenty years ago now—and I'll wonder, "What ever happened to that kid and his family? How is he doing? I hope he's okay."

Even when no report needs to be made, the lives of some students are tragic and chaotic, and we as teachers, principals, and guidance counselors learn about the upsetting incidents our young students have endured. Some students live in group homes; some kids have sick parents or have parents who have died; some live with an aunt or grandparent because their parents couldn't keep them. Some kids have new stepsiblings, and they don't quite know how they feel about that yet. Some have a lot of trauma, and they live with trust issues, anger issues, and fear.

Sometimes I'll have a student approach me before class begins to ask, "Can I talk to you in the hallway?" I might learn that a close friend of hers is in danger or that a sibling was just diagnosed with a serious illness or that a grandparent has died. I don't take this story and plan of action on myself. I am simply the first part of the relay to getting the student a professional who can help, but my sensitive nature may struggle to let this student's pain go. These are the moments I feel for this young person carrying such a weight, and these are the moments I have to categorize the hurt and step back into the classroom to teach a full class waiting for me.

Knowing these stories—being brought into these stories—is an honor in that we can help support the student. It doesn't mean the stories aren't heavy for the teacher to carry. Some stories are so sad that they can stay with us long after the school day is over. Stories I heard over 10 years ago are still in my mind. Those students are well into adulthood now, but they are forever 15-year-olds to me and struggling under an unfair burden. As teachers, we can do and handle pretty much anything. But there is an accumulation effect of sadness and confusion when we hear stories of heartbreak.

Teachers didn't always hear these stories and they weren't always brought into students' personal lives. The ways in which students see teachers is different than how students saw teachers 30 years ago. This all contributes to the emotional fatigue of teaching because we are both supporter and teacher, content-deliverer and nurturer. The roles can get demanding.

From myself and from thousands of other teachers, I know we wouldn't want it any other way. We want to show up for our students and for our work in more ways than

> KNOWING THESE STORIES—BEING BROUGHT INTO THESE STORIES—IS AN HONOR IN THAT WE CAN HELP SUPPORT THE STUDENT. IT DOESN'T MEAN THE STORIES AREN'T HEAVY FOR THE TEACHER TO CARRY.

pushing content. That doesn't mean, though, that we are adequately prepared to emotionally support *and* teach our students. Trying to maintain all of this and do it right contributes to a teacher's sense of "I am just one person."

I know I have felt this. In the last five years alone, I have had more students talk to me about situations in their lives, ranging from heartbreak to grief to insecurity to homelessness, than I've had in the previous 15 years combined. It makes me feel good knowing I can be a safe starting point for a student—to listen without judgment— and that I can be part of the process of connecting them with the professionals in the building who can offer help. This makes me feel like my personality is serving exactly as it is supposed to; yet it is emotionally challenging when I have a heavy conversation or need to make a phone call to the Childline Office to report an incident of abuse or neglect, and then within minutes, I am greeting a group of 25 students filing into my classroom for fourth period. There isn't much time to reflect, think, or shake it off. Over time, this can result in feeling both gratitude and emotional heaviness. I sometimes drive home trying to simplify the complexity, baffled about how much happened in a single school day. I'll ask an unanswerable question: "How did it come to be that so much expectation is on teachers, when each teacher is 'just one person'?"

UNEXPECTED GRIEF

Then, the worst of it. Despite any training or attempt at preparation, nothing will ready teachers for when they lose a student. When a current or former student dies, there is a distinct strangeness and pain that is difficult to explain to others outside of education. This student isn't your family. This student isn't your friend. But they were your student. You shared space with them, interacted with them daily, watched them grow, saw them, and encouraged them. Now, they are no longer here. They are gone, and the potential and hope for what they would have been never materialized. Their empty desk, or when thinking about them sitting in your classroom, leaves a lingering feeling in one's spirit.

I have lost five former students at the writing of this book, and I've only taught half a career. One was especially painful. I adored this student, and we had such a good relationship. I was an integral part of building her up while she reset her life. We spent a lot of study halls together. She shared her poetry with me and the essays she wrote for her English classes. She was such a thoughtful writer. We laughed over funny greeting cards I'd buy at Walmart. She showed me funny comic strips she'd find online. She told me I was the first person who believed she could do something important because she could write and because she was a deep thinker. After she graduated, it was hard to keep in reciprocal contact.

She took her life when she was 23. I don't know why or what happened to her after high school graduation. Getting that email was a crush to my entire spirit. I heard she died in the late evening. I can remember exactly where I was when I read the email. My eyes darted through it, shocked at first, hoping I had read the name incorrectly. I remember getting up and walking downstairs like a normal person, as if I hadn't just read this sad, strange, unexpected news. My daughter, a baby at the time, was napping on my husband, who lay on the couch. It was dark outside, and the TV was on low. I went into the kitchen, aimless, and then came back into the living room and said, "I just read my email, and, well, do you remember the girl at school who I used to spend a lot of time with? She died."

What do you do with that information after you read it in an email that was sent to all staff? Our jobs are so personal and so emotional, but we can't get *that* personal or *that* emotional, so we end up hearing tragic news in an email. I understand why we hear it in an email, but it also doesn't seem to fit. If it were my family member, I'd get a phone call or I'd be with the person. Same for a friend. A student? It's in an email because that is what makes the most systemic sense. And at the same time, it doesn't make any sense at all.

The next day, I taught my classes trying to be "on," but my heart wasn't in it, and my pretending didn't get me very far. The students I had at that time didn't know this person. She had graduated years before they even came to the school. I didn't have it in me to spend energy explaining why I was upset about a student I had many years before, whom I hadn't even spoken with for half a decade. I guess I thought it would be easier if I didn't talk about it than to try and explain it. I was in a strange limbo.

When students die, even former students, it causes a difficult-to-explain feeling of loss for the teacher. Grief is experienced just as grief would be experienced for something else. To reduce this person as "just our student" is insensitively unfair, but as teachers we don't know how to be a part of the loss. It causes us to move on from the grief perhaps a bit faster than we should, even though it all stays in us somewhere.

These things happen. Teachers in the profession can share these stories, and they can feel their pain—pain from their job. The job is hard, and can become even harder when the teacher, who is human and is just one person, has personal stresses. The teacher gives, but, when is in need, may not always get back what she gives. Some examples make my heart heavy. No one is to blame. It's just the way the system is, for now anyway. Yet, I have hope that progressive conversations will change some of the landscape.

TEACHERS' PAINS

The teacher's day of giving and being amongst a lot of need doesn't stop, even when the teacher has a life-stopping circumstance.

Some teachers enter their school day holding grief and stress on their shoulders, but they must put on a brave face because the show must go on. They can't hide or quit or not show up. Each person in the classroom is relying on the teacher to arrive and to deliver.

One of the worst examples I have ever witnessed of managing life with teaching occurred years ago when I worked with a teacher so sick with cancer she struggled to walk in the hallways. This teacher was always friendly and thoughtful, asking how you were doing or giving a complimentary word, even as she faced the defeat of cancer.

She had a teenage daughter and was the only person in her daughter's life who could provide financial support and medical benefits. So, she made the brave and dauntless decision to show up and to teach for as long as she could. She did a heroic job and is still someone I consider a leader.

She died about a week after she couldn't come to school anymore.

O O O

Teachers come to school in pain or in distress. Teachers have depression and anxiety, too. Teachers have spouses who get sick or pass. Teachers go through divorces or have difficult home lives. Teachers take care of the children in their classes all day, and then take care of aging parents into the night. Teachers have kids who get sick or go through a crisis. Teachers having problems and still having to deliver is nothing new. But it is fatiguing and emotionally daunting with sometimes no light at the end of a very long tunnel.

I know these things happen to all professionals everywhere. It is not isolated to teachers.

> *THE TEACHER GIVES, BUT, WHEN IS IN NEED, MAY NOT ALWAYS GET BACK WHAT SHE GIVES.*

Teachers have an energy-filled job that is fully reliant upon them. Thankfully, there are substitutes, but that is a short-term solution. Just like a parent in a household, no one can, in an instant, replace the classroom teacher and start the next day on the back of the day before. Teachers' jobs are demanding and high-energy, even when life gets big.

Teachers going through a crisis prepare lesson plans from hospital rooms and doctors' offices to keep their school life going because what else are they going to do? They may need to for financial stability or because they know being in school is easier than being out of school, as many of us say when we attempt to make lesson plans for a substitute. Teachers grade in doctors' waiting rooms. They talk to colleagues on the phone while they sit with their sick loved ones in the hospital.

Teachers delay important appointments and try to accept appointments during their planning period or after 3:30 p.m.

I am not discounting any professional whose job does not stop because of a life event, and my intention is not to have a comparison-competition amongst professions. Systemically, as a culture, there are problems with the demands of our work when we are not well. We can only be in balance when all parts of our lives are going well and easy. Something isn't right about that.

It may seem like teachers should rely on colleagues to pick up exactly where they left off, so they could return to school when it's right for them. But it's not like that, at least not in most cases.

For one, the teacher has, per the system, been the dominant leader in the classroom. Now the leader is not there. Teachers also don't always teach in teams. There isn't a free team of teachers who can simply pick up that teacher's caseload and schedule. Their colleagues are teaching their own classes and balancing their own days. To step into someone else's work is possible, and we do it for our colleagues because we want to support them, but it's a challenge, nonetheless.

The teacher could say, "I am not available, and I'll catch everyone up when I get back." But that leaves groups of students with an open period each day. Where do these students go? Are they able to stay cooperative? Are they safe and monitored? It brings up a lot of potential problems.

Thus, the teacher who really should be focused on his life is now also focusing on lesson planning, communicating, setting up, and figuring out.

One more item: in most school districts, as per their state's guidelines, teachers get three days of paid "grief leave" as I'll put it. Your spouse dies. It's October. You get *three days* of paid time off. I understand this may be more than other professionals get or it may be par for the course of most professions. It just stinks. Anyone, despite where they work, would probably agree.

While I wasn't shocked, I was saddened when I heard someone lament that she was thankful her mom passed in the summer, because then at least she could manage everything with her mom without also managing school.

One teacher I "met" in an online forum shared that his health had gotten so bad from a reaction to mold he may have developed from his classroom, that he had to resign his teaching position. He could not maintain the doctors' appointments, chronic fatigue, and joint pain with teaching full days. I know of others who experience serious life events, and they just can't manage the life crisis *and* teaching. So, they resign.

To be snarky, is it true, then, that only the most robust and luckiest of us can reach a teaching career that spans three or more decades?

Each teacher is just one person managing *a lot*. All of this is what drives some teachers away from teaching. I argue that we don't necessarily have a shortage of teachers because teachers don't want to enter the profession, or because they want to leave the profession.

I argue that we have a *teacher emotional support problem*. This emotional support problem has caused teachers to leave, or to never begin, or to resign before they intended.

One progressive way school districts can improve teacher emotional support is to offer an assistance program for teachers, called TAP. Many schools, including mine, have a Student's Assistance Program (SAP) or some variation of student support within the school building, which works to mediate conflicts and provide students with crucial mental health support during the school day. SAP is for students. TAP—Teacher's Assistance Program—is for teachers. I want to acknowledge that schools and businesses have the Employee Assistance Program (EAP), but that requires employees to call and to determine services. TAP would be in school buildings and would provide direct counselors for teachers within the school day.

Some teachers are in abusive relationships, or are going through divorce, or have financial stress, or have aging parents, or have children who have special needs, or have depression, or have anxiety. Teachers are people, too. Finding a mental health professional or seeking advice about tough life stuff is not always top on the list of things to do for teachers because of everything else they are managing and because of the rigid schedule in which we work.

TAP would make a significant positive shift in teacher mental health. These mental health professionals would offer immediate support and connections to teachers that would alleviate teacher overwhelm, and they would be available within the teacher's school day.

This is progressive for education, I agree, and would require a complete shift in how communities and schools support teachers. But it's not so progressive when we consider how our world has changed and progressed and how teachers can feel overwhelmed by their jobs and lives. Wouldn't it be appealing to teacher candidates if districts could boast on their employment page about the unique ways in which they nurture and care for their teachers by placing teachers' emotional health as a priority?

Providing mental health professionals to teachers and having these professionals interlaced within the school system sends the message that school leaders hold their teachers' mental health as a priority. School leaders want healthy teachers. When teachers are healthy and feeling well, there are fewer sick days used; teachers are less stressed and more content; there is a higher overall morale; and teachers are seen as valuable.

I think the majority of our administrators and school leaders truly want us to prioritize our needs and take care of ourselves and our families. I believe they care about us. I know my administration does. I believe school leaders are trying to acknowledge the difficulty teachers have in balancing their lives in and out of school. But the education system is not set up to actually *support* this, and, so far, the majority of school districts continue to offer what they are required to offer without being able to do much else.

So, for teachers—and many other professionals—it turns into: "I'm so sorry for your crisis. Please take care of yourself. Communicate with your colleagues, students, and families about your classes and lesson plans. We will figure out coverage, until you get back." The care and condolence is there *along with* the expectation that the work is maintained and communicated.

When there are no solutions to the big stuff that happens in a teacher's life, the teacher ends up trying to balance the big stuff and the school life, while also immersed in grief and worry. That is overwhelming for just one person.

This causes teachers to scoff at the concept of a work-life balance or in rolling eyes when anyone

WHEN TEACHERS ARE HEALTHY AND FEELING WELL, THERE ARE FEWER SICK DAYS USED; TEACHERS ARE LESS STRESSED AND MORE CONTENT; THERE IS A HIGHER OVERALL MORALE; AND TEACHERS ARE SEEN AS VALUABLE.

preaches self-care as *the* solution to teacher stress. I appreciate advocates telling teachers to "take a bath, get a massage, watch a TV show, go for a walk, or eat well" because they are at least recognizing that the teaching profession is taxed, and teachers need to attempt a balance within their lives. I love these self-care ideas and I relish when I get to do them in my own life. These would be more effective if there were *also* a modification to the stress of the day, but that comes from administration and school district leaders, not from self-care advocates. The teacher's mind is fatigued, her emotions are stretched, and her overwhelm is high. Being told to get more sleep will help to calm these feelings, but it will not solve the actual problems.

The balance, instead, comes in the summer when teachers have time to focus on big ticket items. The scales aren't balanced though. It's more of a game of averages. Any balance comes in waking up even earlier to exercise or meditate, or in staying up even later to catch up on that show or read. The balance comes in scheduling time to talk to a spouse or to play with children. Items get put on the backburner until a better time to deal with them.

Being just one person means it's on us, no matter what is happening in our classroom lives or in our personal lives. It also means we get the gift of being *the one* who can change the trajectory of a student's life.

GRATEFUL

I am lucky to have many examples of students and families who have appreciated me as their teacher and who have allowed me the experience of being just one person who can make an enormous difference in another's life. One such instance stands out clearly to me when I was told by a mom that I was the reason her child came to school and stayed in school. When people say things like "If you only reach one person, you're doing your job just right," it can be difficult to value the impact you're having when others resist you. But truly, there is nothing more right than this statement.

Before graduation that school year, this mom asked me to meet her near the school. She hugged me so tight, and we stood together with tears in our eyes as she told me that her son was alive and would be graduating because I had been the teacher he wanted to see each day. "You were the reason he even showed up," she had told me, and she ended with "We will never forget you!"

How could I care about student eye rolls or scoffs or disengagement when I knew I was part of saving a person's life? Those other instances fade and become the color of gray in a dense fog, absorbed into nothingness.

I served. I helped. I gave. And I did it by being me and I did it for someone who needed me.

Yes, I'm just one person and I feel all the stresses and emotional fatigues of teaching. I also feel all the joys and complications and happinesses and gratitudes, too.

This happens when I think about my favorite teaching moments, knowing that being just one person can make so many others feel good in their day. I'm just one person who gets to introduce students to many experiences and life conversations. Some of my favorites being when we have "expert panel," which doesn't happen all the time, but usually a spontaneous moment in class when students are shining in their wisdom about something we've read or have been doing, and we quickly get a few desks organized into a panel, and suddenly we are running expert panel, and this kid or these kids sit there taking questions and comments from the other students in the audience as if it's a post-game interview. Students feel great when they get swooped into being in the expert panel.

In a similar fashion, students offer intelligent, wise-beyond-their-years thoughts, and every now and then "Wise Words by _____" lands on my board and then more and more students try to get a quote on the board.

I love when I take a walk through the hallways and, in that short time, I can have 10+ students give me an exuberant "Hi!" and be genuinely happy to see me. How lucky and how blessed!

Or when I'm just one person, but I celebrate my students in S.A.D., which for me is Student Appreciation Day, and I bring in snacks and candy and we play games, and I tell students "That on this S.A.D., I'd like to thank you for all your hard work and attentiveness and giving to our classroom space." I always have a student enjoy the acronym not at all inferring what is actually happening, and students leave my room feeling seen and loved.

I think about when I make students write two drafts of an essay before they can give it to me, which they abhor, but then I sit with each student as they praise themselves on how well they've done and improved. Or when I print out a student's writing pieces from September and compare it with the writing pieces in January. Often, I'll catch the student looking admiringly at the differences after I've walked away. Or when we talk philosophy through literature, and students start thinking about human nature and what it means to navigate growing up, and I see lots of arms in the air. I love lots of arms in the air. I wish I could freeze those moments. Or when I have upperclassmen pop into my room and say, "I miss it in here! This was my favorite class!"

I love when I introduce poetry, and the majority of students go "*OH, God!* Poetry?" And then within a week, I have student after student visiting me in study hall to share with me their beautiful and personal poems about life, love, loss, and growing up. I tell them they are genius, masterful, and should absolutely not deny themselves the depth of their written word.

I'll smile as I drive home, remembering how I had my fun music booming—music from the 1900s, as my students never forget to remind me—and I'm singing and dancing and then a teacher comes in from the hallway, singing and dancing, and then sometimes, just sometimes, I'll have a class or a student or a group of students also start singing and dancing. The energy in the room feels *good*, fun, ready, and positive, all because I have chosen, despite some hard teaching moments, to enjoy my day and to spread that to as many as I can. I'll smile knowing it's not likely ninth graders would start dancing in the room if it weren't for that room being a most comfortable and positive space.

I'll laugh recounting stories to my family or colleagues about some funny thing that happened in class that day or how some of my students are so funny and are just absolutely enjoyable to be around. I will smile, reflecting on the moment earlier in the day when a student left exclaiming, "That was so much fun. I loved our class today!"

There are so many more examples of gratitude. Some are so small they are only meaningful to us, and some are so big they get noted in newsletters. It doesn't matter the degree. They all matter.

I'm just one person. You are just one person. I've felt the overwhelm and the difficulty, and I've felt the triumph and the gratitude. It's not easy to balance it all with grace and sensibility when we are just one. Sometimes teaching can feel great. Sometimes teaching can feel painful. That's the truth of teaching. I don't know if it can be summed much better, but I do know I am so appreciative of the positive moments because I know how tough the tough moments can feel, especially when they come as a surprise or when they come at us in waves, and we feel overwhelmed and alone.

CRYING. IN CLASS.

SIMMERING

The weight of teaching and being just one person can be enough to make teachers highly emotional. It might be enough to make them angry or cry.

Sometimes students have trouble controlling their talking in class, and they are so enrapt with socializing that they talk the day away. They talk through you, over you, alongside you. They simply won't stop talking, and they, therefore, can't listen to directions or the intent of the lesson.

It's especially tough when there are a lot of students like this in one class period. After 15 minutes of showing step-by-step guides, models, and plans, these students will go: "Wait. What are we doing? I'm so confused." It's unnerving, and it takes a lot of energy to stay patient

> THE WEIGHT OF TEACHING AND BEING JUST ONE PERSON CAN BE ENOUGH TO MAKE TEACHERS HIGHLY EMOTIONAL. IT MIGHT BE ENOUGH TO MAKE THEM ANGRY OR CRY.

with this each day. It's challenging to teach through these behaviors, and to maintain composure for the sake of the students who do track you the entire time.

I had a student who would recognize when I had things under control and then start rapping just to disrupt the class or to get attention. If he wasn't rapping, he'd turn to anyone near him and say, "Yo, look at this video," and then laugh really loud.

An outsider could think he was being playful or just wanted some attention. When these considerations are given, and the behavior continues or gets worse, the classroom teacher can feel even more walked on and stressed, as I did.

When working with that student, I thought about "behavior is communication." I reasoned with him, and asked him privately, "What is making you rap when I am talking? What is making you want to interrupt the flow of the class when we are about to start something? Is there something you need that I am not giving you in here?" Asking these questions with this student only seemed to amplify the behavior, and that made me feel more out of control and weaker.

When students continually misuse our classroom space for *any* personal gain, and are unable to redirect, it leaves the teacher feeling helpless and defeated. Over time, this creates fatigue and frustration.

It's way too easy to tell the teacher to brush it off or not to care. Most human beings are unable to blow things off that easily. If teachers were able to do this, we would not hear teachers protesting over student behaviors or quitting their jobs. Teachers, I argue, can do the hard work of teaching. They don't want to do all the hard work of teaching while also playing the losing game of behavior management.

Trying to keep off-track energy managed while teaching is sometimes just as hard as trying to get students to engage and actually talk in class.

Some of the hardest classes I've ever had included students who walk in looking miserable. They walk right past me, making no eye contact as I greet them with a cheerful "Good morning!" Having a class full of students who claim they have no interests, no hobbies, no extracurricular involvement, and no job interest is so very hard. The energy is flat and uncomfortable, and they don't even talk to each other, let alone to me as the

> [TEACHERS] DON'T WANT TO DO ALL THE HARD WORK OF TEACHING WHILE ALSO PLAYING THE LOSING GAME OF BEHAVIOR MANAGEMENT.

teacher. Sometimes this type of class includes students who refuse to do work or refuse to move into groups or engage in the planned activity.

I once created my personal version of an activity called "Character on Trial," with scripted roles and a pre-designed structure. It took me two weeks to plan, with most of my preparation time at school as well as some time at home dedicated to organizing step-by-step structures, so all students could feel confident doing this activity. It went awesome with my second period class, and many students "fought" over who could have which role. Students in that class asked me if we could do the whole thing again with another literature piece and a different character, so that students who couldn't be a lead would get the chance to be a lead. "Wow!" I thought, "This is amazing, and I'll do this every month if they love it so much!" Some students even brought in props from home! It was inspiring to observe students research, plan arguments, practice tone, and perfect interrogating a witness, like courtroom lawyers. One student "lawyer" even came into school wearing a shirt, tie, and suit jacket—for his English class! I was so honored!

I gave this same activity, all directions and suggestions, to my first period class, and, aside from the time of the day, the class was the same grade level and academic level. I thought by having the step-by-step breakdown and attainable directions I'd be able to get half the class with me to generate some energy. Nope. It was an utter failure. Most students refused roles, refused groups, and wouldn't consider speaking out loud. Not every student in the class acted this way, but the majority did, and it made it impossible to pull off the activity. In hindsight, I wonder if I should have even tried something like that with how that first period class acted. But then I'd be left in the middle of a tough philosophical question: Do you deny *all* students in a class a possible experience because of the resistance of some, or even most? I don't have a clear answer to this, as sometimes things turn out better than expected, and other times it is a predictable response of, "Yup. Already knew it was going to be that way."

I expend more energy in classrooms that are stiff and uncomfortable or won't engage. I try to be overly enthusiastic, loud, energized, and interesting, just to change the personality and culture of that room. I spend most of my time working to build relationships to get students to at least try the lesson planned for the day. Often, the efforts fall flat and can make me feel deflated. Day after day of that kind of acting and overextending is exhausting, and I leave school at 3:15 p.m. at a code-red energy level having used up all my energy. Sometimes I think, "And I did all of that and gave all of that for what?"

It's amazing how the overly talkative class period and the completely silent class period can be so equally hard. When I experience a quiet class, I'll find myself wishing I had people talking, even over me. When I experience an off-task class, I find myself wishing they would just give me five minutes to get through something without interruption. In both extremes, I find myself racing, hustling, over-working to make things go well. No wonder I'm in low-battery mode by the end of the day.

It can also be just as difficult to manage students who hardly ever have their materials, don't have a charged computer, or who require you to sit next to them to complete every sentence in an essay or on a test, or else it won't get done. Sometimes you want to scream, "JUST WRITE THE SENTENCE!" "CHARGE YOUR COMPUTER THE NIGHT BEFORE!" "PLEASE... PLEASE STOP TALKING!!!" "PLEASE, WILL SOMEONE SAY SOMETHING? ANYTHING?!"

In one school day, I can feel all over the place and have emotional swings that feel like whiplash. I can feel all of this even in a single class period, given the many varieties of students that comprise one class. Trying to hold all of that together, bottle it up, and shove it far down for the sake of a controlled presentation or teaching lesson, especially for those kids who are causing no problems at all and deserve a quality education, is exhausting, and it has its accumulated effect.

I can feel that teacher-guilt when I think about some classes as a whole and realize it's hard for me to give the proper attention to the quiet, cooperative students. Some of these students never raise their hands and never ask for help. They do good work and always follow the directions, but they don't get much personal attention, if any, because I am overburdened by too much stimulus in other places. The right attention isn't always placed in the right places.

It is in these times, I think to myself: I was expecting so much more from this profession, and I need much more from this profession. The day can become something to dread, instead of something to look forward to.

BOILING

This is when teachers cry. Sometimes even in class. There is a building of stress and unsettling that causes deep, deep overwhelm in this emotional profession. There is the one thing that boils all the water over the pot. Perhaps it's that student acting out *again*. Perhaps it's unnecessary attitude from a student. Perhaps it's uncooperation in an activity. Perhaps it's a criticizing email from a parent. Perhaps something is changing that you don't want to change, and you have no control over it. Perhaps you carry something from home into your teaching day, and the emotional bags are just too heavy to carry on that day.

Something happens that adds a layer to all that has already been layered. And, you cry. Or you become angry. Sometimes I cry when I'm angry. The emotions of frustration are too big and they come pouring out of my eyes as if I'm sad or distraught, when, really, I'm angry.

I cried on the way home when my course schedule was changing for the following school year from teaching mostly eleventh grade classes to teaching all ninth grade classes. I had nothing against ninth graders or the course I was being moved to. I was most excited about being part of the welcoming committee for our newest high school students, a role I knew I'd be good at, given my enthusiastic and warm demeanor. I was upset because I was at the end of my sixth year of teaching, and I had already taught a lot of courses, but that eleventh grade course was the one consistent course I taught. I had *finally*, I felt, gotten to the point

> ...THE EMOTIONAL BAGS ARE JUST TOO HEAVY TO CARRY...

where years of crafting my resources and modifying my materials and plans had brought me to a confidence in teaching. I felt so good in my teaching and in my materials that my certainty as a teacher was growing exponentially. Colleagues were using my resources or complimenting me on my materials, which made me even more self-assured. I was doing it! I was doing this teaching thing after some painful experiences, and then, bam, major course change.

A lot of teachers change courses or grade levels each school year. Some handle it better than others, and some aren't even affected by it. Some see it as a new adventure and look forward to journeying into new content with different types of students.

Me? I cried on the way home, and when I got home. I cried when I found out about all the new work ahead of me and when I realized I'd no longer be teaching some of my favorite pieces. I was sad when I gave away the course materials that had taken me years to develop and when I gave student projects to colleagues to use as models. Part of me was glad it would all be reused. Part of me was disappointed. Part of me was tired. Part of me felt used. Part of me was nervous. Part of me felt this was yet another unexpected teacher challenge.

Despite these feelings, two special gifts came out of this change, for which I will be forever grateful.

One of my best friends in all of life also teaches the ninth grade level at my school. What cemented our friendship early on was our shared experiences as newer teachers and her willingness to take me under her wing as I learned a whole new set of standards and materials. If I had never moved to this grade level, I do not think I would have become as close as I am with this friend. The decision to move me was the end of me teaching a certain curriculum, but it was the beginning of a most treasured and precious friendship, and I have been so lucky.

Second, it is a special honor to watch ninth graders mature into seniors and then graduate the school. Watching a person grow from the beginning of a school journey to the end of a school journey is a special privilege that not every teacher gets to experience. When I had the chance to experience ninth graders graduate as seniors, I was moved as I stood with colleagues at graduation that year with my participating graduation ensemble on. I had these students as *kids* and now they were *adults*, heading out into their exciting, brave lives. I realized then that I was truly part of a vulnerable and unique journey, though ninth graders can be challenging sometimes.

Even if circumstances have their way of working out, or even if teachers are willing to see the bright side, changes can still be enough to set the emotions to boil, just as can some student's words. I left school one afternoon literally mumbling aloud to myself about the ludicrous events we go through and if the job were worth all the stress and pain. What caused this? When I was pointed at in front of a classroom of students and called "a fucking closet bitch." That one set me off, and as I drove home, I willed myself to let it go. I almost made it home, but then I started crying, unable to accept that it hadn't bothered me deeply.

I squeezed the steering wheel in frustration on the way home after a particularly trying day when hardly a student had their prepared rough draft completed and my lesson plan went to hell and each class was uncooperative.

I sat in sad silence on the way home when I learned a kind and thoughtful student was being abused at home, now understanding why this student would sit closer to me during study hall and tell me how much she liked my classroom and how it seemed like a home.

I sat in defeated silence on the way home when I reasoned to myself that I feel more like a "tryer" than a "teacher," and I wondered how many more years I could endure just being a tryer when I actually wanted to be a teacher. I remember trying to explain some of this to my best and deepest friend during one of our BFF chats on my way home, and her telling me, "You know, Diane, you sound so tired. I don't think I've ever heard you sound so tired."

> *IF YOU HAVE CRIED IN CLASS, IN THE BATHROOM, IN THE LUNCHROOM, IN A FRIEND'S CLASSROOM, ON THE WAY TO OR FROM SCHOOL, OR TO YOUR PARTNER AT HOME, YOU ARE NOT ALONE.*

I was—tired. And bothered. And overwhelmed. And not at all understanding how teaching was such a surprise from what I thought it would be.

If you have cried in class, in the bathroom, in the lunchroom, in a friend's classroom, on the way to or from school, or to your partner at home, you are not alone. You. Are. Not. Alone. I safely bet that all teachers at some point or another have cried or have felt so angry because of this job that was supposed to be so good and so rewarding, not so overwhelming and painful.

As already shared, I have cried over my teaching job in my car, in my house, (almost) in a principal's office. And, I have cried *in* class twice.

BOILED OVER

The less embarrassing time I cried in class was in front of a group of 15-year-olds early in my teaching career. I was behind in my work and didn't have time to read a rather long story before class. I had no other choice but to finish the story alongside the students. As I approached the end, my eyes raced ahead, and my heart pounded. No. The author didn't kill the boy. Why?! Why would the author let this sweet, loyal boy die? I was shocked and saddened by the insensitivity and loss of hope and potential. The shock of the story was so surprising that I cried.

The students sitting in front of me were shocked. The realization that I was crying spread through the room quietly, but with stunned intensity as each one of those students stared at me in disbelief and helplessness. I'm sure they were thinking, "Why is she crying? Did something happen?" I stumbled through telling them that the story is so sad, and that I wasn't expecting the ending.

One kid spoke up and asked, "Have you never read this before?" I said, "No, I haven't, and I thought I could fake it in here today because I'm so behind on my work and I'm so tired." Confessing this and bringing it to the surface just made me cry harder. What a disaster I'd become!

As I tried to gather myself, I heard some of the students say things like, "Oh, Mrs. Manser, the story is sad, and it's okay to cry. I cry, too." and "Do you want us to do something for you?" What kind, thoughtful, understanding students.

The story was the catalyst for the crying. But it wasn't the only reason I was crying. I was tired. So tired. I was stressed, and I was behind in my work, which was why I had no idea the boy died at the end of the story. I was sad about the boy. I was sad about myself. I was sad about how hard teaching was, and how nobody seemed to get it. I was sad that I saw teachers leave at 3:00 p.m. without papers in their bag, while I lost night after night of sleep lesson planning and grading. I was sad that I felt so out of control, and I was sad thinking I'd never figure out this teaching job.

I felt like a little childish baby crying with all those eyes looking at me, stupefied and helpless. At least they didn't laugh, I reasoned. Thank God they are nice and understanding and see me as a human, having a moment.

I calmed myself down and was able to teach the rest of the class. Before the period ended, I teased the students that they'd better bring in more tissue boxes the next day because tomorrow's story was even sadder. I was only joking, but it helped to ease the room. I thanked them for being so mature and understanding, and I apologized for being a mess. I promised there would be a reset to Mrs. Manser the next day.

A teacher crying in class goes right back to "behavior is communication." I was communicating that I was stressed and overwhelmed and completely at a loss for how to manage workload like a tsunami overtaking me with waves of powerful water pushing me under. My communication was, "*Please*. Someone, help me. What do I do?"

Sometimes the work becomes overwhelming and drowning and the stress is thick. When lesson planning collides with grading and grading collides with reports and reports collide with communication home and communication home collides with getting students who are failing into study hall, it can feel like there couldn't be enough time in a day to get it all done properly. I have seen veteran teachers come into lunch with five minutes to spare looking frazzled and stressed because they just can't get out from under the workload. "Where have you been?" someone will ask. "I just couldn't get it all done in my prep period, so I needed to work over lunch," the teacher will say. "I still didn't finish. I have classes all afternoon, and I don't know when I'll get it all done."

This isn't just an overwhelming situation for new teachers. Veteran teachers—who have been teaching similar contents for years and years—are saying these things. Do you know how many times I have heard teachers say when they are feeling especially unsettled and stressed that they wished they had a cubicle job, so they could come in, do their work, and not have to play pretend games while feeling on fire on the inside? A lot. A lot of times.

Teachers wouldn't be making comments like this if the job were easy and if they weren't emotionally affected by teaching, which is an emotional profession. Teachers make these comments because they realize they have no escape when they feel tough feelings, and they don't have a choice to show up or not to show up. They must show back up. They must do the work. The job is a lot, and we must recognize what we need to do for ourselves to manage it better, so we don't boil over and feel out of control, which is what happened in this instance and in the more affecting time I cried in class.

This time (and the last time) I cried was during my fourth year of teaching in front of 17-year-olds—that eleventh grade course I so loved. Some of these students had beards and were six months away from voting for the first time, and they witnessed their adult teacher lose it and cry right in front of them.

I was fighting such resistance in that particular class, and the students were not cooperative. They were harsh and mean—to me and to each other. Each day was a new unpleasant challenge, and it seemed they came to school just to mess around or to mess with me. I dreaded that period before the period even started. I'd lose sleep over it, and the feeling of that class crept in on me at all times of the day.

This day was like way too many other days. Some students were disengaged, some were arguing with me over what I was teaching, some had their heads down, some were sarcastically telling me this class was "so worth their time," and others were embarrassed by their peers' behaviors and were cowering smaller in their desks.

After minutes of trying to get everyone's attention to no positive movement, the frustration and anger bubbled up in my chest. I lost control. It was the first time, and the only time since, I have ever yelled at a class. It didn't feel good in the moment, it definitely didn't feel good in the moments after, and it doesn't feel good now admitting the story.

I slammed my hands on my desk, and as the sting reverberated through my palms, I shouted, "THIS IS THE WORST CLASS...*EVER*! STOP TALKING! WOULD YOU JUST STOP TALKING?! IS IT EVEN POSSIBLE FOR YOU TO LISTEN? YOU ARE THE WORST CLASS I'VE EVER HAD AND YOU ARE AN AWFUL CLASS TO BE WITH! STOP BEING THE WORST!" My face was bright red as I yelled, and my cheeks quivered with anger. My voice was shrill and high and strained, and I felt my chest, neck, and face hot with uncontrolled emotion.

For seconds, the room quieted, and everyone stared at me, shocked. Then a group of boys looked at me, looked at each other, and laughed. One even pointed at me as he laughed, and then corralled his friends across the room to mock my misery. What the serious hell? The yelling was such a surprise fit of emotion, followed by the bitter embarrassment of being laughed at, that I cried.

I was crying from anger and frustration. I was crying from indignation. I was crying from shame. I was crying for feeling weak and embarrassed. I was crying because teaching is an emotional profession, and I hadn't yet seen it from that angle.

I was crying because they absolutely bested me. I was crying because they knew it, and they enjoyed it.

It was like a 1980's movie scene when the high school girl is bullied and finally steps up, only for it to turn on her worse than if she had kept taking the bullying.

The moments after weren't pretty, as if the moments before were pretty. I'm embarrassed to confess this story, but I share it to illustrate that teaching can make us act

> I WAS CRYING FROM ANGER AND FRUSTRATION. I WAS CRYING FROM INDIGNATION. I WAS CRYING FROM SHAME. I WAS CRYING FOR FEELING WEAK AND EMBARRASSED. I WAS CRYING BECAUSE TEACHING IS AN EMOTIONAL PROFESSION, AND I HADN'T YET SEEN IT FROM THAT ANGLE.

and think in ways we'd never expect. I threatened those students through tears still coming and through an attempt to wipe tears on tissues with, "Oh sure, laugh and disrespect me. Maybe I will fail you, and then you can do this all over again next year when you're a senior. Then *I'll* be laughing. I already passed high school. You're the ones who still have to do this."

It wasn't pretty. Not at all. I negated any attempt I had made to build a mature role-model reputation with that class, like an enormous balloon popped and swirling wildly through the air into an open window and plopping deflated and useless on the ground. Those students brought out the worst in me and caused me to behave like an immature child looking to force my anger on those in front of me and seeking to take them down with me.

But they weren't taken down with me. They didn't care about my words. My words and my threats only made them mock more. "Yeah right! You can't fail us. Just try and do that and see what will happen to you," they retorted. Just like with the coffee student, my emotions got the better of me, and the group I was going against was way more powerful than I was. I stood there, defeated and embarrassed, with some of the class looking at me like "What are you going to do now?"

Still angry and ashamed, I left the room and stood by myself for a couple of minutes deep breathing with my hands on my knees and feeling tremendously unsure what was going to happen to me afterwards. Would these students ever consider coming back around with me, or was I going to have situations like this for the rest of the school year? Were parents going to call me, demanding I explain why I lost it in front of their students?

How do you recover from something like that? How do you continue teaching that class? How do you graciously go forward with the rest of your day? Sure, having a come-to-Jesus, *Full House* conversation in that classroom is probably the best option, but that only works when the receiving party is open and compassionate. I wasn't going to get that from those 17-year-old boys who thought my emotional struggle was their playground.

After a few moments, I gathered myself. I was no longer crying. I was no longer trembling. I pushed my shoulders back and decided I was going to walk back into the room and teach the class.

It was the bravest action I could have done. I opened the door, took a deep breath, and walked to the front of the room. Everyone was quiet. Fortunately for me, no one continued ridiculing me. I stood there, took a breath, and held my hands together in front of my body, saying, "Okay. Obviously I lost my cool and that was a mess. You got the best of me. This class is hard, and I am not liking how you treat me or how you treat what I'm trying to do.

I am frustrated and I got really angry. I'm sorry for losing my cool and crying. That's not right for a teacher to do. I feel embarrassed and stupid. But I'm moving on and I'm teaching what I had planned to teach."

If I remember all of this correctly, we were learning about frame stories in *The Canterbury Tales*, and I was using a non-Chaucer example to illustrate the literary method. I don't remember teaching this with confidence or strength. I remember feeling vulnerable and exposed, like I had just shown back up to a group of friends after I had caught them talking about me. No one really knew how to handle the situation. My feelings were hurt, my ego was bruised, my confidence in my patience was damaged, and I just wanted the entire day to be over.

Days later, I heard a student in another class tell me these boys bragged that they had made me cry as they had made other teachers in their lives cry. I was another tally in their record-book, and they held my embarrassment as a badge of honor.

I told a few teachers about this incident and each met me with sympathy and understanding. "Of course," one said. "This class sounds awful. I think I would have lost it and cried, too." All of this made me feel comforted and validated, but it didn't make the incident go away. All I could do from that point is consider what had led me to that breaking point, and what I could learn from it for the future.

LESSONS LEARNED

It's interesting thinking back to my early years in teaching. I've grown in immeasurable ways since these experiences. I'm so proud of how much I've grown and how much I've learned. Much of my growing and learning, though, has come on the backs of such painful, embarrassing moments, which is unfortunate. I wish there were easier, calmer, less embarrassing ways for me to have learned these lessons. Perhaps this book is part of that process for you.

I'm not proud of losing my cool in front of a bunch of 17-year-olds, nor am I proud of how they acted in my class. I am proud of walking back into that class. I was young at the time, and I had had few experiences working with tough groups. I had few experiences managing my own emotions while working with tough groups. I didn't handle it well, but I took ownership, and I showed back up.

I didn't run away for the rest of the class period or find a place to escape. I didn't make someone come back with me and teach the class with me. I did it myself. I lost my cool, and I recovered.

I wish I could go back in time and give myself some advice. For starters, I would never allow a class or group of students to get so disrespectful and unruly today. I still have students misbehave and act up in my classes, but I quickly communicate respect and a standard. Does this always work? No. But I'll have more students come along with me than not. I do what I can, and I implement what I have available to halt, or at least slow down, situations I know are negative and bad news before they get worse.

I talk to the student—or the group—before or after class as soon as I get a sense of uncooperation or disrespect. If things continue, I call home. I don't always know what I'll get when I call home, but I do it as frequently as I need. To layer more steps, I get the guidance counselor involved and the administrator who handles discipline for that grade level. I may even ask for a co-teacher or an assistant to help me divide-and-conquer. There are a lot of things I do now that I didn't do when I first started, because I had little understanding to the strength of these strategies and I was still suffering through trying to handle everything on my own, thinking this would give me the reputation of a solid teacher.

I try to remind myself I am here to teach, to be a teacher. I am not here to only be a behavior manager. There are supports in the school that I can lean on, so I do what I can to engage those supports.

To additionally help me manage the overwhelm, I have learned not to misuse my prep time. If I have time in school to do work, then I am using that time, and I try to protect that time from other distractions, such as social talking or looking at my phone. I always make a plan for what I need to get done in that time, and I check those items off my list as I complete them.

There are times when I do work at home, though I don't love when that happens. But if I do, it's always to get ahead, so I'm not stressed at some later date. If I have a meeting or I have essays to grade, then I am sure my lesson planning is complete, so I can focus on just one thing at a time. I have my lesson plans for the upcoming week on my calendar with all materials associated with those lesson plans ready to go by the time I leave on Friday afternoon. I spent many Friday afternoons early in my career in the copy room. That doesn't happen anymore, but I did that to get ahead, so I could focus the week on grading, communicating, and organizing the next week's lesson plans.

I have also learned that some parts of the school year are going to feel more overwhelming than others, and that I can mentally prepare for this. As one semester ends and another is about to start, I know I will be juggling many different aspects of work. This can feel overwhelming. I try to get ahead when I'm able, but sometimes, I just need to reason that this will be a lot for a period of time, and then it will flow back out.

I am lucky in that my administration does the best they can to get us our teaching schedules by the time we leave in June, if not even earlier. When I know what I'm teaching the following school year, I use the time in June when things are slowing down to plan for the next school year. My friends tease me for this: "It's June 10th, Diane. How many weeks of lesson plans do you have ready for next school year?" I proudly joke that "I have four weeks ready to go at this point, thank you very much!" I know this may seem unnecessary. I've heard a lot of remarks about my over-planning. But it helps me to stay in a healthy mindset when I know a lot will be expected of me in late August when we are about to begin a new school year. If I can have a strong baseline of lesson plans ready, with the intention of modifying those plans for student and class period needs, then I am way ahead and feel much calmer and less stressed. The efforts don't always translate as I'd like, but working with a balanced idea in mind sure does move me in a more proactive direction than reacting to the waves of work coming at me.

Each of us figures out what works to keep ourselves as balanced as possible. Usually, we learn what works better for us because we have been through painful moments in our job, just as I have. I know I am not the only teacher— or only professional—who has cried in their classroom, in their car, or in their office. We cry because we are out of control and because we are weakened by what we have been experiencing. Our behavior is communicating something.

ACTS OF BRAVERY

When teachers cry on their way home from school or lament their anger to a safe person, the night eventually ends, the morning alarm goes off, and they have to get back in that classroom. No one can take the burden off their shoulders. They are the show, and they can't not get on stage.

If you have felt like this sometimes—if you have cried or gotten angry—because of the workload or because of how some students, parents, or administrators have treated you, you are not alone. We have all felt like this, even if we don't openly share it.

Just because we cry or get angry, doesn't mean we are defeated. I've been through a lot of moments in school I would refuse to relive, and there have been embarrassing moments I had prior to writing this book that I've worked to keep quiet. But I'm still standing, and I'm still showing up ready to go and ready to teach, even when I question why and when I doubt the point.

> JUST BECAUSE WE CRY OR GET ANGRY, DOESN'T MEAN WE ARE DEFEATED.

You may feel lonely, but you are not alone.

You are not alone in any of it. And, if you made the decision to pick yourself up, brush yourself off, and get back in that classroom to face those students and try again, then you are my hero.

Take a moment, please, to consider a time when you left your classroom nearly in tears or so red angry, and then you showed back up the next day to do your job. You are *the only one*—the one with the highest value—who can do your job the way you do it.

It's of utmost importance we show back up, for ourselves and for our students. Some of the students in the classes that are difficult need us, even if they don't openly admit it. Some of our students need a visual of what it means to fall down and get back up and to admit when we could have handled something a different way.

In spite of it all, it matters that we show back up. When we show back up, we may be emotionally limping, but we are also growing stronger because we keep learning through these situations, continually getting more proactive, more strategic, and more aware of how to manage the nuances of teaching. It matters that we show back up.

So, when you show back up, take a moment to applaud yourself. I didn't do this all those years ago. I had my tail between my legs. Now I'm applauding myself. I know how hard it was for me to step back into that classroom.

I was resilient and I recovered from a tough situation. Do you know how easy—how safe—it would have been for me to quit?

Some teachers need to quit because their mental or physical health is at such risk. This was not me. I was experiencing ego bruising and needed emotional management.

Quitting wasn't something I *wanted* to do, and I instead showed back up. I did something that is worthy of praise and commendation. I know you have, too.

Perhaps you, too, have woken up after an especially bad school day, gotten dressed, gotten to school, and walked into that classroom. Maybe a little shaky. Maybe a little unsure. But you did it. Only YOU could do that. No one else could do that for you! No one else could take your place. You did that.

Do you know why? Because you are *brave*. Every moment in a tough classroom facing tough students is an act of bravery. Do people say this about teachers? No. They don't because they don't see teaching this way. People see teaching as a physical, results-oriented

> EVERY MOMENT IN A TOUGH CLASSROOM FACING TOUGH STUDENTS IS AN ACT OF BRAVERY.

profession. They do not see it as an emotional profession, in which we experience acts of bravery every single day.

It's an act of bravery and resilience to *show back up* after crying or feeling shame or feeling angry from the heat that comes from our classrooms. It's an act of bravery to face something head-on that makes us feel insecure, angry, or uncomfortable.

Classrooms shouldn't be this way, but, unfortunately, sometimes they are, because teaching is an emotional profession and it, therefore, affects us emotionally. When students "best us," it's important for us to remember that we are not alone in these feelings, and it's most important to remember that this is the unfortunate, unfair part of teaching that is not isolated to you.

So, if you cry or you get angry, you are not alone.

But you are so brave. And you are so awesome. And you are my absolute hero.

Great job. Keep showing up. Just show back up. You can do that.

HIT BY A BUS

SHARING

There aren't many veteran teachers or teacher-leaders who say things like: "Let me tell you some stories about the vulnerable or tough moments I've gone through, so we can all learn from them." Or, "Let me advise you to do some intrapersonal work before you start that first day in the classroom." I argue the stories and experiences are so personal that most people keep them closed or only share with a trusted few, knowing the uncertainty of what could happen if their lowest moments were exposed. Many of us don't want to talk about this publicly, because it's embarrassing to admit that we are part of a problem in our classrooms that we can't fix.

It's a lot easier and more comfortable for people not to see it or hear it. So, we stay quiet about it. We didn't *start* the problems, why would we want subsequent judgment from the problems? Vocalizing the problems, our reactions, and feelings could possibly create more judgment and stress for us, and since we don't know what happens when the paste is out of the tube, it's easier to keep the lid screwed on.

Sharing the stories and validating each other in specific ways will be, in my estimation, what changes education and changes how teachers and teacher-leaders view education. Teaching is an emotional profession that has a high potential to make us feel valued and worthy and insecure and inadequate. The more we see teaching as emotional, the more we can identify the situations and emotions that most affect us, and the more we can find solutions that work for us. If we stay quiet, then we remain isolated, silently questioning ourselves or quitting.

The tough stories aren't easy to read or hear. I don't like living them, and I don't like hearing about them from my colleagues and friends. We deserve better than to live tough stories in our days. But they are there, as are the good stories. They hold an importance to expressing what it is like to teach today, so that we can work toward solutions—whether within ourselves, or within our classrooms, or within our school buildings. Arguably, if we don't share the stories that impact us emotionally, how can we celebrate our successes, triumph in our growth, and resolve the emotional pain points?

SOME EXAMPLES

We experience wins during our days with examples of working with thoughtful, cooperative, and interesting students, while we also experience losses during our days with examples of disrespect, entitlement, criticism, and disengagement. These have their way of seeping under our skin because we don't know how to view them properly and because we haven't trained ourselves to work through them in such a way that will "lower their volume"—a guiding line of wisdom I was taught by my therapist.

It may be easy to dismiss the negative situations with "Who cares?" or "What does their opinion matter?" or "Consider the source." That's way too easy, and if it were that easy, we wouldn't have teachers in therapy, or quitting, or college students not joining the profession, or so many news reports covering the "teacher crisis." I argue that it all matters, and that it can be the death by a thousand papercuts metaphor. Teaching is emotional and the tough situations *do* matter.

Stories and examples help validate a larger truth that we will experience all the emotions, good and bad, from teaching. Good and bad happens, and it can happen in the same day. If I'm lucky, the bad doesn't happen in my day at all, or it's few situations, and I'll hear myself saying things like, "This semester has been so great. I have the best, sweetest, most awesome, hard-working students. I am so *lucky!*" I usually continue with some foreboding fear of, "I am a little worried about next semester. What's my luck I'll have it this good again? I wish I could just freeze things right now as they are." With all the work and time we put into our teaching day, it is amazing that so much of our professional job boils down to *luck*.

Learning all of this has been a turning point for me in realizing that teaching is not just an art that requires performance, skill, experience, compassion, and "bettering" of one's content, but it is also a profession of customer service. I've had students threaten me in email that "I'd better not email their parent again about their failing grade." I've had students command me in email to grade their work immediately, and I've received emails that contain an attachment with the only message in the email: "print." I've had students school me: "Your job is to grade my work and leave me alone. Do your job." Sure, sir. Sure, madam. Right away. Whatever you wish.

After learning more about myself and seeing the profession from a broader viewpoint, I decided a long time ago that I don't get commanded, though some students and parents think they can command teachers. For example, when a student has completed an assignment late, for whatever reason, and expects the grade to be updated immediately, and he or she says to me with charge, "Grade it before the end of the day," I now say in reply: "Excuse me. I decided a long time ago I don't get commanded. Would you like to try this conversation again with respect as the driving factor, or would you like me to get to your completed work when it fits into my schedule?"

Teachers take a lot without any way of defending their honor, correcting the record, or sending a clear message that they will not tolerate certain abuses. In some cases, teachers give second, third, and fourth chances, as if what they are receiving is acceptable, as if what they are receiving is simply a manifestation of young people learning. Teachers can't remove students from their classrooms or say they won't have this person in their space.

I've had students assert their opinion that teachers shouldn't make more than $50,000 a year because "Your job is easy, and you get summers off." What would these students think of me, and how would they judge me, if they knew I made more than $50k a year *and* I cherished my summers off?

Students have told me "I don't do assigned seats. I sit where I want," or that it won't matter what I do, they aren't going to work in groups or with partners. Probably one of the most demoralizing feelings is when I've worked hours on a lesson that includes group work for sharing, extending, and collaboration, but I have students refuse to move their desks or bodies to join the group, or they refuse to speak in the group. I can continue this lesson with fewer students, but, unfortunately, the message reverberating through the class is that some play by the rules while others do not.

Teachers set all of this up and are excited for the magic. But the magic doesn't always happen.

Students stare awkwardly at each other, not talking to each other and not engaging in the work. Or they say they are done before they've started, or that they are confused, and, therefore, can't start. Or they don't join the group at all. Or they choose to do the work as an individual, even though it was group work. I thought my directions of this being a collaborative activity were pretty clear. I'll find myself encouraging, redirecting, clarifying, re-explaining, asking, pleading, begging. But the lesson was never the problem; it was the behavior of the people engaging with that lesson. Nevertheless, it was a lot of wasted time coupled with feelings of inadequacy, disappointment, and hopelessness.

Similarly, this feeling of purposelessness occurs when I teach plays and have few or no volunteers for parts, or I have a few eager students and no supportive cast. Such a bummer for something that could have been so cool, so fun. Anytime a lesson is dependent on students to launch it, the teacher enters uncertain ground. It may go great with period 1, and it may crash and burn with period 2. I joke with my next-door neighbor at times, asking if he heard the crash and smelled the burn. I've asked him this so many times, he can finish the joke for me now. Kindly, he always tells me "No" and reminds me I'm doing a great job.

I witnessed one of my colleagues in a tough moment, trying to keep students in her room before the bell at the end of the day. These twelfth grade students would push past her or each other to leave three or four minutes early to get a jump on the parking lot. For this teacher, after a long school day, it made her feel like she wasn't valued and that her directions could be ignored. These students felt *they could do this to her*, even though it was wrong. What a way for her to leave the school day.

Years ago, I happened to be in a faculty lunchroom I'm not usually in when an easy-going colleague barged into the faculty room, screamed and cursed about a kid, slammed his hands on the counter, and then stormed out.

I sat there shocked. *What happened? What was this kid doing?* I felt so bad for this teacher and so relieved (sorry to admit) I didn't have this kid in my class. It was only October. A lot of time left. I learned later it was a student everyone in the school knew, whether you had him or not. He ended up being a problem in the community, eventually serving jail time. But, while in the school, this student was so difficult that he caused many, not just this teacher, to have outbursts of reactions.

This experience had echoes of another I had with a student, who was tough and was surely feared by his classmates. He had openly mocked me because of an email I had written to his mom about his behaviors in class. The email was about him leaving class frequently and for long periods of time, about his eye-rolling, scoffing, and unnecessary, attention-seeking comments, such as "This class is so stupid," or "I hate this class," or "How much time do we have left?" and about his refusal to engage in some of the class activities.

As I came into the classroom after greeting students in the hallway, I walked in on him laughing and showing his friends the email and saying how ridiculous it was. Then he laughed and said that his mom also thought it was hilarious and mocked me. According to this student, his mom said about me, "Wasn't she an adult? Wasn't she the teacher? Shouldn't she grow up?" I felt targeted by his mockery and poking fun, and I was frustrated by his attitude and daily behaviors. I reacted, instead of pausing and gaining my composure, when I heard him talking about me.

I hadn't at that time learned about "behavior is communication" or about the introspective work I needed to do to become a stronger teacher. I didn't handle myself maturely, and told him with an attitude that there would be no such email if he weren't disrespectful and rude each day. I encouraged *him* to grow up and reminded him that he had walked into a high school that day, not a middle school, but maybe he wasn't aware of that. Finally, I challenged: "How about I get your mom on the phone in front of the class to see if she *really* does think this is all so funny?"

My sarcasm and my reaction made this student push back harder, and the semester remained uncomfortable. Unexpectedly, years later, he asked me if I would write him a college recommendation letter. At first, I wondered if he was messing with me. But he was serious, making me curious if some students have any idea how they treat adults, and how those consequences feel. I wasn't rude in my reply to him, but I sincerely asked him why he would choose me for a letter when we didn't have a good situation in class and when I had hardly seen him in the years since. He just responded, "Never mind, forget it," and walked out of my room.

As teachers, we know the difference from how we handle negative relationships in our personal lives to how we handle negative relationships in our professional lives. If there is an ongoing negative pattern in our personal lives, we could have the opportunity to put boundaries in place or end the relationship. Within the classroom, though, the issues can continue until the semester or school year ends, and a lot of emotional baggage can be carried as a result.

The great situations in my career far outweigh the tough situations. I am lucky for that, and I know it is not this way for every teacher. For me, it's the few, the very few, that can keep me up at night or make me feel inferior. Within these few, I've been ignored, I've been stonewalled, I've been glared at, I've received eye rolls, I've been shut down, and I've been called hurtful, insulting names.

Honestly, I didn't sign up for *that*.

Thankfully, though, I have been called *way* more nice things than bad things, and I have had *way* more students adore me, as I do them, than I don't. Because I have people in my corner and because I believe in the good I do, I am able to weather the storms, even if the storms still affect me.

The difficult situations may be but one part of an otherwise very good or even great day. Just as I have students resist a lesson plan, I'll also have students enthusiastically jump into groups and dive into discussing, drawing a scene, creating a prequel or sequel, or making the best darn movie trailer ever. I'll have classes ask if we can read more plays, so everyone can have a lead role. I'll have students so eager to tell me their thoughts on what we are reading that they email me in the evening because class time wasn't enough time for them to share. I am moved when I see students welcoming a quieter student into their group, and I am so impressed when students research a supplemental idea to what we are learning and are then excited to share.

> *...TEACHING CAN BE MORE ABOUT
> SELF-MANAGEMENT THAN IT IS ABOUT
> CONTENT MANAGEMENT.*

The teaching day can be inconsistent, and this is what causes us to say, "This job isn't what I thought it would be." I concede that teaching can be more about self-management than it is about content management. Precisely, this is why it's important we continue to train our minds to focus on the good and to remember that we are part of a system, and we are doing the best we can to improve the situations that are difficult.

THE COOL TEACHER AND THE MUSIC TEACHER

I was lucky to reunite with a teacher at a community event, who I had met years earlier at our kids' soccer league. This teacher has eight more years of teaching experience than I do in a neighboring state. He's a cool guy who laughs easily, is funny and charismatic, and makes you feel comfortable in his presence. It seems to me his students would love him and would love to be in his class. I think at some point they really did.

He shared with me that the last five years of teaching have driven him to early retirement webinars and to seek employment at any place other than his classroom. He said he didn't care about the higher teacher salary he spent years waiting to get—or his pension. He just needed out and felt he couldn't do X more years in the classroom with the way things were going. He told me how the stress from the school day was following him home. He was not the person he wanted to be for his kids or his wife.

He admitted it wasn't always this way for him, and that he used to be the favorite teacher in the building and even had a few yearbooks dedicated to him. He said that years of student disengagement and disinterest coupled with more work have made him angry.

He told me about the agonizing class periods of begging kids just to take out a pencil, or to read a few paragraphs, or to put their phones away, or to not go to the bathroom every single class period. He said the hardest part for him was being "ineffective." It wasn't something he was used to being, and it wasn't something he could accept. "I used to wake up excited about the day, and I was one of the first people in my building," he said. "Now I get to school just a few minutes before I need to be there, and I don't stay after anymore."

As our conversation about school started to end, he turned to me and said, "You know, when I'm in my classroom, I can feel like a total loser."

That got my attention. Yes, I've felt that, too. Sometimes the situations in my classroom can make me feel like a loser, though I never feel like a loser in other parts of my life. I also never would have guessed this fun-loving, smiling, cool guy had ever known the cold sting of feeling like a loser.

It resembled a similar sentiment I heard at a teacher's retirement speech when the teacher commented that his fine-arts department saved students year after year. His department saved the kids who felt they had nowhere to go or who felt they didn't fit in. People nodded along to his speech, affirming all the good he had given to these students over a 30+ year career. Then he said something that torpedoed right to me: "Unfortunately, I am leaving my course and my extracurricular in worse shape than when I found it." He said, "It's been a struggle since COVID getting kids to reengage with music and the fine arts and it's been a struggle getting them to challenge themselves. We have the lowest numbers of participants now than ever in my career."

Then, to my dismay, he blamed himself. We all knew this wasn't fair. We've all struggled in recent years, including club sponsors and sports coaches, and it saddened me to see this teacher confess these thoughts during his retirement celebration, and it saddened me to think about all the teachers who retired or resigned within the COVID years, with their teaching careers ending before large systems have had the chance to reset and replenish.

I've realized after so many conversations and experiences over the years that the emotional stress that comes from teaching can happen to anyone or at any point in their careers, and I started to wonder why we aren't talking about these things more openly and why we aren't warning our newer teachers, who may not expect emotional triggers in their workday. I wondered why we were allowing teachers to enter the profession and struggle in the profession without telling them that these things may happen to them, too, despite how much they loved school, or how much they are prepared in their lesson plans, or how confident they are in their personal lives.

Teaching will enrich your life and you will in turn enrich the lives of others. Teaching will also make you doubt yourself and will make you feel like you are doing it all wrong. It will be both, and sometimes it can have a sudden change.

BETRAYED

A pivotal moment for me to understand how quickly things can change occurred a little over a decade into my teaching career, when I ignorantly thought the years of experience and service would build a thick enough shield that I wouldn't be affected by petty or mean circumstances. I was wrong, and I'm glad I was wrong. After going through the situation, it helped me to accept that teachers should always be building and nurturing their emotional strength, just as a body builder lifts daily. The emotional work shouldn't end or decrease simply because of accumulated years of service or because teachers get better and stronger at their teaching. They have to continually work on themselves to maintain their emotional strength.

Being emotionally strong comes from learning about and doing the inner work.

I had a student, with whom I previously had a really good relationship, tell another teacher that she hated me and wished I'd get hit by a bus and die. Yikes. *Really? Die?* I have so many people who love me. I love so many people. I never thought that anyone would want me to die a premature, violent death. Despite living a life in which I have so many who love me, this kid started to hate me

> ...IT HELPED ME TO ACCEPT THAT TEACHERS SHOULD ALWAYS BE BUILDING AND NURTURING THEIR EMOTIONAL STRENGTH, JUST AS A BODY BUILDER LIFTS DAILY.

and then wished me dead. Certainly, with the enthusiasm for which I started my teaching career, I never would have thought this would be said about me.

This colleague, who happened to be a newer teacher, got an up-close look at a crack in my foundation. Learning about this student's wish caught me off guard, as if I were actually hit by a bus, and it triggered my insecurities of seeking approval and needing to be liked.

I wish I were the type of person who could have easily and flippantly blown it off to show this young teacher that I was invincible to such nasty comments from teenagers. I wanted to be a superhero with a tough exterior, fully in control and unstirred by such temper-tantrum comments. But, instead, I was upset and hurt. Betrayed. It made my stomach sink and my heart pound. My face got red, and I felt the sting of tears. No time for that, though. I had class in five minutes.

When teachers get upset, they have nowhere to go and nowhere to hide. Their private office is their public classroom, and they are the show that must go on. So many times I've thought it would be nice to every once in a while work in a cubicle, where I could hide as an individual in a bigger system, and put my head down and do my work.

Though I wanted this teacher to see me as capable and in control, I was unnerved by this harsh comment. "Kids are dumb and say dumb shit," is what I wanted to say. I wanted to laugh it off. But I felt defensive, thinking to myself how I go above and beyond with my time and kindness to give students the best I can. I so absolutely did not deserve to be killed by a bus. Moreover, this same student came into my study hall with her friend multiple times a week to talk and eat lunch. We had a good relationship, and it was great being in class together. For a time.

When she declared me "dead by bus," I felt betrayed, which is so bewildering and peculiar to one's psychology because I was an adult teacher and this was a teenage student. But that is how this student's rejection toward me felt. I learned years later with my therapist that what triggers our emotional pains can come from anywhere and anyone, despite age difference or authority expectations.

The helpless feeling started to creep in, knowing that once someone *like that student* makes a strong negative assertion, it's nearly impossible for them to publicly admit they are wrong. This student held social power and was popular, with many in the class looking for this student's permission to engage or disengage. The heat from this student wasn't going to quickly reset to normal. Before even walking back into class, I already knew how it was going to go.

This younger teacher asked me, "What are you going to do?" truly curious about how more experienced teachers handle situations like this. Contrasting how I felt inside, I calmly stated, "I need time to determine how I am going to handle this." Then, I walked into my classroom, and I taught, like I had planned to do when I woke up that morning, not dead by bus.

I was proud of myself for taking the necessary pause, for not losing my cool, and for not crying. Look at how far I had already grown.

I knew why the student felt upset with me. After she had finished giving a presentation a few days before, I shared that her picture content was extreme and that she needed to be considerate of her audience and what they can visually handle. It wasn't critical, and I was simply providing a suggestion for future experiences. Her pictures weren't inappropriate for school, but she chose them for shock value, and this needed to be considered. I provided her feedback, but I embarrassed her because I gave the feedback at the end of her presentation in front of the class.

This was something I could work on. I could have been more delicate in the timing and delivery of my feedback, and I could have used the opportunity to give a whole-class lesson outside of this student's presentation. I didn't think about these options in the moment of giving the feedback, as I was more focused on giving the feedback, and I didn't feel it was that big of a deal.

From my perspective, I was her teacher, and I was giving a point of consideration. Additionally, I had built a good relationship with this student and the class, so I didn't think my feedback would be seen as threatening. Never did I intend to embarrass her. While I can accept that all these situations are ways to learn and do better next time, I'll never accept her vehemence and words.

For the days following her presentation, she either rolled her eyes at me or totally avoided eye contact. She didn't return any hellos or attempts to discuss the situation rationally in a one-to-one way. She didn't budge when, the next day, I attempted to speak with her individually to share that I didn't intend to cause her embarrassment or overt-criticism, and that I could learn other methods of delivering feedback for next time. She gave me the cold shoulder as a response. She told me "Whatever," and she refused my fist bumps at the door. Eventually, her anger grew until she informed a fellow teacher that she wished I were dead by bus. Wild.

> *I WAS IN THE CLASSIC SOCIAL WHIRLPOOL SYNDROME, WHERE STUDENTS LOOK TO THE ONE STUDENT TO DETERMINE HOW THEY ARE ALLOWED TO ACT TOWARD A TEACHER AND IN A CLASS.*

Unfortunately, this student held a lot of social power, so her friends in the class couldn't like me or work with me while all this was going on. They needed to ensure their own good standing with their friend, who had now reneged the figurative permission slips that she had signed and given out that allowed liking me and my class.

I was in the classic social whirlpool syndrome, where students look to *the one* student to determine how they are allowed to act toward a teacher and in a class.

When I think about that student, I wonder what it was like to be her classmate, or in her circle of friends, or in her family. I'm sure she generated a lot of fear. The silent treatment—just one tactic she used to indicate her disapproval of me—is emotional abuse meant to manipulate. It is painful to the receiver, no matter who is giving it, whether that person is 15-years-old or 40-years-old. It is a go-to method used by abusers because it can make their victims jump, apologize when they've done nothing wrong, and puppy-dog to regain the abuser's approval.

For my situation, I'd like to say that eventually it smoothed over, but it didn't. I was able to take the threat as far as I could to illustrate that saying those types of things, whether with intent or from embarrassment, is never acceptable, but the student never did apologize or come back around. The parent shared that his daughter was upset over a comment regarding a project she had worked hard on, and that she was merely "expressing herself." The semester ended, and that was that, but the class was never quite the same.

Whenever I saw her over the following months or years in the hallway or otherwise, she was sure to laugh with her friends, and tell them I was "The worst teacher she ever had." This student who had once sat with me in study hall eating lunch now rolled her eyes at me, ignored me, or walked coolly by without any eye contact. I had been teaching for 12 years at that point, but it felt like I had just started, and it was like reliving high school mean girls, only this time it was in my job.

After the sting lessened, I did what I typically do when I want to lighten a situation, and I began jokingly using the phrase "hit by a bus" for other instances when I'd be blindsided, suddenly betrayed, or when I'd feel so overwhelmed by my own expectations or others' expectations that my emotional or physical state felt like it had figuratively been hit by a bus. Those in my life who know this story understood why I'd choose that phrase, but in many ways, the phrase fits because sometimes our teaching lives are so overwhelming that we can actually feel like we've been hit by a bus.

Joking aside, experiencing this situation, the way her friends reacted, and then having to see her from time to time for four years eventually propelled me to accept that

I needed to work on my reactions to these situations that were out of my control. I knew I needed to learn *how* to place these situations behind me much sooner if I was going to keep my peace of mind, my confidence, and my joy. As I became curious about how much this one student's words and actions had affected me, I began to see that I was not the only one, and that we need to talk about these situations openly to learn solutions and to hope for changes.

EXPECTATIONS

A betrayal and a shock can come from poor student behavior and from a misalignment of teacher values and societal expectations. Hannah Natanson[10], journalist and reporter covering K-12 educational issues, shares this exact feeling in her September 2023 *Washington Post* article about Advanced Placement English teacher Mary Wood from South Carolina. Ms. Wood introduced a diverse text to her AP English students, and some of her students "reported her to the school board for teaching about race," claiming Wood had "violated a South Carolina proviso that forbids teachers from making students feel 'discomfort, guilt, anguish, or any other form of psychological stress' on account of their race."

The dialogue about appropriate or inappropriate classroom content is not the premise of this book. What I want to share is the aftermath for Mary Wood, who felt "'defeated and betrayed'" and was even "'scared to go back to school'" when entering the next school year, given her story reached national attention, angered parents, gave students reason to criticize, created a community uproar, and teetered on her possible firing.

She was scared to go back to school. *Scared.* Some of us have felt this, or we have at least felt the tension in our bodies when we are in conflict with our students or our school system, as was the case for Mary Wood or with another teacher I learned about, who struggled to get out of her car in the parking lot because she was scared about what she'd face that day with a bad class.

As the article continues, one comment by recent graduate Audrey Hume who had Ms. Wood during the time of her reprimand painfully resonated with me. In stating her reaction to whom she had as her English teacher that school year, Audrey Hume recalls, "'Oh, I got Ms. Wood, and now I have to scoff and roll my eyes because she's going to teach me things I don't want to learn. A lot of kids did not like her.'"

Despite your opinion on Ms. Wood's decision to teach Ta-Nehisi Coates's *Between the World and Me*, to put it plainly, it is nearly impossible to teach people who don't like you, even if their dislike has nothing to do with who you are as a person. It could be something completely outside of you, but for reasons that are beyond my understanding, some students will put that conflict to the teacher in the room, and then will behave as if they can treat the teacher with unworthiness.

Ms. Wood's story affected me for a couple of different reasons. Most notably because of expectations. In reading her story, I know she wasn't expecting to have her entire life flipped upside down because of a literature piece she planned to teach. We don't purposely do things that will upend us. The examples that come from my own life are not as severe as from Ms. Wood's, but it touches on the same point. Often, I have expectations of how something will go, and when that does not occur, I become disappointed and hurt.

Thinking my expectations should be fulfilled, simply because I created them, has repeatedly been an important lesson in my personal life and in my teaching life. I still fall into the trap of expectations, but I can at least now identify when I'm creating expectations, and I can evaluate if those expectations are *reasonable* or just me wishing and hoping.

I had a classroom neighbor years ago who never seemed bothered by anything, even when he had harder classes or students. Watching this person react calmly to crappy situations and maintain an even-level of satisfaction in his day was an enigma to me. I wanted the secret. I wanted the answer. "How do you maintain your composure and not get frustrated when you have students who don't turn in their work and ask for multiple extensions, or when they have their heads down while you are talking?" I asked, with full anticipation of the wisest answer. He replied, "Oh, that's easy. I have no expectations. At all. I never set myself up with expectations, and sometimes I'm wildly surprised and it's a great feeling."

I decided in that moment this man had been a past-life monk.

No expectations. *What*? That didn't even seem possible. Our jobs as teachers demand that we have expectations. How else could we predict and determine how a lesson or an assessment or a meeting will go? We are doing all this work expecting and planning for it to go a certain way.

Psychotherapist Moshe Ratson[11] has a series called "The Wisdom of Anger" on the website *PsychologyToday*, and in one article published September 2023, Ratson offers the subtitle "Unrealistic Expectations are a Happiness Destroyer." He continues by sharing that our expectations are a "standard for how we would like people to behave and how we want the world to be… [and that when] we become disappointed or frustrated, it's often because an experience or situation does not fit our expectations. There is a gap between the reality we face and the way we think it should be."

I considered what my neighbor taught me, and I witnessed the healthy result of him having no expectations. It seemed to me he had never felt figuratively hit by a bus. Perhaps I had entered the wrong profession because I reasoned that I like predictability and expectations and control. I don't know if I will ever be able not to have expectations, but I recognize the problem isn't necessarily expectations, but rather when my expectations are unrealistic or unreasonable, or when I hold so fast to my expectations that I am bothered when they aren't met.

Ratson writes that "expectations are normal, but the attachment to them creates suffering." Certainly, there were times when I was suffering, and I figured changing my approach to expectations would be key in my path to happiness.

Learning how to moderate expectations, though, is very difficult, especially for teachers, or at least a teacher like me. Expectations are built on hope. We want our students to achieve, and we want them to see the value in what we are teaching them. We hope what we do matters, and we hope our students allow us to lead them and not resist us. When students give us far less than their potential or are downright uncooperative, we have to, at least, consider if our expectations are intersecting with their effort, their care, and their ability. How to meet students

> *HOW TO MEET STUDENTS WHERE THEY ARE AND MAINTAIN HIGH STANDARDS, SO WE DON'T ACCEPT MEDIOCRITY—OR WORSE—IS A FINE ART IN TEACHING...*

where they are *and* maintain high standards, so we don't accept mediocrity—or worse—is a fine art in teaching, and I am constantly reconsidering my philosophies.

Expectations are also built on patterns. Something in our lives consistently shows itself a certain way, and we create the expectation that it will always go this way. I have learned to stay open to the possibility that patterns can change, sometimes for the better and sometimes for the worse. If I have a tougher student, and I feel the student is open to the conversation, I will let the student know I am open to the pattern changing. If I have a good student, and I see the student is starting to shift, I will acknowledge this with the student and maybe even the guardian and guidance counselor. I will try to encourage the student to come back around, but I don't hold it against the student that they are suddenly different. That is out of my control.

These are all things I've learned along the way— usually from mistakes—and that I continue working through.

BALANCE

To expect more sets myself up for frustration and sets students up for pre-determined expectations. Balancing our reasonable expectations with the high expectations we have for ourselves and for our students is difficult because we shouldn't expect the bare minimum from students; yet that may be all they can give sometimes. We also shouldn't expect our high-achieving, good students to be more than they can be.

I met a teacher friend who taught seventh graders, and he told me how, that year, a group of kids refused to talk to him, whether it was over school-related things or friendly check-ins. They "stonewalled" him as he put it, and they pulled others into this nastiness. They enacted the silent treatment to show this teacher they didn't like him.

I asked him why he thought they acted this way toward him, and he responded, "Because I am the 'hard' teacher in the grade, and I make them do work and I don't give high grades." He told me that students "often show up to [his] room already having an opinion, but the ones who are open-minded thank [him] for being a teacher who taught them more than anyone else."

He continued by telling me he didn't really care, but that it had affected his enjoyment for teaching and that he was looking forward to retirement. "When will you retire?" I asked. "Oh, about 10 years," he declared. Ten years. That's a long time to continually show up to a job that you don't want to be in anymore.

I understood what he meant in this student-teacher dynamic, as I had gone through my own experiences of students not liking me because of holding an academic standard with assignments and grades. I had experienced my own examples of stonewalling and dissatisfaction from some of the best students I've ever taught, which was terribly confusing and upsetting for me. Teaching being emotional doesn't always come from poor behaviors or disengaged students. Sometimes it can come from our best-behaved and caring students, who feel rejected when they receive anything lower than an A.

It took me school years to figure this out. When I had the highest expectations for my students to succeed and exceed is when I was met with the most hostility. I was battling two different educational philosophies. Maintaining high standards to increase rigor conflicted with the message that good students should get A's for their achievements. I was prioritizing student skills and growth in a world that was placing "what I look like on a college application" as its top priority. I was not recognizing that my expectations and my students' expectations were unaligned.

Many of us fall into this conflict, and if we do not strike a healthy balance between competing educational philosophies, we risk giving away grades for work that is not up to par, which Frederick Hess[12] calls an "educational crime."

Senior contributor Frederick Hess titles his September 2023 article from *Forbes Magazine* "Grade Inflation is not a Victimless Crime." He starts with "America's high schools have just endured a decade of dramatic grade inflation, according to a new study from ACT," and that academic achievement has notably declined through retention measures, SAT scores, and state standardized scores while GPAs and graduation rates have increased, allowing "students to graduate without essential knowledge or skills." He admits that teachers and school leaders have decided it's easier to give in than to fight, but he presses that "it's crucial to appreciate that grade inflation isn't a victimless crime [as] it sends a false signal to students and families... [and] can be difficult [for teachers] to hold the line on high expectations."

Giving away grades and baselessly passing otherwise failing students is identified as an *educational crime*, according to Hess, and it feels many in education have been thrust into that lose-lose corner. I have been guilty of this, too. It took some growing pains for me to balance

> *...IF WE SWING TOO FAR TO ONE PHILOSOPHY, THEN WE ARE GIVING AN INHERENT "NO" TO THE POLAR PHILOSOPHY. AT BEST, WE MAGNETIZE OURSELVES TO THE MIDDLE...*

high expectations with student growth, and I have now struck a much better and healthier balance meeting students where they are while also trying to maintain high standards.

In teaching, we must keep in mind that if we swing too far to one philosophy, then we are giving an inherent no to the polar philosophy. At best, we magnetize ourselves to the middle, always willing to move a little this way and a little that way to blend philosophies and champion the most valuable aspects.

Finding the balance in all things teaching, including grades, is difficult and takes a ton of trial and error. Standards matter, rigor matters, achievement matters, teachers matter, and so do students and their needs. We shouldn't accept stonewalling because we want our students to achieve, and we also shouldn't accept giving out grades that provide an inaccurate description of success because our students demand that.

NOT OUT, BUT THROUGH

Given teaching is an emotional profession, the hurts that come from teaching feel more personal, in my opinion, because we are leading and nurturing the classroom environment, expecting that students will treat us with dignity and value due to what we are giving to them and to the space.

Ask any teacher, and they will say that "Teaching is hard." I often hear this phrase, but we aren't quite phrasing it right. We don't mean the work, necessarily, though the sheer workload can be overwhelming and nonstop. Most teachers are hard-working and have always been hard-working. We aren't afraid of the work, nor the fine balancing of our executive functioning abilities. In fact, there are aspects of the work that are enjoyable and exciting. It's the emotional toll that is hard.

It's showing up pleasantly and enthusiastically day after day, and having some students or classes meet you with blank stares, miserable faces, no eye contact, lack of cooperation, or disrespect.

It's waking up knowing a student or class is very difficult, for a variety of reasons, and you're the classroom teacher needing to manage it for the next eight hours.

It's putting hours into lesson plans, new curriculum designs, new assessments, models, real-life connections, video supplements, and activities, only for some students not to engage or to dismiss the work.

It's trying again—creating work for the next day's lessons, knowing the same bad things may happen, but hoping they won't.

Teachers feel the inner struggle when they give the best of themselves to a class because many students in that class deserve it, though they sit amongst students who don't appreciate it and abuse it.

Teachers feel the challenge when they decide they won't even own a white flag for surrender.

Teachers lament that they wouldn't feel the exhaustion from teaching if they could just *teach*. Yes, they'd be tired because presenting and managing all day is tiring, but they wouldn't be *exhausted*. There is a difference between tired and exhausted. The exhaustion comes from the defeat, which is where our focus should be to lessen.

I wish it weren't part of teaching, and I wish our days were filled with "just teaching" and only with the joy that comes from teaching. I wish we didn't say and feel things like, "I didn't sign up for *this*."

Teaching can be like taking hit after hit, while also getting build up after build up. The emotional body is confused, unless it's given language and identification. The stories

> *LET'S LIGHTEN THE TEACHER EMOTIONAL BAG. MAYBE EVEN PUT THAT BAG DOWN. WE DON'T HAVE TO CARRY THAT BAG ALONG WITH US.*

stick with us, though we have moved on to new school years and classes. We carry these stories and place them in our figurative teacher book bags, where they sink heavily to the bottom, allowing room for more to pile on top, compacting each layer as we carry them on our shoulders.

These emotional tolls are what make us consider quitting or what do make us quit. They are what make us think, "I have to get out of teaching." Let's lighten the teacher emotional bag. Maybe even put that bag down. We don't have to carry that bag along with us.

I like to think about Robert Frost's[13] advice from his poem "A Servant to Servants," from which is cited his famous quote: "The best way out is always through."

He advises us that the only way out is through. It's not actually getting out, but rather, in going through.

For me, it's helpful to see the painful parts of my day *exactly as they are*. In this way, I don't hide from them, I don't repress them, and I don't gloss over them. Adding layers of false positivity or untruth to something that is hard will only make it harder.

I see the difficult parts of my day, wherever they may come from, as disappointments for what I had hoped for and as lingering grief, so I can then work to effectively cope with these feelings, instead of repressing them or turning them into anger. When I experience pains from teaching, whether it's from my highest achieving students or from the student who wants me killed by a bus, I identify that hurt being a form of disappointment and grief.

It's worth it to consider that our unmet expectations from teaching are a form of disappointment and grief, even if universally they are not seen that way. We know what it feels like to enjoy teaching a class and to know our contribution as the teacher was valued. We know what it feels like to experience the opposite. We also know what grief feels like. Grief can be experienced from our jobs, too. We had expectations. We were looking forward to it going a certain way. We worked for it to go a certain way. And it didn't go that way, maybe some of the time or a lot of the time. That's disappointing. The result of that disappointment is grief because the result of any disappointment is grief.

I have learned to see some of my teaching life as a disappointment and a grief, not because I *want* to see it this way, but it helps me to see it this way. It helps me to name it. There are times I am disappointed. There are times when I cry, in grief, over what it was supposed to be and what it is. I don't quit and I don't give into the "Why bother?" but I have to let those other feelings out or else they will fester into resentment, and I don't want that.

I want to say disappointment from teaching happens to all of us, no matter who we are or where we've come from or where we teach. The disappointment and grief surprises us and catches us off guard, especially because it's not the totality of our teaching day. Some situations make us feel great, and some situations make us feel bad *all in the same day.*

After we take a moment to accept this, we do the best we can to understand ourselves. We try our best to determine why exactly we feel the way we do. Then, we try as hard as we can to implement mindsets and strategies that alleviate disappointment and shift grief, so we can be the people we want to be and do the work we were made to do.

We can improve this heartache by having open conversations and sharing strategies about how it will feel when kids reject our lesson plans, or when the social power of the class is against us and we can't "make" students do what we had planned or wanted, or when we have created something that should go a certain way, but it doesn't because of things we can't control.

There are many teacher stories, and it takes us to be emotionally strong and brave to admit, "Yes, I've been

> *DON'T EVER RESIGN YOURSELF TO CLOSING, BECAUSE NOTHING IS WORTH CLOSING YOUR HEART, ONLY TO LEAVE ANGER, DISAPPOINTMENT, AND RESENTMENT INSIDE.*

part of the problem" or "Yes, I've had some teaching losses." We can't hide from the truth, even if the truth is painful to hear. We can talk about how the difficult student or group has tornado energy that pulls in others, and it's hard to untangle from them, or how the social power of the difficult students is strong and they "whirlpool" other students into their vortex, who would have otherwise been fine, or how even our best students can struggle with us because we are trying to challenge them.

Instead of "Teaching is hard," the phrase should be: "Teaching is emotional."

If you love teaching, and you truly believe you have something to give as a teacher, then stay open. Don't ever resign yourself to closing, because nothing is worth closing your heart, only to leave anger, disappointment, and resentment inside.

There are ways through the emotional stress of teaching, not out of it. There are ways to deal with it, not avoid it. Unless there are monumental shifts in accountability and expectations for public school systems, the issues are here, but so are we, and the waves that have come to my shore haven't knocked my castle down.

The only way out is through…the only way out is through. It is not getting out, but rather going through. How do we get through when we just want to get out?

That answer, first, requires deep understanding of ourselves, and then implementing that learning into our classroom lives. This has led me farther down the teacher's happiness path, as I hope it will you, too. Thankfully, I don't have as many buses in my view now—though they do still surprise me from time to time.

SEEING

THE SNACKY GIRLS

After I was through the initial years of teaching that get redefined as "the survival years," I naïvely thought I had made it—that I was *there*. I had experienced some tough situations, tough students, tough parents. I had worked through constructive feedback, and I had developed content for numerous courses.

I was right, in a way, that I was making it because I had improved greatly in the physical parts of my teaching abilities. But I was wrong in that I had yet to understand the emotional impacts of teaching and why these happen and what to do about them. I had still a long way to go in understanding any of that.

While I'm a work in progress and I have to reset myself from time to time, I didn't fully see teaching as the emotional profession that we should all see it to be, until I had "the snacky girls" in class. This group of girls, who combined with previous years of painful experiences, finally catapulted me to *knowing* that I needed to understand the "why" behind my emotional reactions if I was going to be an effective teacher.

On the first day of a new school year, this group of girls came in, yelped that they were all in the same class, ignored my seating arrangement, and talked over me and through me, so they could have their social hour. I didn't even know their names, yet, or if this first day was a strange occurrence or if this would be my entire semester with these girls. I did win out on that first day by making them sit in the assigned seats, but they figured out ways to communicate across the room, so my assigned seats were meaningless.

Because they dismissed me and were disrespectful before I could even get ahead of it, their force pervaded the rest of the class as well, and on the first day of the semester, I was asking student after student to take out headphones and to put phones away and to shut computer lids. Their energy disrupted the class and made cooperation, let alone learning, optional.

I couldn't believe it. Here I was *again*, faced with the predicament of the power-struggle and the lose-lose. The only difference now was regarding my fatigue and my annoyance because I had been here before, and I was tired of being in this position. I also already knew that I could do 1,000 good things and the situation could still possibly stay the same. I didn't have a fresh perspective. I was going into the game with tired legs and a losing record.

It wasn't long before this group came into each class period late, so they could get snacks from the vending machine in the cafeteria. They would casually walk into class late, without any consideration to how they disrupted the environment, noisily squeezing bags and chomping snacks, talking with mouths full of Cheetos, sometimes even with a pass from a well-intentioned teacher, who didn't recognize he was being used, or who cared more about being a friend to these students than upholding a colleague's requests for assistance.

The irony wasn't lost on me that I got cursed at for enforcing a school rule of no food or drinks outside the cafeteria on my first day of school, and years later, after that school rule dissipated, I was facing disrespect because of snacks outside the cafeteria.

Telling them they couldn't show up late to get food from the vending machine was met with a defiant talking back of, "We're not late. We have a pass. That kid came in with a pass and he wasn't 'late.'" Or, "What?! You're telling me I can't eat? Yeah right. I can eat if I'm hungry. You can't stop me from eating."

I tried talking to each one individually to share perspectives and to elicit cooperation. One girl wouldn't even talk to me and refused any conversation. We were still in mid-September at that point, just to give context. I have no idea why she was so haughty to me within the first two weeks of school, and when I asked, I didn't get an answer. A few seemed more willing to cooperate after individual conversations but wouldn't change their behaviors once they were reabsorbed in the group.

If they didn't stop at the vending machine first, they'd come into class on time, drop their bags and go to the bathroom; then, of course, come in well after the bell. Asserting to them that "No, you cannot drop your bag as if you are on time, only to come into class whenever you like" was met with eye rolls and scoffs: "I was in the bathroom. What's your problem? I can't pee or poop? I can't use the bathroom?" If I responded that they could use the bathroom one at a time, but that the classroom expectation was to be in class before the bell rings, I was met with, "I can pee whenever I want. Sorry if me having to pee doesn't fit into your schedule."

It was unreal to me how there was no regard for language, respect, or awareness within a classroom system or community. Even if I managed to get them to cooperate with arriving to class on time, they were uncooperative in the classroom space, talking over me to each other, glaring at me, and making learning for everyone nearly impossible.

I was tangling myself in my own fears of disapproval as well as the philosophical idea for teachers to understand their students. I was, therefore, restricting myself from taking a direct approach to end these behaviors.

If I tried to understand them and approach them with, "I'm curious why you act this way in here; help me understand more, so we can figure this out," I was met with "What is your problem? I get my work done." This is a dangerous mindset amongst some students, who think if they're getting work done, they are allowed to act and do whatever they want. They do not recognize how completing their work is the basic expectation of being in school, and that much more beyond that is expected of them.

I talked again with these students individually and as a group. I modified class expectations and work expectations. I called home. I involved the administrator who works with my grade level. I informed the guidance counselors. I recorded information and sent through behavior examples. I tried to use the side-door method by building positive relationships, resetting expectations, and attempting to understand what they needed and how I could be part of a positive restart.

While administrator and guidance counselor support made the biggest difference and the girls started showing up (and staying) on time, they soon replaced that behavior with other behaviors, like laughing out loud in the middle of class for no reason, using their phones and having the volume up, dancing to music in their desks, or blowing their noses or clearing their throats right when I'd start talking. One problem ended, and all I did was substitute that problem for a bunch of other problems. Every day, new problems and new frustrations.

By the time I reached the middle of October, I was entering that class stiff, nervous, and trying to think of ways to respond that would keep the class managed without making anything worse, given there were 20 other students sitting in that room who deserved a good, organized education. In all of this, I had to teach the course content of writing and literature and speaking skills. That part of the job didn't stop simply because this was a tremendous challenge. I also had to shake that class off when it ended, so I could be the enthusiastic and capable teacher I wanted to be for the rest of my classes. My other classes didn't include any groups like this, but they weren't that great, either. I was losing my grip, and the stress was building.

I remember telling someone outside of the education field about my first few weeks of school that year, admitting it was awful and I was considering a new profession. He was shocked. He looked at me while he lightly grabbed my arm and proclaimed, "But you love teaching! You always tell me how much you love your job and the students and what you get to do."

After sharing some examples of what I'd been dealing with for a number of years, he innocently asked, "Isn't there someone in the building who could take them out of your class, or isn't there somewhere else you could send them?"

I tried my best to explain that supports are available, but they aren't long-term solutions. "The only lasting solution is if the students *want* to start acting better and start having decency, or if they get into a lot of trouble for acting out and this turns them around," I explained, "and that may not happen until they are older, or if someone gets involved, or if they are separated from each other in future classes." He responded, "No, I mean, can't they go to a different teacher or a different school?" I really appreciated this friend's care and questions because it was obvious he was feeling for me and just couldn't understand how this could be happening in schools, or to any teacher. I shared that, "No, they are enrolled in this school because that is where they live. I am the teacher on their schedule. Even if I were to remove them from class, such as through security or an administrator, they would be back, either in 20 minutes, or the next day. I can't request students be removed from my class long-term. That would require a lot of data collection and a willing administrator to determine where they could go. Plus, in this case, there are like six of them. It's not that simple."

His response: "It should be that simple. This sounds crazy."

I told him it *was* crazy, and I thanked him for listening. That was the first time in my teaching life, that I can recall anyway, in which I had ever told anyone outside of my family or a few trusted friends that school can be downright abusive, and that teachers are expected to take it. It was the first time I was ever solely negative about school without any feel-good, optimistic add-ins, like "But I have this other class that..." or "Yeah, it'll be okay and work itself out."

Nope. I didn't have anything good to say, and I didn't want to dig deep to find something. The situation and the sheer amount of stress and work it was causing was unfair, undeserved, and I was done with it all.

It's possible there would have been movement in the right direction if they weren't such a large group. But there were too many of them, and I entered a power-struggle every day. It's possible there would have been movement in the right direction if there were clear and organized systems in place to handle things like this, or to handle any student who consistently, year after year, chooses to disrupt classrooms or who constantly refuses work, requiring one-on-one attention from the teacher for the student to do anything.

I don't know what made these students act this way or what they were trying to communicate through their

> *NO PERSON WANTS TO GO THROUGH THEIR DAY*
> *FEELING WEAK AND POWERLESS.*

behavior, given "behavior is communication." Even if I knew why, it wouldn't excuse any of it, and it wouldn't preclude me from feeling affected. In this case, I was a victim of the circumstance and of *their* choices, yet I had to somehow figure out how to teach them through their behaviors. In the end, their choices caused the greatest impact on me—not on them.

None of this was a matter of better lesson planning, or understanding the curriculum design, or enacting best practices, or incorporating a recent professional development initiative; nor was it me refusing to try strategies that had previously worked with tough students. These kids got enjoyment out of being powerful, and their unstoppable, negative behavior went right on my back, resulting in me feeling like a weak doormat, who still showed up smiling, trying to pretend I was impervious and ready to teach. But inside, I was angry and exhausted. No person wants to go through their day feeling weak and powerless.

"Don't let people rent free space in your head" and "Just let it go" sprang from people who didn't really get it.

Even if those words could work, they were like a garden hose to a raging fire.

People can feel this way when they get cut off in traffic, when they ask someone nicely (or not so nicely) to stop talking in a movie theater and the person ignores them or mocks them, or when they do a favor for someone and don't get an acknowledgement afterwards. It's an indescribable feeling when you are used, stepped on, and disrespected.

I was completely entangled in this situation, and it followed me everywhere—on my drive home, when I was making dinner, while watching my kids' sports game, before going to bed, and when driving to school. My chest and shoulders would tighten, and I became easily agitated from things that wouldn't typically agitate me. This group of girls invaded my life and my mind, and I was completely out of control. They intensified my internal fears, and I felt taken advantage of and used. I needed some real help.

REALIZATIONS

Not knowing it then, but learning about it soon after, these girls hit my most vulnerable emotional triggers: my insecurity of being disliked, my fear that I wasn't good enough, and my need for approval. In a weird way, colliding with this group of girls, despite being the adult teacher with a solid reputation, launched me back to my 12-year-old self, trying to negotiate my survival in a harsh middle school world. Asserting yourself could lead to more problems and trusting that others would be nice simply because you were nice was never a guarantee.

In the situation at school, when I tried nice, they saw weakness, and they attacked even harder. One of my dear friends reminded me I could be the juiciest peach, but there are some people who just refuse to like peaches. I appreciated this love and reminder. Unfortunately, though, the situation was affecting my work, my class period, and my peace of mind. No one can do their work well when their peace of mind is disturbed. I felt uncomfortable teaching in that class. My teaching was not at its best. I knew it, and I felt guilty because of it. Seeing myself as an adult person being treated with disregard and hostility by a group of teenage girls made me feel shame and anger.

It also made me feel like quitting.

Who wants to be in a job that triggers you and hits your emotional stuff? Who wants that ever, let alone every day? I felt exposed and mocked; yet, I had to show up and do my job, and I had to do it well. I couldn't run away or avoid the class or hand it over to someone else. Each day for an hour and 20 minutes, I was in the thick of that class period.

I chose to show up pleasantly, trying my best to be there for the other students who didn't cause issues. Talk about acting. Talk about exhaustion. Because in one's teaching day, "the snacky girls" aren't the whole day. They are just a portion. To reiterate, that is why a teacher's day is so confusing and unsettling. And that is why teaching is emotional.

So, at first, I did the thing that I knew how to do, and that I'd done so many times before I'd worked through my introspective learning. I doubled down on my control. I reworked lesson plans. I reworked my classroom seating arrangement. I reworked assessments. I tried to rally other kids behind me. Ugh. So much re-working! So much energy wasted. Of course, it didn't make any difference because that wasn't the actual problem.

The actual problem was with *me*, and the inner work I had yet to do.

Their behaviors hit me deep. These girls had gotten far under my skin, and I couldn't shake it. I began to see the emotional reality of *who I was* and what I was dealing with. It was through this painful introspection that I learned an invaluable lesson.

Here was my perception turned reality: they saw me, and *I saw me in my school environment*, as someone *they could do this to*. They saw me as a nothing, a valueless person. They saw me as someone they could pick on, laugh at, mess with, take advantage of. Bully. I never saw myself as valueless or as someone who could be bullied. But in this scenario, I saw myself as someone who couldn't do much about it. As the teacher, I couldn't block them, tell them off, distance myself from them. I felt powerless, and I allowed myself to feel powerless. They decided they wanted to treat me like this, and I took it. I saw myself as powerless to their power. I detested the all-familiar lose-lose corner.

In this case, and in so many like it, these mean students have the upper hand over the teacher, or at least that's how we've allowed them to act to some teachers and peers. There are some teachers that these same students would never treat this way. Why is that? It's hard to define, but it's true. Maybe if I were male?—no, that doesn't seem fair because I know males have these problems, too. Maybe if I were stricter and meaner?— no, that doesn't seem fair because my kindness and gentleness and enthusiasm are why so many love me, and students don't work well with the strict, mean teacher either.

How about this one?

Maybe if I didn't feel inferior sometimes. Maybe if I didn't feel not good enough sometimes. Maybe if I didn't hustle for approval.

Oh. Ohhh. Okay. Yeah. There we go. There it is. These are the problems. These are the lessons.

These insecurities are inside me, and outside experiences brought them all to the surface, causing me to feel rejected, used, and bothered.

I was the teacher. I was the one who was supposed to be in charge, in control. But I was out of control and hustling for approval from every person in every part of my day, whether student, parent, colleague, or administrator, because I was trying to protect myself from my insecurities, and I was trying to ensure the world around me didn't see those insecurities.

No wonder I was so damn tired. No wonder I was so overwhelmed. No wonder these girls bothered me so much.

This group of girls who took advantage of me brought attention to something I had carefully hidden deep inside of me, something I could no longer afford to ignore. Recognizing this was just the first step. The real work came after in figuring out why it was all there and what I was going to do about it.

I had hit a low spot that was a new feeling for me. I remember on a Friday in October of that school year slowly walking out of the building, as teachers howled around me with excitement, thinking that I wasn't even excited it was Friday because I'd have to come back on Monday. I drove home with vibrant gold, yellow, red, and orange Autumn colors adorning the branches of large trees, blazing like a

> *I COULDN'T RELY ON SOMEONE ELSE TO FIX THIS FOR ME. NO ONE ELSE COULD FIX HOW I WAS FEELING INSIDE. ONLY I COULD BE THE ONE TO DO THAT.*

sunset—a sight that usually brings me such anticipation and happiness—just wondering if I had it in me to get home and act like everything was fine. I didn't want to see anyone including my own family, and I certainly didn't want to socialize. This was all a very new feeling for me.

I was beginning to dread my days, all because of feeling so drained by the emotional fatigue of my job. No job—no matter how much one loves it or wants to love it—is worth feeling dread. I was beginning to feel like I'd been handed an injustice. How unfair, I thought during this self-pitying drive home, that my day sucks while other teachers have good days, maybe even easy days. I knew I was a loved person and teacher. I knew that I had many blessings. I also knew that this school year would have its way of repeating for me again, and I didn't know if I wanted to keep going through school years like this.

Did this mean I was done with teaching? Did this mean I'd be looking for a new job? What job? Did this mean the lifestyle I had created would change?

That seemed so messed up. So unfair, when I really loved being a teacher.

This was on me, I reasoned. I couldn't rely on someone else to fix this for me. No one else could fix how I was feeling inside. Only I could be the one to do that.

At the next red light, I took out my phone (not something I'd recommend) and I researched "therapist near me." I was looking for a name, not a company, and I clicked on the first name that appeared. The therapist's face looked calm and inviting and intelligent. His business was close to my house. The website said he took insurance. Some boxes were checked.

I left that Google page open on my phone. I finished my drive home and pulled into the garage. I took a deep breath, and walked into my house with an exuberant, "HIIIII!!! I'm home!!! Who's ready to have a great weekend?!?!"

More hiding. More pretend games. I knew there was no way I could keep it up.

PART III:
EPIPHANY &
EMPOWERMENT

THE CALL

I called Lou on a crisp Tuesday afternoon in the late Fall. The blue sky was bold, vibrant without a cloud, and I remember looking up at that sky with the sounds of kids playing throughout the neighborhood, thinking it was almost so perfectly blue and remarkable that it was demanding why I couldn't get out of my head to appreciate it. The chill in the air was such that you could snuggle into a soft, nice-smelling long-sleeve shirt over yoga pants, and all the moms were excited about the beautiful weather, the established school routines, and planning for Thanksgiving. The atmosphere was relaxed, anticipating, joyful.

I played along as I typically do when I want to hide my real emotions. But that game was getting harder. My spirit was bothered, and what usually worked to get me out of school moods, like playing with my kids and socializing with friends, was no longer working as effectively. It was another tough start to the school year, and I had driven home defeated and tired.

What was I going to do? How was I going to get through this one?

So, I did the thing I had been thinking about for a few weeks yet hadn't done. I called that therapist's office close to my house. *He answered on the second ring.* I couldn't believe it.

I was so not expecting an answer that I stumbled through why I was even calling, and I even considered just saying, "Hey! Thanks for answering! This is actually way too scary, so never mind. Have a great day!"

But I hung in there with that phone call, and he got me scheduled for an appointment two days later. I know. I can't even believe it as I'm telling you the story. No one's attempts at mental health services seem to go anywhere as smoothly as this.

I informed my husband of my crisis and plans, and 48 hours later, I was driving to meet Lou for the first time. Lou was a "homerun first at bat," and I am so lucky I got him in my life. After just that initial appointment, I left his office feeling much better and standing much straighter. Complete appreciation, admiration, and gratitude to you, Lou!

Lou wasn't one to mess around or to allow you to go on and on for too long. He was exactly who I needed at that time. As he listened to me trying to dissect my life's dichotomies and paradoxes, I watched him relax back in his reclining chair, touch his fingers and thumbs together like a prayer, nod to me, and then say, "Stop."

> *I HAD POSITIONED MYSELF IN A PLACE OF AUTHORITY, BUT THAT I HAD NO AUTHORITY OVER MYSELF, SO MY LIFE IN TEACHING AND OTHERWISE WAS GOING TO CONTINUE BEING AN EMOTIONAL DISASTER UNTIL I DECIDED TO BE... EMPOWERED.*

I was sure I had done something wrong. Like I had screwed up my first attempt at explaining why I was in his office, if a person could even do such a thing. What followed was the best understanding of myself, and I remain infinitely grateful to him for seeing this in me so quickly and for being honest with me.

Lou told me that I was dishonest with myself and with most people in my life, that I didn't trust myself, and that I was disempowered.

Having no prior experience with therapy, I laugh now thinking how I thought Lou was going to feel bad for me and side with me, not tell me that I was wrong. This direct approach was exactly what I needed. He told me I had positioned myself in a place of authority, but that I had *no authority over myself*, so my life in teaching and otherwise was going to continue being an emotional disaster until I decided to be...

EMPOWERED.

While he explained the concept of empowerment vs. disempowerment, my mind raced to example after example after example of the many times I had protected myself by choosing approval from others over approval from myself, and that each time I made the decision to choose what I thought someone else would want over what I wanted, I was giving away my power and showing myself over and over again that I was weak and powerless.

At my core, I was protecting myself against rejection, but I didn't know I was doing it.

I attempted to reason that he wasn't altogether correct because I wasn't a submissive, weak person, and that I had accomplished a lot in my life, including a college athletic career, degrees, awards, a teaching job with a respectable reputation, a loving family, close friends, and happiness.

He responded with a confident smile. "No?" he questioned. "Why are you here, then, lying to yourself and choosing denial?"

I thought he sized me up too quickly and couldn't possibly be right. "What do you mean, 'choosing denial'?" I retorted defensively. But he just stared at me, and threw the question back, asking me why I thought he would say that I was in denial.

I fell into the strategy, and explained that he would see me in denial because I was holding all the good things in my life, including my positivity, like a shield in front of me, so no one, including myself, could see that I was actually insecure, and that I was afraid of people's disapprovals, which would lead to a false perception of who I actually am.

There was no way I could have people seeing me for something that I wasn't. No way could I have people disapproving of me or disliking me. That would be too scary for an insecure person, who didn't feel like enough.

In no way could I be *powerful*.

I was denying who I really was, and how I really felt. I was hiding. I was lying to myself. And, I was so good at it, I had even deceived myself.

I had constructed such a thick, confident, people-pleasing, people-approving mask over the years that I didn't know if I could even take it off.

He then asked me to be truthful. He said, "Tell me. What does it feel like to be *you*?"

I shared that it felt confusing because I *really* am a genuinely happy, joyful, loving person, and that I love my beautiful life and I am so thankful for the people I have in my life. "I love people," I said, "and I love making people happy and being a sunshine in people's lives."

I confessed that I knew I was successful in my life, but that I always feel like I am not good enough, even though people in my life wouldn't agree. "I feel like I am working to prove myself, and that I am working at a 150% level, but getting 40% level results," I expressed, "and that I sometimes hate teaching when I have students who are mean and don't care, and that I hate how teaching can make me feel and that no one seems to care that teachers get abused, but that I keep teaching with joy because there didn't seem a better option." I told him that I say yes to things when I want to say no because I don't want people disappointed in me, hurt by me, or annoyed with me.

I lamented that I am downright exhausted and frustrated, and that there are times when I just want to hide in my bed, where no student could say "F-you" and I wouldn't be banging my head against a wall at my job or wishing my life could speed up a couple of decades, so I could retire.

I tried my best to explain how I feel like I am two parts that sit side-by-side, never blending, with one side feeling denied and neglected as the other side feels happy and confident. I admitted there is a part of me that feels resentful and angry in teaching and in other parts of my life, but that I choose to act or play pretend when I downright dislike something because it seems simpler and easier this way.

He responded with powerful, important questions: "Really?" he asked. "Is how you are choosing to live *really* less stressful? Is how you are choosing to live giving you what you want in your life?"

In other words, was my denial and disempowerment serving me?

After a few moments of silence, I quietly shook my head and answered "No," while looking down at his carpeted floor with my throat tightening and that burn of tears shocking my eyes.

AWARENESS

The choices I was making weren't serving me, probably had never served me, and certainly weren't going to serve me in the future.

I realized I had made a choice without even realizing I was making a choice. My choice was to pick the comfort and happiness of others—as well as their expectations of me—over the comfort and happiness of myself and the expectations I had for myself.

Truly, I was living disempowered.

Lou joked that "the teacher was getting homework," and that I had an assignment to complete before my next session with him, which he scheduled for later in the week. The homework included finding a book about empowered women, identifying my next example of disempowerment, and journaling about my thoughts from our first session. The beginning of that journal, which I was fairly consistent with writing at the time, is now the book you hold in your hands.

I left his office thankful and bewildered at how so much had happened in just 45 minutes.

I also left his office mad. That did surprise me. I was mad. Not at Lou. At myself. How could it have come to this? How could I have allowed all of this? I had been so loved growing up and had troops of friends. I was an athlete, the captain of my college volleyball team, a Varsity high school volleyball coach, and a high-achieving student. I adored my teachers, and they loved me. I was always a leader, and people looked to me when there were conflicts to help mediate.

People love me, think I am funny, and trust me. I am a parent to young children, teaching them to believe in themselves and to remember that they matter and not to let others boss them. Yet, here I was, not even valuing myself the way I deserved to be valued. Unbelievable. It was playing out in so many ways and in so many places. Example after example swarmed my mind like angry bees around a fallen hive.

I was furious at myself for getting tangled into this pattern. I was furious at systems and expectations and lose-lose situations. I drove home with my hands gripped so tightly on the steering wheel that my fingers went numb.

> ## *I WAS CHOOSING MY FEAR OVER MY VALUE.*

I replayed all those times when I didn't speak up as assertively as I could have and didn't put a stop to nonsense behaviors or situations because I was choosing my fear over my value. I was choosing another person's wants, and/or my fear about their possible reactions, over what I knew was best for the situation or for myself.

I was choosing being liked by *others* over being liked by *me*. How weak of me not to just cut it off. How weak of me to just allow it in my space.

In my teacher life, I was, in essence, handing over my approval of self and personal sense of worth to teenagers, instead of holding it close within.

How disempowered of me.

I recalled with resentment the hours I consumed myself with schoolwork after teaching a full day to make my lessons more effective, my units even better, my assessments even stronger, and my grading more precise, and how in so many instances I just handed that hard work from those long hours over to others who asked for the lessons and assessments and packets, when I wasn't getting the same work back in return.

I regretfully remembered the days when I had sick babies and chose to go to school because I was overwhelmed with creating solid substitute lesson plans. I was worried about how my students would act with a substitute, and I was worried about the transition back to school after being out. I'm lucky—my sick babies could stay with my husband, their dad. But they weren't with their mommy. Why would I choose work over my baby, when I'm privileged enough not to have to do this?

I reflected on the sleepless nights grading, planning, or ruminating about an issue. I resented those accumulated hours that I could have given to something else in my life. I felt angry about not just saying "No." I felt angry about the consequence of weight gain and some distanced friendships.

How disempowered of me.

I recognized my role in allowing certain behaviors in my classroom because teachers are set up to be perceived as "in control," and they are also set up to be powerless over someone else's choices. I realized I was allowing, instead of putting some things to an end.

How disempowered of me.

I thought about the many examples of me giving my time and energy to some school-related thing without thanks or recognition or acknowledgement, and yet how I continued to do this, even knowing the end result would be the same.

How disempowered of me.

Over and over, I confessed to times in and out of school when I hustled for approval, trying to feel like I was good enough, and how I willingly gave my power away—consequently, also giving away my energy and my value.

I saw it all for what it was, and I admitted my role, my allowance, in all of it.

Eventually, I made my way home to my concerned husband, who knew something was up because my 45-minute appointment turned into me being gone for over two hours as I had been sitting in a nearly empty grocery store parking lot contemplating my life. I didn't know what the next steps were going to be, but I did know I was done feeling like this, and that I was eager to learn how to reclaim my power and the value I deserved to have in myself.

CONSCIOUS TEACHING 11

BEING REAL & BEING VULNERABLE

I started with Lou and I did the work with Lou. God bless that man who was a gift from Heaven to me. Week after week. Book after book. Podcast after podcast. And I grew, and grew, and grew. I read a lot, and I listened a lot. I still do.

Once you start doing this type of deep, inner work, you learn about yourself and the reasons behind your behaviors. You don't go back to the way you used to be. You are the same person and a new person all at the same time, and it's an empowering rebirth. You become *conscious* of all that had previously been *unconscious* within you but was causing so many points of pain and stress.

I echoed Maya Angelou's[14] self-forgiving words: "Do the best you can, until you know better. Then, when you know better, do better." I needed these words, and I willed them into myself. I had to hold myself accountable for the things I had allowed in my teaching life and my personal life while giving myself grace for doing what I thought was necessary in those moments. Now, I know better, and I do better.

I read about boundaries, empowerment, vulnerability, self-love, our soul's purpose, God, spirituality, the shadow self, fear, the inner child, the trap of perfectionism, manifesting, simplifying, transforming one's life, meditation, and so many other topics.

I devoured as many books and podcasts as I could. It gave me the gift of some of the best life teachers on the planet. These are people we all have easy (and in some cases free) access to, thanks to today's technologies and availabilities. People like Rob Bell, Michael and Monica Berg, Kate Bowler, Brené Brown, Michelle Chalfant, Glennon Doyle, Jim Fortin, Carolyn Myss, Mel Robbins, Michael Singer, Jay Shetty, and Oprah Winfrey. There are so many others to add to this list. Check them out. Read and listen for yourself. You won't be disappointed, and you, too, will grow and understand yourself so much better.

If you read and listen to Brené Brown, you will learn, spiritually and scientifically, how necessary it is for us to be honest with ourselves and about ourselves. As she says in her book *Daring Greatly*,[15] "Vulnerability is not weakness, and the uncertainty…we face every day [is] not optional. Our only choice is a question of engagement." Vulnerability, as defined by Brené Brown, is "our most accurate measure of courage."

Vulnerability is not inferiority. Only through being vulnerable and honest with ourselves and about ourselves

VULNERABILITY IS NOT INFERIORITY.

can we begin to identify what is not going well for us. Only through identification can we then begin to change.

Brown titles her book *Daring Greatly* after the infamous speech by Theodore Roosevelt[16] that has come to be known as "The Man in the Arena," where he proclaims, "It is not the critic who counts; not the man who points out how the strong man stumbles, or where the doer of deeds could have done them better. The credit belongs to the man who is actually in the arena… who strives valiantly; who errs… because there is no effort without error and shortcoming;… who spends himself in a worthy cause; [and] who…at the worst, if he fails, at least fails while daring greatly."

This is a valiant spurning of the outside critic who isn't doing the work. It is also a spurning of our inner critic that lives in us, oozing doubt and hesitancy.

If we don't do the honest work about who we really are, then we stay trapped in the same cycles and patterns. Even worse, we stay disempowered. So, the first thing we must do, which is the most crucial, intimidating step, is understand ourselves on a deep level, perhaps deeper than we've ever considered. It requires an admittance that we have played a part in what is not going well in our lives or what is holding us back. It requires a long look in the mirror. It requires no blaming to anyone else. It requires us to self-forgive, and it requires us to be willing to do better.

THE CHILD WITHIN US

Lou introduced me to the psychology of the inner child. This inner child is in all of us. He/she is our emotional state, and he/she is meant to protect us from harm or danger, and to alert us when something is amiss in our life. When we are angry, for example, it is like an alarm system for us to perk up, pay attention, and work to resolve whatever it is that is bothering us. We aren't meant to stay bothered or angry or insecure.

The inner child, according to this psychological theory and my interpretation from learning about it, is our alert system, our alarm. *Our inner child is our emotional state.* The inner child's needs are very strong, just as an actual child's needs are very strong, and these needs show themselves in varied ways depending upon what it is that affects us emotionally.

As adults, our inner child can run rampant and be in the driver's seat of our lives without us even being aware that it is happening. I call these adult temper tantrums. We can respond the same ways over and over again to similar situations, not even realizing we are doing it because we, the adult, aren't actually in control. Our inner child, full of unregulated emotions, is in control. We just keep spinning our wheels, getting nowhere.

We have to take back the driver's seat and place our inner child safely in the backseat. We don't want to kick our inner child out of the car. We need the inner child in the car with us because they are our alert system, and we need to feel our emotions. But we don't want the child driving the car, and we don't want our reactive emotions running our lives.

To calm our inner child—to take control of the driver's seat—and to reach peace, the inner child has to be nurtured, validated, soothed, and loved. There are lots of ways to do this. It works best for me to take a breath and then to talk to myself in my head when I recognize I'm having an emotional response. I give myself pep talks and reminders that what I'm experiencing is my inner child getting my attention because something has flared me up and triggered me. Like any good parent, I give the child attention, and I—the adult—try to fix the problem.

To do this, you have to:

1. Recognize that something has occurred that has made you flare up emotionally.
2. Identify precisely what that something is.

3. Ask yourself questions about how it makes you feel and why you think it makes you feel this way.

4. Enact your plan on how to handle it, how to reason it out in yourself, how to love yourself through it, or how to better it. Enacting a plan helps to calm the emotional, inner child side of us because then he/she doesn't have to be in charge. There is a plan in place that will bring relief.

When we learn about the inner child and we learn about the most vulnerable parts within ourselves, we are on the path to becoming empowered and conscious. The goal is to be a conscious person. For teachers, the goal is to become a conscious person, who is also a conscious teacher. To reiterate, our personal lives are wrapped in our teacher lives because teaching is emotional, and we are emotional beings.

Good teachers know how to get their content to their students so effectively that their students could teach the content. Great teachers do this *and* understand

> FOR TEACHERS, THE GOAL IS TO BECOME A CONSCIOUS PERSON, WHO IS ALSO A CONSCIOUS TEACHER.

themselves on a deep level, so they can resiliently handle the emotional stress that comes their way. It's not enough to have a bunch of good teachers who can't do their jobs effectively because they are dealing with emotional stress and fatigue. The education system needs to have great teachers. What the system needs to do is establish, build, and nurture "conscious teachers."

PERSONAL TRIGGERS

I learned from Lou to consider times in my life when I was bothered, defensive, hurt, or angry. In other words, to think of a time when I was emotionally triggered, and I had a strong reaction to something or to someone, even if that reaction felt justified. Sure, I could do that. How many weeks was he willing to give me?!

- *Who were the people?*
- *What were the events?*
- *How did it feel?*
- *How did I handle it?*

I learned this and I still ask myself these questions because what emotionally affects us in our personal lives will somehow and some way come to us in our teaching lives. You may not think it will, but it will, and it's best to expect it and then to have a plan. I didn't think of teaching in this way until years ago when I started my introspective journey. I also didn't think that young high

> WHAT EMOTIONALLY AFFECTS US IN OUR PERSONAL LIVES WILL SOMEHOW AND SOME WAY COME TO US IN OUR TEACHING LIVES.

school students would emotionally affect me, until I was experiencing the effect. I remember trying to reason this out with Lou.

"But I'm an adult," I'd say to Lou with as much charge as I could muster, "and they are young adult students. I have a family and a house and a life outside of school. These are kids."

I'd ask him, "How could I be affected by *kids* in my job? This makes no sense to me."

His reasoning was that we are human, and it doesn't so much matter where the emotional trigger comes from. "It could come from anything or anyone, including kids," I remember him telling me. I learned that if we are people, working with people, then we will, at some point, experience our own emotional pains that we have hidden carefully, so they aren't exposed. For me, I had done a great job hiding my insecurities—or shadows as they are also called. I had hidden my fear of inferiority, my fear of disapproval, and my fear of rejection so well that I didn't even consciously know I had these. I had to learn how to become conscious of these in my personal life and in my teaching life to be a strong emotional teacher.

I'd drive home from my weekly sessions with Lou acknowledging that it didn't feel good to admit that 15-year-olds emotionally affect me because I was still battling that internal conflict of being the adult in charge and being in control as the adult teacher. I was also still trying to understand how to balance accepting that 15-year-olds can emotionally affect me while holding them accountable for their behaviors. This sometimes requires outside assistance, such as from a school administrator or the student's parent.

As my sessions with Lou continued, I began to accept that this is part of teaching. I began to see that teachers don't have as much control as they think they do, and that teaching is emotional, but we have somehow forgotten to include these very important aspects when learning how to become a good teacher. I realized that *every* teacher needs the benefit of this work and this knowledge as so much of our day affects us, not so much from the physical work of the job, but from the emotional impacts of the job.

Therefore, I will ask some questions, just as Lou did for me, with the intention of allowing an opportunity for your own introspection. Consider your answers to these questions, and consider times in your recent past when you may have been agitated or defensive or bothered by someone else's behavior or choices. Being able to think through these situations will help you learn about yourself and will help you understand what, or whom, may possibly affect you in your classroom.

- How do you react when people purposely don't do as you say or don't listen to you?
- Do you get defensive when people judge you or criticize you or give you feedback, especially if you didn't ask for advice?
- Do you have trouble following advice or direction from an authority figure who doesn't also do your job?
- How do you feel when you are dismissed or invalidated?
- Do you have trust issues?
- Do you hold grudges?
- Does it take you a long time to let things go?
- How do you act when you are mad? Why do you act this way?
- Do you take revenge when an injustice has been done to you? If so, what do you hope to gain from taking revenge?
- Do you have different expectations for girls than for boys?

- Are there any kinds of people who make you feel less comfortable? If so, why? And what is your response?
- Do you need to be liked?
- Do you need to be seen as cool or popular?
- Do you often or always have to be in charge? Do you assert your power over others to stay in charge?

I am affected in class when I have students flat out not listen to me or not cooperate. I am affected in class when students refuse to stop talking when I am talking. I am affected in class when students continue to play computer games or message on their phones when I am teaching, or when they are supposed to be discussing in a group and are instead disengaged. I am affected in class when I know a student isn't happy with me or the class and refuses to say hello to me, make eye contact, or brings other students down. I am affected in class when parents don't help me figure out their child's behavior, so the onus falls on my shoulders. I am affected in class when students use my class time to go to the bathroom only to socialize with friends or make TikTok dance videos. I am affected in class when I have a student who tells me my class is stupid or boring. I am affected in class when I communicate how their behaviors affect me and I seek solutions, but am met with uncooperation, disrespect, or refusal.

These examples make me feel inferior, like I am not good enough, and like I am a doormat. I seek approval, so I see defiance or refusal as rejections of me, causing me insecurity. I don't like to feel like a doormat. I don't like to be taken advantage of. I don't like to feel not good enough. I don't like unnecessary conflict or problems. I don't like when I am not liked.

It doesn't matter if the person is a teenager and I am an adult. Defiance flares me up. Backing down to defiance and avoiding conflict to move along with my happy life may work in low-stakes settings, like the grocery store or in a parking lot, but in my classroom setting, letting these kinds of behaviors go will only cause me more of the same problems and then consequential negative emotional feelings.

I value people, like myself, who are team players, cooperative, supportive, givers before takers, and who choose to improve the quality of situations vs. choosing to tear down the quality of situations.

Other teachers don't get as upset about the situations that affect me, just as I don't get as upset by situations that affect others. I don't get affected, for example, when a student needs help *again* or is incredibly dependent on me to do work. I see this as the student feeling insecure and wanting to get the work correct. I don't get affected when students enter my room a few seconds late to class,

> RECOGNIZING AND ACCEPTING OUR SHADOWS
> AND THEN WORKING THROUGH THEM MAY SEEM
> LIKE PERSONAL WORK, BUT IT'S ALSO PART
> OF TEACHING. IT HAS ALWAYS BEEN. WE JUST
> HAVEN'T YET SEEN IT THIS WAY.

especially if they acknowledge the lateness and give me a greeting. I don't get affected when students seem disinterested, as long as they aren't pulling others down. I don't get affected when students question their grades or my feedback. I don't get affected when a parent wants to talk to me on the phone or needs me to explain something over email, even if the email is curt. I don't get affected when someone in authority says, "I think you can do better." I don't get affected when students are cooperative but will never engage beyond basic cooperation.

Recognizing and accepting our shadows and then working through them may seem like personal work, but it's also part of teaching. It has always been. We just haven't yet seen it this way.

Teaching is a people profession. Obviously. But we have to remember that people are emotional. They are also self-centered. How do we navigate our own emotions and self-centeredness in the midst of others' emotions and self-centeredness, while also teaching them skills and concepts and going home in one emotional piece?

There are lots of ways to do this, and working through our inner child to achieve empowerment is just one way. If you want to know more about the inner child, look up Michelle Chalfant[17], who is an expert in this field. She has a podcast called "The Adult Chair" and has other invaluable tools that will teach this to you and provide examples of how to make this work in your life. In her podcast, she has hundreds of episodes that teach how to connect with our inner child and how to take back the driver's seat. In her coaching and therapy practices, Michelle teaches "using three different chairs, a child chair, an adolescent chair, and an adult chair." She walks listeners through when they are in each type of chair based on what they are experiencing and how they are reacting. The hope is that we can recognize when we are in each "chair," and that we can bring ourselves to our "adult chair."

Lou introduced me to the inner child psychological theory that has changed my personal and teaching life and has helped me to better regulate my emotional triggers. Michelle Chalfant, through her podcast and guidance, has been my side-by-side mentor in applying this philosophy to my life.

LOWER THE VOLUME

Lou gifted me the best phrase to help me look upon instances that trigger me as he coached me to "lower the volume." I love this. What a gentle way to place the things that hurt us in perspective. It teaches us that these things will come at us outside of our control, and they will sting and agitate and hurt and mess with us. We can't avoid any of that, and we also may not be able to get rid of it entirely. But we can work a strategy that helps to "lower the volume" on that pain, so it's not as loud and in our faces, taking over our minds and our days. This mindset takes the pressure off, and it guides me to focus on something I know I can do. I can definitely lower the volume, even if I can't turn it off completely.

I'd like to share my process with you that has worked for me to "lower the volume" as Lou put it. When I feel bothered by a situation, and I need to calm my inner child from feeling rejected, insecure, or inferior, or when I am hustling for approval, I go through a process. It's not always a set-in-stone process, and it's not always a long process.

Sometimes I need to take a deep breath and remind myself that "this situation is simply me *feeling like* a doormat. *I am* not a doormat." Or this situation is simply a person expressing some anger or disrespect, and the roots don't have much to do with me. I'm just the easiest target, and I can signal to dozens of other people who have not expressed any anger or disrespect toward me. Or this situation is someone not happy with me because I said "No" or I held a line, and I'll remind myself this feeling is temporary, and they will get over it. I hold fast to my "No" because there was a reason I gave it.

I don't hustle for approval, and I don't change my mind. I don't behave the way they want me to behave simply because they are showing me disapproval.

When I have the typical feelings of unrest, I remind myself this is my "inner child alarm" going off, and that I only need to turn the alarm off calmly, compassionately, and patiently. This is enough to put me back on track. It may not be over, and I may need to do this each day if I have a student who bothers me. I don't aim to rid myself of the feeling. I aim to "lower the volume" of the feeling. To me, there is a big difference.

Outlined next is my process of working with my inner child and lowering the volume from a simple, hypothetical example of a ninth-grade student refusing to move into an assigned group for collaborative work. I created this example as it's easy to follow, though I recognize there could be greater emotional stresses in one's day than a student refusing to join a group.

1. First, I recognize that a 15-year-old student set out to dismiss me *on purpose*, and they made that clear in their actions, words, or tone of voice.
2. Second, I acknowledge myself in how this makes me feel physically. I may feel my heart pound, my stomach tighten, or my mouth grimace in anger/ annoyance. I also acknowledge myself in how this makes me feel emotionally. I acknowledge I now feel insecure and bothered and nervous. I don't know how this power-struggle will go, and that makes me unsure how to respond.
3. Next, I tell myself that this person's behavior is unaligned with my core values of cooperation and being a team player.
4. Then, I connect with my inner child.
   a. I take a breath and take a moment to stay calm and not to react. Even if I only have five seconds, I take a breath and take a moment.
   b. I remind myself that this situation is temporary, that I am not in control of this student's choices, and that this student's choices have nothing to do with my value as a teacher or person.
   c. If the situation is fairly low-stakes, like a seat issue or not completing work, I hold off on saying anything to the student, but I look at him, so he knows I am aware of his defiance.

d. When I have time to talk to my inner child, I close my eyes and tell the little girl in me that this student chose to behave poorly in that moment, and it has nothing to do with her. It was the student's choice. I acknowledge that it made her feel disrespected and walked all over.

e. Then, I remind her of what year it is, and that I am the adult in her life, who will handle this situation appropriately. I comfort her by telling her she doesn't have to handle this problem because I am her adult, and I will be supporting her and blocking her from this person and his behavior. Then, I give her some love, and send her to the backseat of the car, and she sits there calmly looking out the window.

5. Finally, I move into my plan with the student:

a. At a time that is right, usually one-on-one during class or after class, I approach the student with calm emotion.

i. I let him know that I saw he did not cooperate in engaging with the assigned group. I ask him if he'd like to share with me why he made that decision.

1. If he has a valid reason, my emotions soften, and I have understanding and compassion. We make a plan for what to do better next time, so there isn't a miscommunication or misperception of defiance.

2. If he has no valid reason other than defiance, then I share with him clearly and directly that I won't (language is important) tolerate or accept blatant defiance to me as a person or in my classroom. "I don't allow that," I say. "I wouldn't allow that," I assert. I inform him of this warning, and that I'll be documenting (FYI-style) it to the disciplinarian should there be a future instance. I then remind him that he now has a choice the next time he comes into my room because he knows my stance on defiance and disrespect.

3. I explain he may not like my reaction, but my intention is to have a healthy, cooperative classroom, and I make that my number one priority. I then wish him a good day, and I let him know I'm looking forward to a fresh start the next day.

4. I make it a point the next day to let him know I am glad he's in my classroom. If the student is cooperating, I acknowledge this with thanks and appreciation.

5. If the student is not cooperating, I have another one-on-one conversation to let him know a reset is expected, and that I will be communicating with the administrator.

Each situation with each student will vary because each student is different, just like every teacher is different. As you come to know yourself and your students, it becomes clearer when you need to directly stop behaviors, when you can enact humor to subdue a problem, and when you need to approach a situation with delicacy and softness.

What I have outlined above is not a one-stop-shop sort of response. The inner child work has been a turning point for me, and it was just what I needed to assuage the fears within. It may not work for you. In the illustration above, I would address my inner child. Every time. But I may not be so direct with a student if he typically cooperates and just didn't on that particular day. I also wouldn't send the issue through to administration if the

> *IF YOU ARE THE TYPE OF TEACHER WHO WANTS TO TEACH AND WHO ENJOYS TEACHING, BUT YOU KEEP EXPERIENCING TOUGH SITUATIONS THAT UPEND YOU, IT IS IMPERATIVE YOU FIND WHAT WORKS FOR YOU.*

student seemed to understand they were out of line and they showed up better the next day.

My purpose in sharing an example of what I do is to give you an option. It may not be the option that works for you, but something will. If you are the type of teacher who *wants* to teach and who *enjoys* teaching, but you keep experiencing tough situations that upend you, it is imperative you find what works for you. Empowering teachers to be emotionally strong may start with what works for the individual teacher, but it must be supported by everyone if it is going to work and be a long-term solution.

One way to be a conscious teacher is to work with our shadows, or our emotional triggers, or our inner child. I love observing people who are full of confidence and who never seem to care what others think. They just do what they do and everyone around them will figure out how to deal with it. These people delight me because I am so not that person. I have to work with what I've got, and I can't wish I were someone else. My shadows are insecurity, self-doubt, and people pleasing. These shadows exist while I simultaneously navigate the world with joy, confidence and satisfaction. There are worse shadows just as there are some who never deal with insecurity as a shadow. I accept these are part of who I am, and I consciously work with them.

Conscious teaching is being aware of what is happening around us and to us, but not *reacting* to what is happening around us and to us. This is the goal because so much of our teaching day causes us to react. We make thousands of decisions in a single school day, and we have students who push our buttons, and we have parents and administrators who push our buttons. Of course we react. None of this is easy, and it takes effort and thought.

Conscious teaching challenges us to look within, and to understand those emotional parts that have been hidden, because those are the parts that are reacting. The challenge is to examine what's within, and then calm it.

From this, we don't react. We respond.

And we stay empowered.

IMMOVABLE 12

A RECOVERING "SHOULD"-ER

On my drive home one school day, I recognized the tight, unsettled feelings in my chest as the result of me hustling for approval that day because I had experienced something that made me feel insecure and judged. It had flared up my fear of rejection and not being good enough. I turned the radio down, took a few deep breaths, and reminded myself that I was learning and doing great because now I could at least recognize when I was hustling or feeling insecure.

Then, I turned on my Bluetooth and the next episode of Rob Bell's podcast, *The RobCast*, came on. Rob is one of my favorite and most revered spiritual teachers. I listened to him share a story, and at the end of the story, he told each listener that we should never, ever "should on ourselves or anyone else."

"What?!" I thought, as I laughed at the play on words. This was new for me, and I loved it. I rewound the episode a few seconds to hear it again, and I again chuckled through the words.

Don't should on yourself. Or anyone else. Stop should-ing on yourself. Don't should on anyone else.

Wise and hilarious! I stopped the episode to think about the word "should," and I realized how often I "should" on myself. God! I was should-ing all over the place. At school, at home, on my kids, on my husband, on myself. No one was free from my should-ing. I was should-ing everywhere!

Pun fully intended—it is a crappy word.

We are should-ing all over the place. If you stop and *listen* to people's language, you will hear people use the word should and it's usually in a sentiment of "not good enough" and judgment. Sometimes, we use the word when we have learned a lesson and we know what we will do the next time to make that situation better. "I should have done…" is so different, for example, than "I should be doing…"

I needed to hear how often we use the word "should" and how it disempowers us and puts unnecessary pressure on us to be more, do more, have more, and get more. The word should most often implies what we are currently doing is not good enough and that we "should" be doing more or having more.

What a mistake in language that we may not even hear ourselves say, but it sends us a powerful message, nonetheless. It's very easy to throw the word "should" around in school because that classroom is *never* done. There is always more that could be done to make our classrooms better, stronger, more efficient, and more effective. I have learned in my years of teaching that we could spend an extra three (or more) hours a day on "classroom items," and still never be at a point where our classrooms are perfect or functioning at high levels in every single aspect. This does not discount working to make something stronger and better. We just need to be careful of our language and not to shame ourselves with the word "should" when there are some parts of our classrooms that are stronger than others.

Before understanding how the word "should" undermines, I'd hear myself saying things like, "I should have a better assessment for that unit," or "I should be on more committees," or "I should be volunteering to help with that," or "I should give better feedback on those essays," or "I should spend more time developing high engaging activities for that unit," or "I should reach out to that parent," or "I should do more teacher-student conferencing," or "I should do some work this weekend to catch up," or "I should connect with that teacher I haven't seen for awhile" or "I should have handled that better," or "I should already know how to do this."

Yikes. That's just at school. I was should-ing all over myself in my personal life, too. I know I am not alone.

In sharing this with others, *many* people admitted to me that they also have a running "should" list, and that it only makes them feel bad, not good enough, and exhausted.

Why do we do this to ourselves? I think, for starters, we don't recognize we are doing it. We don't hear the word "should" as a bad word. We see it as a motivating word to keep ourselves doing more and seeking more. For the people who are already high achievers putting pressure on themselves to achieve—like myself—the word "should" only compounds the pressure with more pressure, and that is not healthy.

Additionally, we live in a society that praises and cheers perfection, high achievement, and the accumulation of doing and having a lot. We live in a trophy society. Teachers have an additional layer to this, in that, year after year, there are new philosophical educational ideas that get stacked on old ideas, so we try to do it all, and we are graded and evaluated on how well we can do it all.

It turns us into "I should be doing this," and "My students should be doing that," and "My life should be this way" in every aspect of our day. For me, all these shoulds were exposing a painful part of my identity: that inherently I believed I wasn't good enough and that I should be someone better. That feeling as well as the "shoulds" were exhausting and incredibly unhelpful.

Some of the hardest working teachers are the ones most in need of should-ing recovery. They carry it all on their shoulders, and they feel they "should" be doing even more. They carry the students whose abilities are grade levels behind. They carry the behavior problems as if it's their responsibility to fix someone else's behavior. They carry the kids who have hard home lives and who need Child and Youth Services to advocate for them. They carry the kids who have been through trauma and pain. They carry the change in curricula designs and their colleagues who are having a hard time. They carry committees and extracurriculars. They carry it all.

Listen to your language and consider how you speak about yourself, in your teaching life or in your personal life. Being reflective allows us the space to improve and grow. We have the opportunity to say, "Next time, I'll do this instead" without having to shame ourselves with what we should have done before knowing what the outcome was going to be.

> SOME OF THE HARDEST WORKING TEACHERS ARE THE ONES MOST IN NEED OF SHOULD-ING RECOVERY.

For should-ers, we need to remember kindness and patience to ourselves and that sometimes "good enough" is actually *great*.

Today, I am a recovering should-er. Perhaps you need to join me in should-ing recovery. While the should-ing is still quite sneaky, I do have the ability to catch myself much sooner than I could years ago. I can sense and identify when I'm feeling agitated by insecurity. I don't like the feeling, but I can catch it. This need for people to like me and this need to hustle for approval is still in me. For Diane Manser, it feels good and secure to be liked.

When disapproval or judgment come knocking at my door, I have to pause, take a breath, and listen. Then, I choose to respond better than what I did before. I work hard not to respond with hustling, and I work hard to avoid that icky, bad word "should." That word is a waste of time.

I admit it's easier to teach a class when students like me and like the class. It's nice to walk confidently into a room knowing I am liked, appreciated, and valued. That's when I shine. Class personalities that allow us to shine

> ...THAT SOMETIMES "GOOD ENOUGH" IS ACTUALLY GREAT.

are fun and comfortable, and I could teach for hours in those classes without needing a break.

That may not be the reality of a full teaching day, though. We may go through a school year and have a mix of classes that automatically make us feel comfortable with classes that require some work to make us feel comfortable. Teaching is both/and. Teaching is two truths in one. This is all part of it. Should-ing on ourselves, our students, or our families isn't going to make the reality of our day any better. It will only admonish us and bring on more pressure and shame.

What we can do is recognize when we are in a should spiral and when the "should" list is growing unsupervised in our minds. We can stop ourselves. We can say this is just a stupid word that people use to compare or to expect more. Then, we can reaffirm precisely where we are enough and where we are doing great.

Our language matters. How we speak about ourselves and to ourselves matters. Don't should on yourself. Don't should on anyone else. The teacher whose classroom was next to mine for years—you know, my friend with the "no expectations"—certainly doesn't should on himself or his students, and he lives quite a content life. For me and maybe for some of you, let's put that "should" word down. It doesn't serve you. It doesn't serve me. Root yourself in empowerment and confidence, and let others hear it, too.

WOULDN'T, DON'T, WON'T

Oprah Winfrey's audiobook *The Path Made Clear*[18], which is a self-help title I listened to when working with Lou, bolstered my strength and purpose. In it, Winfrey offers a guide to live a life of significance. Each chapter has invaluable lessons. For me, at that point in my life, nothing held more weight than the power of Oprah's voice when critics doubted her girls' school in South Africa would remain successful. "How could anyone doubt Oprah?" I thought. But here was this infamous, most powerful, revered woman having to keep naysayers off her back.

Perhaps her words need to be framed on the desks of each classroom teacher who battles self-doubt. She firmly, calmly stated to these cynics, "You cannot defeat someone who knows who they truly are. I know who I am and why I am doing this, so I *would not* bet against me."

Transformative…magical. Those words, along with Lou's teaching of self-empowerment, lodged themselves in my soul, and I knew I had found a rock.

No life can have significance or power if the person is wafting between what they want and what they think others want, or what they believe and what they hope others will believe. That is one confused life, and one unclear path. The clear path is one of self-empowerment

> *THE CLEAR PATH IS ONE OF SELF-EMPOWERMENT AND INNER STRENGTH THAT DISALLOWS ANY DOUBT, WHETHER EXTERNAL OR INTERNAL, IN WHAT WE KNOW TO BE RIGHT.*

and inner strength that disallows any doubt, whether external or internal, in what we know to be right.

Oprah Winfrey's willingness to share how she handled critics gave me a guidebook on how I should see myself when faced with tough students or situations. It also opened my eyes to the most powerful words teachers can use in their classrooms, which I discovered while learning about how to be empowered.

Oprah Winfrey cemented herself in "I know who I am and why I am doing this," and she took it one step further to address those outside of herself with "I would not bet against me." Would not. There is power in knowing yourself and knowing why you are doing something. There is also power in addressing others with definitive language. It wasn't "should not," which gives an opportunity to do something or not to do something. "Would not" is definitive.

When I discovered the power of "wouldn't," "don't," and "won't," it was a game changer for me. These words protect self-assuredness. I know who I am and why I am making a certain choice. I am clear on this. To make others clear on this, whether in my teacher life or in my personal life, I now use these conclusive words, which have become my favorite and most-used strategy. Simply by utilizing these clearer, firmer words, I have reduced or eradicated classroom problems that would have previously lingered.

Whereas before, I hesitated, uncertain how a redirection, request, or discipline would land, I now recognize I'll be in a worse position doing nothing or being unclear. I always knew why I needed something to go a certain way or why I was upholding an expectation, but now I have this knowing cemented in strong language that allows others to know my reasoning as well.

Here is an example. Let's say a student is playing games on his computer when the class is completing work. We are assuming in this example of the playing games that this is not a one-time occurrence and that I have already talked to the student about this behavior prior to this class day. Also, I have a classroom protocol that has been communicated that classwork is completed in class. Of course, there are always considerations to this. I am not unreasonable. But there are times when students will push the boundaries of classwork and do what they want in class, unless the teacher makes it clear it *won't* be accepted.

On this class day, I remind the student two times to complete the classwork, and he keeps his eyes on his computer game and tells me, "I know, I'm getting to it."

The class period ends, and the work is not completed. He gets a 0% for the work.

Fast-forward to later in the week. He tells me he has finished the work. "I have that work done from the other day," he says, "but you still have it as a 0% in my gradebook."

Here is when I'll use my "wouldn't, don't, won't" strategy.

"I know it's a 0%," I respond. "You did that work outside of the class period when you were present in class and able to complete the work. You were playing games and I reminded you two times about my classroom expectation that classwork is completed during the class period. You ignored me. I _wouldn't_ set up a classroom expectation that has a purpose and then refute it. My class time is important. I _won't_ allow my class time to be treated otherwise."

"Wait, you won't take it at all?" he asks me, indignantly. "Not even for, like, half credit?"

"Correct," I say back. "I _won't_ take it at all because I value my class time. I think next time you will value my class time, too."

If the student wants to argue with me, tell me I'm ridiculous, mock that it's a stupid rule, or threaten that he'll tell his mom or a principal, then I stop, put my hand up, look him in the eyes, and calmly say, "I *don't* go back and forth. I know why I have this rule. This conversation is over." I walk away, or I stay where I am, certain not to allow myself to be baited back into the conversation.

In my experience, the student is not happy with me. Of course not. But *I* am happy with me. Most likely, the student completes the classwork the next time around, and things have a way of resettling. If, by chance, an administrator or parent questions me that I refused to give partial credit, I calmly and clearly explain my classwork protocol and share that, "Yes, I *would not* go back and forth with this student after explaining why the work is a 0%. I *don't* give partial credit when the student disregarded the opportunity to earn full credit."

I don't over-explain and I don't over-defend my position. I may not even tell another colleague this conversation happened because there is no point in saying anything. It was a part of my day that I handled, and I don't need someone else's approval or advice. It's over as quickly as it started, and I send the message to myself that "I know who I am, and I know what I'm doing."

In this example, I'm very clear with my intentions and purpose. I want students using my class time for what is planned and for what is important. I have thought it all through. I am not giving pointless busy work.

There is a purpose. I consider all this when I apply my backward design method of classroom expectations and boundaries. I want focus and engagement. I'm clear and I'm *reasonable* with my expectations. I know they won't like my answer of "No," so I prepare myself for that ahead of time, and I speak Oprah's words in my mind because I know what I stand for and why I do what I do. I know what will result in a better-managed classroom and what won't. I know who I am.

If students want to talk back or fight with me, I am clear and kind in my delivery. "I'm stating this clearly and directly one time for you, and I *won't* say it again. From here you have a choice..." is what I say.

If I have students who require frequent one-on-one conversations for behavior or incomplete work, I will eventually tell this student that "I am now finished with these one-on-one conversations. These are taking up my time and you are showing that you are not willing to work on these issues. I *won't* be having any more one-on-one conversations with you. I *wouldn't* continue wasting my time. Any future conversations will be with you *and* your parent or with you *and* an administrator."

I sometimes have students who get annoyed with me when I redirect their behavior or hold them to a standard, as they think I wouldn't do that since I am nice. "But you are nice," I will hear students say. "I am nice," I explain to them, "but you interpreted my niceness as weakness and that is your error. I *wouldn't* allow my classroom to be treated however you want simply because I am nice."

When students ask me toward the end of a marking period if they can complete work from two months prior because they now want a higher grade, I will say, "I *don't* allow work to be completed long after the due date when the learning has passed. I care about the meaning of the learning, not just the completion of the assignments."

I do not use the word "can't," as that gives an opportunity for possibility. If a student asks me to change a grade, and I were to say, "I can't change that grade," it leaves "Why can't you?" with a possibility of options. If my answer is "I *won't* change that grade," the word "won't" has a firmness of already decided with clear reasons behind the decision.

Before, I'd get caught in the confusion of trying to validate students and understand their perspectives while muddling through what I needed from them. I'd say things like: "I see that you want to…but I'd like you to…" or "It would be better if you," or "Can you please…?"

None of that was effective because it allowed permission for other options, and I wasn't being clear in what I expected. Just by using firmer language like "don't," "won't," and "wouldn't," I am asserting my boundaries with what I am and am not willing to stand for. The firmer

> *THE FIRMER LANGUAGE SETS A CLEAR TONE THAT I WON'T ACCEPT CERTAIN BEHAVIORS IN MY CLASSROOM, NOR WILL I ENGAGE IN CERTAIN CONVERSATIONS, AND IT TEACHES STUDENTS HOW I EXPECT THEM TO SHOW UP IN MY CLASSROOM.*

language sets a clear tone that I won't accept certain behaviors in my classroom, nor will I engage in certain conversations, and it teaches students how I expect them to show up in my classroom.

The new language of "I don't, I wouldn't, I won't" is based on *me* and has nothing to do with anyone else's choices or responses.

When I need a reminder of why this is important to me or why I do this, I tell myself I do this because I value my value, and I no longer allow others to devalue my value. Simply put, I *don't* let that happen.

LANGUAGE & THE SNACKY GIRLS

In the case of "the snacky girls" I shared about in an earlier chapter, there was some luck that turned things around for me. But what made the strongest impact on me then, and now, is how I implemented the coaching from Lou and the lesson of language that I had been learning about.

The luck that fell into my lap, and well outside of my control, occurred in December of that semester when the group had a falling out, which meant they now "hated each other," and refused to go anywhere near each other. For months I had tried to manage a classroom in which their distractions and socializing were minimized, and now they wouldn't even speak to each other. On top of that, one of the hardest in that group moved out of the school district within a short time of the falling out. The group that had been so strong was now divided, and I took my opportunity.

I held the remaining group members in the classroom after class, which was before lunch. I told them they would be late for lunch and that I hoped they'd find time to get something to eat when I was finished talking. I started by telling them I noticed their change in behavior toward each other and within the classroom.

I stood straight and tall, looked them in the eyes, and said, "You came into *my* classroom on the first day of this semester acting like you owned it. You took it hostage and you ruined a class that had the potential to be a good class. You disrespected me. You made me uncomfortable. You disrespected your peers and the purpose of this classroom. You chose to handle yourselves poorly."

I took a pause and ended the first part of my lecture with "And...I let you do it."

I continued telling them, "Yes, you may have done the disrespect, and I may have tried to stop it, but I didn't stop it head on because I was thinking you'd realize you didn't want to act this way, and I was thinking you'd realize I didn't deserve your disrespect. It was stupid and naïve of me to think that you would figure it out when you kept showing me you weren't capable of figuring it out. The more I 'let you go,' the worse your behaviors got and the less you respected me and my class."

At this point, one of the girls started crying and another was telling me, "I'm sorry. You don't understand..." Another told me "Whatever, this is stupid, I'm going to lunch," and stomped out of the classroom down the hallway. Two others just stood silently watching me.

They weren't monsters, these girls, or bad kids. Together, they were very powerful, and I was part of allowing their power. Separated, they were kids who took advantage, and they liked how it felt. As individuals, they didn't rise above the social power, and my class was an easy target for their common bonding.

I maintained my stance and finalized by telling them that "I had learned valuable lessons from this experience that will not be forgotten."

"I will never, ever," I asserted, "be disrespected in this way *ever* again."

I told them that I had expectations that as the class continued, they would cooperate, be quiet when I was talking or when others were talking, and that they would engage in the community of the class, and if they were unable to do these things, then I would send them out of the classroom daily, and that their new best friends would be the security guards. I reminded that they'd always have the opportunity to take the class again next year where they could sit side-by-side with the newest freshmen. I established that moving forward, I'd refuse to allow some students to act, do, and get away with whatever they wanted, without at least getting the proper support in place to try and stop it. I finalized with, "I will no longer be both teacher and behavior manager, nor will I allow my valuable classroom space to be someone else's disrespectful playground."

The conversation ended with me telling them I had said all I wanted to say, and that I didn't want to hear what they had to say. I am not sure if I like my choice not to allow them to talk, but that is what I chose at the time. I told them to go to lunch and to come back to me differently the next day. The group walked out of my room quietly. I grabbed my lunch bag, turned off my light, closed my classroom door, and walked down the hallway to the teacher lunchroom.

I felt *immovable.*

The part of me that was willing to hang in there with student behaviors, whether to give chance after chance or because I was afraid of the outcome, was gone. It got smaller and smaller with every step I took away from that closed classroom door.

The next day, each of those girls was different. Even the one who had stomped off. She may not have cared to listen to me, but the others did, so there was no more power, and there was no more misbehaving. The most empowering part was that it didn't matter to me if they were willing to cooperate or not. I knew what I stood for. I knew my plan. I knew what I would and would not accept. "I would not bet against me," I had said to myself earlier that day as I walked into that school building like a lion in a cage, ready to pounce into action if challenged. Any prior nerves I had felt were transformed into power.

If I have situations arise that lean toward something similar—whether it's a student trying to derail my classroom intentions or a group holding power—I now choose every single time to immediately cut off the behavior and to reassert my classroom expectations. After a single attempt at a one-on-one conversation, I contend to these students *within the classroom community* that their current behavior and choices are disrespectful and that their energy is not welcome in the good space of my classroom. Everyone hears my intention and the type of classroom I aim to create. I remind them they have a choice: they can join in the positivity that is happening, or they can choose not to join, but either way, we are moving on, because the rest of us have work to do and have a purpose here. I share that their dissatisfaction is of no issue.

Then, I do something that I feel is most pertinent to my communication. I explain to the class that I see and feel there are issues, but that it is my choice to show up enthusiastically and with joy because that is the person I want to be. I clarify that me being nice and enthusiastic isn't me being unaware, or a person who takes disrespect. It is me showing up how I want for the students who appreciate it and need it. It is my choice to focus on the good, and I always choose the highest ground.

This is what I have learned, and this is what works for me. I over-communicate when necessary what I expect from my classroom space in order to stay empowered. When I do these things, I become a voice not just for myself, but for the other students sitting there, who could never stand up to these kids because it would be a social death. The result is a sturdy classroom with a sturdy teacher.

This process of direct, immediate communication has worked for me, in and out of school. It has provided me with power, control, and solutions. What I have noticed, which is the biggest game changer for me, is that the bad situations don't emotionally last as long when I communicate that I am the authority over myself and my classroom. I have noticed that communicating my expectations clearly and directly lets everyone know where I stand, even if they don't like it. This provides me with the most important need in my life: Empowerment.

REMINDING

Because so much hasn't gone the way I've wanted it to, I have learned a lot about what to try that will make things go better. I've gone through plenty of trial and error, but when it comes to a classroom that comprises uncooperative or dissatisfied students, I have learned it is best to be honest, direct, and clear *at the very beginning* of a situation, before it has a chance to grow or spread. I build a boundary around the issue, and I readjust and reposition that boundary as often as I need.

Sometimes, despite the process or my go-to strategies, the bad situations remain, and the student is a consistent boundary-pusher or toxic person. If he/she were in my personal life, I would determine if this person could stay in my life, or perhaps I'd choose to limit my time with this person. My personal life isn't my school life, though. I can't remove students or people from my classroom or my professional life.

These types of students will always win in a power-struggle game. They have more experience and more years acting this way than I do. I cannot match or win against the personality they have developed (and have been allowed to develop) for years in the few months that I have them. When they push or start with certain behaviors, and my strategies of language choice, whole class addressing, one-on-one talks, seat changes, administrator support, and calling home do not mediate the behaviors, I accept them winning the game. Good for them. They get this temporary win, but I maintain the win within myself.

When I have situations today that are painful reverberations from the past, I see them immediately for what they are. I let Maya Angelou's[19] words come to me: "When someone shows you who they are, believe them the first time." I am always open to someone changing, just as I've changed, too. But I don't expect someone to be different than how they consistently show themselves to me. When it's clear how a person wants to be, I accept this, and I do the best I can to work with it and to manage myself through it. I don't resist it, fight it, or let it aggravate me because I want it to be something different than what it is.

This bad situation is simply a loss in a record that holds many wins. I acknowledge the situation, let the student or students know I've done all I can do, and I tell them I am no longer engaging. I cut the game off, and I no longer play. I directly tell these students, "I don't play games, and I don't play your games. I don't even own a uniform." I congratulate them on their playground win, and I move on as best as I can.

I try to remind myself that the situation will either get better, or it will end, as all school years do. The situation is awful and unfair, and has surely bothered me, but it is temporary, and I can handle it, even if I don't like it. I also remind myself that I've had plenty of tough classes and students in the past, and while I wouldn't want to have them again, I did get through it, and I did it with grace and integrity. I remind myself that, after time's natural separation and progress, I am not holding the anger or bad feelings toward those students or groups years after having them. I am not carrying them with me. I let them go a long time ago. So, any person in my present teacher life who is giving me the same grief, I try to remember that, in time, I'll

> THE SITUATION WILL EITHER GET BETTER, OR IT WILL END, AS ALL SCHOOL YEARS DO.

feel the same and will also let them go. I know, in the end, I'll be okay. It'll all have its way of being fine.

I refuse to let the negative situations grow. I don't allow them to get to the point where my peace of mind is in jeopardy or where my class is taken hostage by a group or by a person. I may not be able to fix the problem or change the student because that is out of my control, but I show up with a stronger response, so the communication and expectations of my classroom are clear, direct, and kind.

Before I start my teaching day, I remind myself that the most important thing I can do is stay empowered. My goal is to be...*immovable*, in the healthiest, strongest of ways. Everything else, including what is not in my control, will work itself out if I stay in control and empowered. I tell myself that—above and beyond anything else—I am in charge of my thoughts, reactions, and choices. That I am ready, capable, and powerful.

There are times when I feel nervous about a situation in school, or something shakes me up. I know I have to execute a strategy right away, or I'll teeter more and more sideways. If this happens to me, I will literally sit in my car before going into the building, and I'll talk to myself. Sometimes using my pocket mirror. Call me crazy—I've been called worse. Now that I'm writing this, I wonder how many colleagues have seen me do this in the morning and have looked the other way, pretending they've seen nothing. Thanks, guys! This strategy works for me. Practicing and hearing myself be assertive to someone who will not easily accept someone being assertive to him/her helps me to stay empowered and in control. It gives me a plan. This may not work for you, but you need to find what works for you because staying empowered within an emotional job is the most important thing we can do for ourselves.

Get to school. Park. Turn your car off. Look in the rearview mirror or a pocket mirror, and assert to yourself:

I am powerful.

I am capable.

I will handle any problems that come my way.

I am in charge.

I am ready.

I am enough.

I am *immovable*.

Then, walk with a stride and a power into that classroom, knowing all of YOU that you have poured into it. Look around and take notice of the hours of planning, considering, and organizing you have done to make that space meaningful and important. When the students start coming in, stand tall, greet them with joy and confidence, and let them know that you are glad they are in your classroom, all the while reminding yourself that you are empowered, you are capable, and you will only allow what you want to allow.

Be proud of how much you have managed, handled, figured out, and improved. Be proud of what was thrown at you and how you caught it. Be proud of the taking on and the letting go, and in doing the best you can to show up as your best self each and every day.

Show your students that you value what you do and what you give.

Choose two times within that same day when you will remind yourself that you are empowered. "I am empowered. I am in charge. I am capable. I only allow what I want to allow." Just say it in your head as a reminder two times on the school days when you especially need it.

When uncomfortable instances come up, as they will, don't panic or stress. Take a breath. Your pause alone will send the message that you are in charge because you no longer get caught up in others' dramas, negativities, reactions, and games. You _wouldn't_ get caught up in that. Remember, language matters. You _don't_ let others pull you into their toxicities.

Remind yourself: I am empowered. I am in charge. Ask yourself: What outcome do I want here? Get a clear answer. Then, work toward that outcome. You know why? Because you are in control of the outcome, and you will get that outcome because you are empowered.

> *EVEN IF IT TAKES ME A FEW DAYS TO GET THERE, OR EVEN IF I NEED TO WORK A FEW THINGS OUT IN MY MIND, MY END-GOAL IS TO BE IMMOVABLE. TO BE EMPOWERED.*

Even if it takes me a few days to get there, or even if I need to work a few things out in my mind, my end-goal is to be immovable. To be empowered. To know who I am and why I am doing what I am doing. To trust myself. To be…immovable. Like the image of someone in a power pose.

The more I learned from Lou and the more I read and listened about "the journey of self," the steadier I became. It is a great feeling, being immovable, and it is an even greater feeling to identify when you're disempowered or when you're not immovable, and you have strategy after strategy to get yourself back to it. Because the goal is to always get back to empowerment and back to immovable, so to live with strength and inner peace.

Every teacher has felt this anguish, this grief, and we need to be brave enough to share our stories, so we can determine what to do about them. The body is keeping score, and all that emotional fatigue, pain, and overwhelm is in there somewhere.

IDIDN'T SIGN UP FOR THIS

Let it out and let it go free.

The problems you come across in your classroom aren't from you. If you are a teacher who loves to teach and who is serving the best way you can *and* you are experiencing tough situations, please know it is not you. It was never you. You just happened to collide with a situation that was already tough, and you've tried your hardest to make the best of it. It is no one's fault. The storm was already forming before you even showed up.

Perhaps next time when you are faced with that same situation—because you certainly will be—you will handle it just a touch better, or maybe even a lot better. And won't that be an achievement and a medal-worthy moment? Certainly, it will be. Look at how much you keep growing and learning and changing.

In any situation that's not going well, it's easy to blame, criticize, and find the negatives. In a job like teaching, which will be imperfect despite any and all efforts, the invitation will always be there to complain, to be cranky, and to see it for what it's not. There are lots of angry teachers out there, who feel justified in holding their anger and spewing their anger. Don't allow yourself to get there. Move yourself as often as you can and as close as you can to being immovable. To knowing why you do what you do, and why you started doing what you do in the first place.

None of this is easy and it takes honesty, courage, and a hard look in the mirror. I don't blame anyone else, and I don't expect others to fix this for me.

It's not easy experiencing a few hard kids bringing down a great class period. It's not easy greeting kids with a smile and hello by the door as they choose to ignore you as they walk into your room. It's not easy to then walk into that same classroom enthusiastic, prepared, professional, and hopeful, all the while knowing this may not go so well.

Our other options—to power-struggle those kids, or to be angry, irritable, and short-tempered—don't lead us anywhere positive either, and we all know that isn't fair to the kids in the class who are cooperative and trying to learn.

It wasn't easy for me to see a therapist, admit my shortcomings, take life's tests one after another and try to pass them. It hasn't been easy to write all these private experiences, knowing they will be out in the world, out of my control, but hopefully helping others feel validated and not alone.

In all, this has been a total act of bravery.

Teaching is not easy. If it were, we wouldn't be in a profession that is in the middle of an epidemic.

We are in a profession that is emotional. It doesn't mean the identification of that makes the tough emotions go away. It only means we now have *awareness*, and we can begin to build strategies.

I can do it, and you can do it. Empowered people express their expectations clearly and they trust those expectations will be met because they value themselves and their expectations. Tether yourself closest to the person you are trying to be each day. That is, finally, where you do have control.

You are a person who is valued. You are a person who is empowered. You are a person who is immovable. Because you are *enough*.

CHANCE MEETING

I left my trailer classroom a few years into my teaching career, and ever since, I have purposely positioned my desk to face my beautiful classroom windows that are lined with a mixture of green and flowering plants on an oversized windowsill.

One morning years ago, I glanced up from my computer during my lunch break, and my eyes admired the green grass and large oak trees. Then, I suddenly realized I hadn't used the bathroom since before first period and my reflective moment was broken by my rush to the girls' bathroom.

As I walked back into the hallway, assuming it would be empty due to lunch block, I nearly collided with a student I had in class two years earlier, who was very, very challenging. My first instinct in seeing this former student was to give an enthusiastic "Hi! How are you doing?!"

But I tempered my enthusiasm, because the situation with this student had been rough, and I didn't know how he was going to respond to me, especially after not seeing him for a couple of school years.

I slowed my pace and apologized for almost running into him. Then, I looked him in the eyes and said with sincerity, "I haven't seen you in a long time. How are you? How are things?"

He stopped, which was a good sign of relationship rebuilding, and said, "I'm doing a lot better now. A lot better than when I was in your class." He asked me how I was doing and how my new classes were. Then, he did the thing that we have all done to someone at some point in our lives, and that we hope others will do to us.

"I'm actually really glad I ran into you," he said. "I want to tell you something. I know I was really bad for you, and I know I ruined your class." He ended with "I'm really sorry."

He told me I was "the nicest teacher he's ever had," and that I was always good to him, even when he didn't deserve it. He told me that I was a great teacher, and that he was sorry for being so hard.

Since I had him in class, a lot of time had passed, and a lot of other experiences had happened. I didn't harbor any hard feelings toward him. My life had moved on, and I had learned a lot about myself and students because of him. I didn't need him to apologize.

But I was thankful he did. I was grateful and relieved that this young person was willing to look me in the eyes and say, "I'm sorry."

I felt seen, and I felt that swell of letting go when stress has finally broken up and eased from our shoulders, like harsh noise vanishing into wind.

I told him that I could have been better, too, and that I continued to learn a lot about myself, about students, and about teaching since having him in class. The interaction wasn't long, but it was meaningful. As we parted, I gave him a high five, thanked him for being so mature and honest, and I wished him the absolute best.

That wasn't the first or only time I experienced a recovery situation. I wish it were every time.

School years are long, and a lot happens in one school year. The recovery was appreciated, but I'd rather not have the recovery. I'd rather have a stable and positive situation from the start. When that doesn't happen as I would hope, the next best thing is a recovery.

As I walked away, I wished all tough situations could move to a better place like this one did. It made me acknowledge how much better our school lives would be if students and teachers could get to this place sooner and without as much damage.

It also made me wonder how often the situation needed to be reversed with teachers apologizing to students.

I never did learn what this student meant when he said that he was doing better now than when I had him in class.

What mattered was that I was reminded of something we hear over and over again, but can have a hard time remembering when we are in the moments of stress, anger, hurt, and frustration from someone else's choices:

We don't always know what someone else is going through.

That doesn't give people permission to treat us however they want. That leads to disempowerment, and we don't want that. But it helps us to remember that some students' lives are hard, not always by choice, but that we have the option to approach situations with compassion and understanding instead of judgment and ridicule. We can choose to accept the "is-ness" of a situation, as Lou told me, and then to improve the situation or accept things as they are, lest you get consumed by someone else's hurt.

It may have been that it wasn't easy being him at that time for whatever reasons. And it may have been that I was an easy target for his anger—for reasons unknown to me and maybe even unknown to him.

> THAT DOESN'T GIVE PEOPLE PERMISSION TO TREAT US HOWEVER THEY WANT. THAT LEADS TO DISEMPOWERMENT, AND WE DON'T WANT THAT.

It may have been that he was at the peak of a most unpleasant time in his life, and I collided with that as I was trying to hold down an English classroom.

Even though we all know this lesson about other people and their hardships, it can be incredibly difficult to keep that in the forefront when we are colliding with someone's bad attitude, meanness, refusal to cooperate, and targeting. It's hard to put our pride aside, remove our egos, and have compassion for that person when we are hurting because of them.

BETTER THE BALL

As teachers, we have the opportunity to leave the situations in front of us better than we received them. Maybe the most we can do is leave things just a small percentage better. My volleyball coach in college would constantly say "Better the ball!" meaning make it your responsibility to improve a broken play. "If there is an errant pass, chase that ball down and bring it back into play," he'd instruct. "If there is an errant set, readjust your body and keep that ball in play with an aggressive swing," he'd demand. "Better the ball," he'd remind.

We can all better the ball. Don't choose to do nothing, and don't choose to make it worse. I loved when he'd say this because I knew I could better any ball. I might not make the play perfect, but I could certainly make it better.

We have the opportunity in teaching to better the situations in front of us. All we ever need and want is a bettering. Not a perfecting. Thanks for the life lesson, Coach Kachinko. We may not be able to fix the situations, and we may not be able to make them perfect. But certainly, we can make them better than how we received them. We can "better the ball" with whatever is in front of us that needs some bettering.

It's not always easy to have this mindset. When we have this mindset, though, we are serving a much larger purpose than ourselves.

Jim Fortin[20], a spiritual teacher who teaches how to transform our lives from the inside out, asks his listeners to consider their own lives and how their choices serve themselves and the world around them. Jim challenges his listeners to consider who they want to be, and if they are living in a way that correlates to who they want to be. Are we being honest with who we want to be, and who we actually are?

> WE HAVE THE OPPORTUNITY IN TEACHING TO BETTER THE SITUATIONS IN FRONT OF US. ALL WE EVER NEED AND WANT IS A BETTERING. NOT A PERFECTING.

"Who would you *be*?" he asks, "And what would you *do*, if you lived for something bigger than yourself?" How would you act if you were living a life that bettered yourself and the people around you? Who would you *be* if you were living a life that bettered yourself and the people around you?

Endeavor to see the profession differently—not as an obstacle in your way, but rather as a gift that allows you to give and helps you to grow. How are you a better person, parent, friend, son, daughter simply because you are a teacher, and because you have had the emotional strength training that only a teacher gets? How has the ball that is your life been "bettered" because you are a teacher? How have you helped others become better versions of themselves because you are their teacher?

That is service.

That is the "why." The reason why we do what we do, and why we continually show up the way we do.

We know on a deep level, much deeper than what we may even realize, that we are giving of ourselves in a way that is making a difference in others' lives, and that is meaningful service.

Why do you teach? Why does *anyone* teach?

It's not to enter a situation in hopes that we get triggered, so we can work on our emotional insides. It's because we are serving others. It's because we are trying to better the ball.

We have an inherent contract: "I have something to give to you. It's important. Valuable. Precious. And I want you to have it, so you benefit, too."

Maybe it's kindness or humor or listening or content sharing or storytelling or confidence-building or patience or compassion or physical fitness or art or music appreciation.

There is something in you that is making you do this job—and do it well—even within all the difficulty.

It's your why. Remind yourself of your why. Hold it close.

In teaching, it's the kind of service in which you use your life for the betterment of others, and you bestow on others, as top influential coach Jay Shetty[21] teaches, the "superpowers that are inside of you."

THERE IS SOMETHING IN YOU THAT IS MAKING YOU DO THIS JOB—AND DO IT WELL—EVEN WITHIN ALL THE DIFFICULTY.
IT'S YOUR WHY. REMIND YOURSELF OF YOUR WHY. HOLD IT CLOSE.

We all have superpowers. My superpowers come from my kindness. From my kindness comes my patience, my listening, my compassion, my encouragement, my happiness, my humor, and my love. My superpower is loving people *as* they are and *how* they are to meet them *where* they are. This gives me joy, and my why is joy.

I give this superpower freely and easily because it's not hard for me to give in this way. The more I give my superpower, the more my superpower comes back to me. The more I hide or shadow my superpower, the more I feel the trudge and the drag. It is in those times that I reflect on what is depleting my superpower, and I work to reclaim it.

Before you begin teaching and as you continue teaching, define your why and identify your superpowers. Remind yourself of this often.

Your why is precious, and it will be the thing that emerges from all the other details. I cannot think of a more fitting profession for one to serve others while simultaneously evolving one's personal growth than being a teacher.

Mother Theresa[22] tells us her why. She calls us to build again, even after what we built was destroyed overnight, just as she did. She dares us to do good, even after the good we just did is forgotten. She encourages us to do the best we can, even if our best isn't good enough for some people.

Because, in the end, "It isn't between you and them," she explains. This entire time—all this time—it has only ever been "between you and God."

You were made for goodness. You were made to serve. You were made to use your superpower for good.

MARY OLIVER

There exists a most important reminder to everything we experience in our day, especially for something like our teaching jobs. We live this life, and this life is built on time. Hours, minutes, seconds. The point is to honor the time and protect the hours. That is what our life is built on, and time is really all we have.

The hours I spend at work—teaching—are hours that make up my life. And yours, too. My precious, precious *life*! Your precious, precious *life*.

I can't just hand something that fragile to someone or something that isn't careful with it. I can't allow my energy and the hours that make up my life to be handed to a student or a class or a teaching task that gets under my skin and irritates me. I <u>don't</u> accept that to be a

> THE POINT IS TO HONOR THE TIME AND PROTECT THE HOURS. THAT IS WHAT OUR LIFE IS BUILT ON, AND TIME IS REALLY ALL WE HAVE.

teacher means we have to be stressed, tired, frustrated, and overwhelmed. I _wouldn't_ allow that. I _won't_ accept that this is the way teaching is.

American poet Mary Oliver[23] teaches me this lesson when she speaks to her reader in her poem "The Summer Day," commanding "Tell me/What is it you plan to do with your one wild and precious life?"

I read those poetic words for the first time a long time ago, and they reverberated in my mind. They nestled there. _My one wild and precious life_, I'd wonder. I'd hear her direct her question "What is your plan?" toward me, commanding me for an answer: "Tell me."

I would think about this on my drive home. I'd think about this when I was making dinner. I'd think about this before I fell asleep. What _is_ my plan? What would I say to Mary Oliver if she were standing in front of me waiting for a reply?

Before that poem, I hadn't thought about my life as wild before. Precious, yes, but not wild. I also hadn't thought about the minutes and hours that make up my life as precious—I only saw the whole of my life as precious. In reality, though, our lives are made up of all these small moments that we can easily disregard or take for granted or not even notice. Most of these moments are really, really precious. How can I give more of my time to the experiences in my life that are guaranteed to be my most favored experiences?

This all helped me to reclaim my power and to see my life differently and more beautifully.

I refuse to enter my school day wishing for it to be over. I refuse to enter a school year not being able to wait until the end. I refuse to look at my life hoping for it to speed up to some other point in time. I _won't_ do that.

Instead, I find moments in my every day that are precious, and I remind myself that these are the moments that build my one wild and precious life. I find the A+ moments. They can be as small or as big as I want them to be, and they may be situations that others would dismiss as typical or ordinary. I look upon them as precious and special, and I'm so thankful I see them this way.

Getting to walk into school with a great friend, knowing our cars arrived in the parking lot at just the same time for a quick hangout before a busy day. That's a precious moment. Having a student stop in the hallway to catch up with me when they could have kept walking. That's a precious moment. Walking out of my building and feeling the weather—crisp or warm—on my face. That's a precious moment. Driving home and seeing bright white snow carefully piled on bare tree branches, so the path ahead of me glistens with sparkling snow glitter. That's a precious moment. Greeting my own kids as they walk through the door of our house with their large bookbags looking cartoonish on their small backs. That's a precious moment.

We can see any and all of this as ordinary. But none of it is ordinary. In any moment, we can see precious. We can give ourselves the gift of perspective. We can see the moments that build our one wild and precious life, like in the poem "Days" by Billy Collins[24], when he illustrates the fragility of our days as if they are stacked one on top of the other in an impossibly high tower, and "Each one is a gift, no doubt,/mysteriously placed in your waking hand/…No wonder you find yourself/…hoping to add one more [day]./ Just another Wednesday/you whisper."

Wouldn't we all plead and *whisper*, "just another Wednesday," if we knew our stack of days was about to topple? It's all precious. This is all a most important reminder.

Our school days may be hard and tiring and frustrating, and they may make us feel like "Why bother?" They are, nonetheless, part of our stack of days and within each are precious minutes and hours that build that stack.

Knowing I have this precious life that is built on time, including time I spend in school, I no longer hand over that time to mean students or to situations that trigger me. These circumstances will happen. I acknowledge them and I try to move through them, instead of fighting them or allowing them to take over. I don't want to spend the precious hours that build my life in conflict, or in anger, or in frustration over something I have no control over in the first place.

So, I have to ask you: How will you treat the *hours* that you spend in one single school day—the hours that make up your life?

You can accept the invitation to see only the negatives, and then you will venture down into a shadowy, ugly, dark world. For sure and without a doubt, teaching is imperfect. There are too many people trying to move something along with too many variables that get in the way. If we wanted, we could find fault with almost all of it. I see all the "realities" of my day, too. But I don't live in the world of negativity. I don't want to do that. I never want to do that. I choose to put my attention to something else.

I prefer to identify and recognize the realities, while moving myself as often as possible to the light and to the joy of what is around me.

Dare to be different from the norm. Dare to challenge what has occurred too many times with teachers everywhere, who get jaded and frustrated. This is your life. This is your one wild life. Dare to make it something precious.

THE POWER OF GRATITUDE

How can we promise we will dare to live a life that is precious and wild? My answer is through the two ways that are the highest guarantee: gratitude and giving.

> ### DARE TO BE DIFFERENT FROM THE NORM.

While I wouldn't have thought it at the time, I am so thankful for "the snacky girls." They were a gift to me, because they forced me to look inside and to accept that I may have been showing the world a happy, confident, capable person, but I was actually struggling inside. I was living half a truth. Now, I can take a deep breath, acknowledge when I'm hit by a force (or a bus) that makes me feel insecure, and respond with love and compassion for myself. I now do this in my personal life and my teacher life, all because of hard examples I've shared with you.

I think of myself in this big, massive Universe, floating on this Earth bubble, appreciative that some of my best friends are the people I work with, and I even get to eat lunch with them every day. I am grateful I have people in my life who understand how hard the day can be, so I never feel alone in any of it. One of my best friends wrote me a card acknowledging I choose to be positive and a light, even though I was struggling with classes and parts of my school day. I was so grateful to receive that card. I do the best I can to find anything small that I know could be overlooked, but that actually brings me a lot of happiness.

- Seeing students sitting in my classroom space, smiling and laughing, enjoying the class and each other. *Gratitude.*
- Sitting with a small group of students each week in my school's "Book Club," as we dissect and analyze cool books. *Gratitude.*
- Learning from the student who says to me, "You know, Mrs. Manser, I was thinking about what you said the other day about Squealer in *Animal Farm* and did you know that…" *Gratitude.*
- Former graduates coming back to do observation hours in my classroom because— guess what?—they want to be future English teachers. *Gratitude.*
- Having my own classroom with large windows that give me a view of grass and trees. *Gratitude.*
- Seeing teacher friends everyday who are my real friends. *Gratitude.*
- Having a healthy body that can stand and teach all day and endure long hours in my job and my after-job life, and having fingers that can type fast for feedback on essays. *Gratitude.*
- Owning a car that I know will work. *Gratitude.*
- Walking into a grocery store at 8 p.m. on a Tuesday because that is the only time I can go that week, knowing it's open and knowing there are workers

who will help me, and seeing the splash of beautiful cut flowers when I first walk in. *Gratitude.*

- Talking on the phone on my drive home to my best friend who lives across the country in a different time zone while she's on her lunch break, knowing how hard it would be for us to talk as frequently if we had the same schedule. *Gratitude.*
- Getting to live in a beautiful neighborhood and being lucky enough to have neighbors who have turned into best friends. *Gratitude.*
- Sharing my kids' lives with my parents, who try to attend all the events. *Gratitude.*
- Having a husband who believes in me and doesn't let minor things get in the way. *Gratitude.*
- Being blessed with sweetheart kids who I can tuck into bed at night. *Gratitude.*

It's everywhere. It's in everything. We just have to take a small, short moment to see it and to notice it and to recognize the gift that it is. If our minds are taxed with what we need to do next, or what is not going well, or what we "should" be doing or "should" already have, then it's much harder for gratitude to break through that thick barrier. Gratitude is like the blue atmosphere above the clouds, as Oprah Winfrey shares from her perspective. "No matter how often I fly," she says in her *Oprah SuperSoul* podcast and in a 2018 *O, The Oprah Magazine* article[25], "I still look forward to the moment when the airplane pierces a shield of clouds and is met with radiance on the other side."

The clouds will be there, and they may be thick on their own or we may thicken them ourselves. If we flew through and past those clouds, we'd be in a beautiful blue atmosphere and the sun would still be shining—steady, dependable, never wavering. Gratitude is always there and always ready to meet us where we are. We just need to see it for what it is and try our best to loosen those thicker clouds.

THE POWER OF GIVING

Sometimes we want the thick clouds to remain because that makes us feel better in the moment, and we need to feel self-pity for the hand we've been dealt, or it's not easy to loosen the thicker clouds. I've been there. When gratitude isn't that easy to find or when it

> GRATITUDE IS ALWAYS THERE AND ALWAYS READY TO MEET US WHERE WE ARE.

feels forced and fake, I turn to giving. When I give—anything—it lets me get out of my own way and focus on someone else. It loosens those thick clouds and the next thing I know, gratitude is pouring back down on me.

I have always lived a life that is centered on gratitude and giving and helping. These things aren't new for me. But prior to doing my introspective work, I didn't see them as tools of empowerment. When we are grateful, we are reminded of what we have in our lives that we own, and that is personal empowerment. When we give, we are reminded of something we have that we can share with others and that is personal empowerment.

Gratitude and giving are tools to a better life, an empowered life. Now that I see them this way, I realize their power, and I realize how lucky I am that I can do these simple things that have a big impact. Throughout my day, I give a lot of compliments, high fives, fist bumps, hugs, and encouragement to those around me. I love building people up and being a cheerleader for people. I have always loved doing this. This is not new in my

> GRATITUDE AND GIVING ARE TOOLS TO A BETTER LIFE, AN EMPOWERED LIFE.

personality, but now I see it as a gift I get to give and as a part of my empowerment.

We have some awesome people in our lives, both students and adults. Why wouldn't we celebrate them and acknowledge them? When I hear about an accomplishment or when I notice a positive effort in a student, I do my best to acknowledge this and build it up. I give that praise to the student. After a student has said something wise and profound, I'll take a moment, wipe a dramatic, invisible tear from my eye, and share that those words were the most inspiring words I'd heard all day, and I might even ask the class to clap for those words and for the student who said them. "Give it up, people. Let's get a clap going. Did you all hear *that*? I mean, really! Those need to be printed in some publication." This is genuine, and the students know it. It makes everyone feel good, especially the student who said the words.

I am giving something I can give. I am giving acknowledgment, credit, confidence, and community.

I stand outside my door between classes to greet students and to take that short amount of time to say hello and to ask how people are doing. I always stand at my door before the class ends, and I give a fist bump as each student leaves. I take this time to make eye contact and say, "Have the best Monday you've ever had in your life," or I'll take that time to give individual praise for something great that a student did that day, or I'll take that time to wish them good luck at a game or performance, or I'll take that time to tell them I look forward to seeing them the next day.

I tell students individually, in small groups, or in whole-group classes how much I appreciate them and exactly why. I give them my gratitude. Being specific is important because it acknowledges students' behaviors and their ownership over those behaviors. They feel good about themselves, and they are likely to keep doing it, simply because they were acknowledged, seen, and thanked.

The first period of the day in my school starts at 7:30 a.m. Despite the early start, I may have a first period with students smiling, talking to one another, greeting me, willing to move desks, responding to philosophical questions about literature and life, and writing paragraphs. I tell them as a whole group, "I am so grateful to you all. You are an AWESOME way to start my day! Do you know how lucky I am to start with a group like you? Thank you! You are choosing to bring the best of yourself to me this early in the morning, whereas you could use the early start as an excuse to disengage. You are the reason why this is going so well, and I know I am really lucky."

I will take the time to walk over to a few students, who are especially energetic, and let them know that I see them and their efforts. I tell them they are giving the other students permission to step up and engage, and if it weren't for them being so vibrant, the class may otherwise be flat.

If there is a fundraiser in school, and I have been giving to many fundraisers, I always try to contribute something to the overall fund, even if it's only $5.00. I can do that. I may not be able to buy the $15.00 t-shirt or the $20.00 program book, but I can give $5.00 to an overall fund because this activity is important to my student, and it's important for me to give.

I give my gratitude and my acknowledgement and my praise. I can do that. It makes a big difference. I wonder if we, too often, assume things "should" just be this way. We "should" have students who engage and we "should" have a car that starts, for example. Maybe. Or maybe these aren't guarantees. So, giving our thanks and giving our acknowledgement sends the message that we aren't taking these things for granted and that we see them for the high value that they are.

I *mean* my thanks because I know it doesn't have to be as good as it is. I thank the student who is willing to walk another student to the nurse, or carry their bookbag for them to the elevator. I am sure to thank students who lead class discussions, who make the choice to work on a skill that was harder for them, who give themselves to my lesson, even though they were having a tough day. I thank individual students or small groups of students for being people who are easy to talk to or who make me laugh. I thank whole classes, and I thank individuals. All day long.

I don't know how often we, as teachers, thank our students, or give them compliments and acknowledgement. We may not think of it, or we may not think of it very often, because we have a job to do and content to cover and emails to get through and grades to manage and student absences to figure out and reports to complete and meetings to attend and next week's lessons to plan.

But we all like to hear when we are doing well. We all want to be seen, acknowledged, and appreciated. It makes us feel good, and it gives us a boost that we are doing something bigger than ourselves, and it's making a difference for someone else. Our students feel similarly and giving that is one small thing I can do to make a big difference.

Giving a compliment or thanks—giving something sincerely from yourself to another person—is what reminds us of our own blessed life. Giving and gratitude are in the same family. They are both powerful. Being grateful is, research proven, the number one mindset that will change the energy of your life. If you could slow your pace for a moment, and *deeply* think of something—just one thing—that you are grateful for that could otherwise not be there, then you may experience the sensation come over you that is gratitude and love and happiness. I cherish this feeling.

If we can find it in ourselves to give this feeling to someone else, especially when it's hard, then we are honoring the service we can give to others. I may have to force this sometimes. But better to force gratitude and giving than negativity. At least I'll be moving in the right direction.

Mindset shifts, gratitude, and relationship-building are all ways I stay empowered. They are all ways I look at myself from a distance and I see a teacher who knows who she is and knows what she stands for. It's clear in my mind, and I stay immovable.

Sometimes, when I find myself teetering or I'm feeling unsteady, I seek the people in my life who are funny and who I know will cut a joke for me that will make me smile despite feeling frustrated, angry, or disappointed. Just that one smile or laugh can reset me and remind me that "Hey, this problem sucks. But it's small. There is still a human separate from this school world inside of me."

Find the people in your life you can count on to make you smile and laugh. Find the people in your life you can be *honest* with. They are your treasures. Hold on to them. They will keep you empowered.

The tough students are there, and none of this may help them at all. But it will continually remind you that we are in an emotional profession, and we can choose not to live in their negativity. Instead, we can choose to live the most important reminder of a space that is light, healthy, grateful, and good.

THE REMINDER

Through this learning and improvement, Lou did caution me that we all have an autopilot setting, despite our growth trajectories, and that I would find myself defaulting to some of my old patterns, but that now I would have awareness and a plan full of strategies.

He was right because there are times, even in recent days, when I have that inner struggle of insecurity and disempowerment, when I want to be liked, when someone upends me or flares my nerves, and I don't want to cause "problems." The old feelings come back where I am placed in a lose-lose, and I know a situation won't be as good as it could be. I get defeated, frustrated, and nervous.

When someone disrespects me, makes me feel inferior, is dismissive, doesn't listen to me, or blows me off, those old feelings are the first to invade. They come at me hard, and I am like, "Geez, am I not past this already? This feeling again? This person in my life again?

C'mon!" I then must go back through the steps to remind myself that I am in an emotional profession, but that I give myself value, and that I am not seeking value from anyone outside of myself.

I get curious about myself and why I feel the way I do. When these negative situations happen, and they are handled, it doesn't mean they don't hurt or bother. I still get affected by these situations, even while trying to work through them better than I did years ago. Just last year, even as I was working on this book that shares the emotional impacts from teaching and ways to empowerment, I felt the sting of tears when a colleague acknowledged it looked as though I was stressed. It was the end of a harder day, and I was so close to exiting that building. Her kind, caring words were the push over the edge, and I felt that chest-tightening burn. In telling her why I was stressed and disappointed, I choked up.

Certain stresses, pressures, fatigue, and overwhelm we experience daily in our individual classrooms hurt so much, touch so deeply, and blindside us so suddenly. Some people even leave teaching because of them. Professionals leave their *careers* because they are hurting from the mean voltage of others, who seem not to care that they do this to people.

This is all part of teaching. Teaching is both/and, not either/or. It is rewarding and hard. It makes us feel good and bad. We can't pretend it's something that it's not. What we can do, though, is learn about ourselves and do that inner work. It won't make the problems go away, but it will make our response to the problems stronger, stabilizing us more and more each day and each school year.

So, while I have the cognizance of what I've learned about myself and how it plays out in my life, it doesn't mean all tough situations go away or no longer bother me. These things still upset me, because I'm human.

I think this is the whole point—to recognize the price we have paid for the life that wasn't serving us. To see it and to do something about it. We are supposed to grow and evolve, and we really can't do that effectively without lots of practice and lessons. Lou reminded me time and time again that my purpose in all of this was to "lower the volume" on the situations that negatively affected me in my life.

From there, I have learned many strategies that work for me. Some of them I always had, like gratitude and giving. But now I see them as tools of empowerment that bring me back to the most important reminder.

> [TEACHING] IS REWARDING AND HARD. IT MAKES US FEEL GOOD AND BAD. WE CAN'T PRETEND IT'S SOMETHING THAT IT'S NOT.

> *...THIS IS THE WHOLE POINT—TO RECOGNIZE THE PRICE WE HAVE PAID FOR THE LIFE THAT WASN'T SERVING US. TO SEE IT AND TO DO SOMETHING ABOUT IT.*

JOY IS MY ANSWER

My day is made up of moments. I can choose to see those moments however I'd like. I can choose to hold them or let them go. I can choose to give them a lot of power or to reason that it's all just part of it. I can do whatever I'd like to do with the moments that build my day. My choice is to see as many gifts as I can.

I choose to use my superpower to find the joy in the life that is around me. Joy is everywhere, and it's not that hard to find. When you find it, you get to delight in it, and you get to chuckle that you found it again.

Rob Bell's "An Introduction to Joy"[26] on YouTube is what anchored me in seeing the power of this word. Rob wants you to have this lesson to learn precisely how to live a life relishing the joy of all that is around you.

Sometimes joy is easier to find in my personal life than in my school life. It may be harder to find joy at times in my school life, but it is always there, and I remind myself to find joy, and to share my superpower to be the person I want to be.

Joy, in my teaching, is when I have meaningful conversations with young people, and I get to be part of watching them grow. Joy is the number of graduates who find me to say goodbye before they walk across stage. Joy is when a student tells another student how lucky they are to have me as their teacher. I know then that I'm on track with my superpowers, and I also recognize this commendation made me feel good.

Joy is when someone tells me I am exactly who they needed to see that day.

Joy is now knowing I don't *need* these external validations because I have my inner validation that knows I am giving of myself and serving just as I am supposed to.

Joy in my teaching is knowing I am one small part of helping a student see that she is valued, she is wanted, and she is in control of making the choices to live a good life. Joy is expressing to students that they are good, and that they will be just fine.

Joy, to me, is seeing that there is abundance all around me, and I lack for nothing. Joy is remembering to keep my #1 priorities as #1, and my #2 priorities as #2, and so on.

Joy is seeing students grow up from 14-years-old to 18-years-old. What a difference those years make. Not everyone gets to bear witness to that. It is seeing these

> ## *JOY IS DARING TO BE DIFFERENT.*

kids not just grow taller and older looking, but it is proclaiming that they are growing in self-confidence, in service, in accomplishment, and in leadership.

Joy is being open to young people changing, showing up better, being different. Joy is being open to this in myself.

Joy is choosing to see the joy in the world. Joy is moving my attention to find the joy.

Joy is choosing to celebrate my contributions, instead of thinking "I'm not enough." Joy is not being a victim.

Joy is being sunshine, happiness, love, and warmth.

Joy is working toward and maintaining inner peace.

Joy is daring to be different.

○ ○ ○

Joy is that I can now give my answer to Mary Oliver if she were standing in front of me, anticipating an answer. I've wondered about my answer for years, knowing I couldn't give an answer to the profound question "What is it you plan to do with your one wild and precious life?" when I was feeling disempowered, unsteady, and fatigued. Giving an answer in that emotional state would be fraudulent, and my answer wouldn't match my reality.

But now I can give my answer to Mary Oliver because I know myself, including my shadows. I have experienced emotional fatigue, and I have tools that now lead me through to personal empowerment.

Thank you very much for the question, Ms. Oliver. It's a good one and it's one I've puzzled over.

My answer is to live my life—my one wild and precious life—in school and out of school with as much joy as I possibly can.

To me, that is the answer to what we are all here to do.

To me, that is a life of honor.

To me, that is a life well-lived.

To me, that is exactly what I have signed up for.

I hope it is for you, too. I hope you find, in your trial and error and self-discovering, your "answer" to this most profound question. When you do and when you let go of everything else, you will find your own version of joy.

> TO ME, THAT IS EXACTLY WHAT
> I HAVE SIGNED UP FOR.

Teaching is everything we knew it would be and so much more. We know it once we start, and we can be braver in sharing our stories because we don't have to be afraid of them. We can be empowered by them and by how far we have come.

Teaching is an emotional profession that will give us the opportunity to journey through our best and hardest emotions. It will be fulfilling. It will be painful. It will teach us a lot about ourselves.

But you've got it, and you're doing great.
Because guess what? I am, too.

ACKNOWLEDGMENTS ♡

There is a special bond and love that happens when people step up for you and give you something—time, advice, a listening ear, expertise, help, connections—when you know, as the receiver, there is very little you can give back in return, except your heartfelt and endless gratitude.

There aren't enough pages in the world to allow me to do this properly, as I have received encouragement and assistance from so many throughout this entire book writing process. Each word of encouragement, each word of enthusiasm, and each word of advice is appreciated and valued. Please know there are more words I could write in this section, and there are many people I will continue to thank long after these pages end.

A thousand times…NO!…an infinity times THANK YOU to…

MY FAMILY AT HOME.

Thank you for being patient and understanding as I squirreled away for hours on my computer when we would typically use that time to play and have fun. Shane, thank you for the many rollercoaster rides you took with me as I oscillated between self-doubt and worry and excitement and elation. Thank you for loving me and for staying up late with me when I needed reassurance. Thank you for reading sections of this book in draft form, even when the score was tied, and the game was down to the final seconds. Thank you for being proud of me and for being so happy for me when good news was filtering in. Thank you for excitedly sharing what I was doing with everyone you'd run into. Thank you for exclaiming, "You wrote a book. You have a logo! Wow!" I shall get you that "Teaching is Emotional" hat someday. Leah, thank you for loving me as much as you do, for caring about this project from the very beginning, and for genuinely wanting to know the latest updates. You were the first one who knew when I had an editor and a website. Thank you for the surprise notes and gifts you'd leave me. You are my treasure. I am so lucky to have you as my girl. Eric, I don't think I've ever felt such a swell of surprise pride as I did that afternoon in your 3rd grade classroom when one of your classmates shouted out, "I heard you wrote a book!" right when I was about to start "mystery reader," setting off a clamoring of excited chatter and questions from each of your classmates. "Of course I told my class, Mommy! You are awesome and you wrote a book! I am so proud of you," is what you said to me in the car on the way home. Thank you for always saying "I love it" as new pieces came into view. You are my treasure, and everyone who gets you in their life is lucky to have you.

MY PARENTS, BILL AND DEBBIE LUCAS, MY BROTHERS MATT AND ADAM LUCAS, AND MY SISTER-IN-LAW MARY LUCAS.

Nothing quite says love like one of your brothers stating, "I haven't read a book cover to cover in a long time, but you'd better bet I'll be reading every word of this for you." To my mom for being proud of me, for reading the end before the beginning, and for assuaging my doubts by simplifying my over-thinking and reminding me not to worry about what people might think because, "What if it's great and you help lots of teachers? Take me when you go to meet Oprah." To my dad for those playtimes in the basement when you were my only real-live student, sitting amongst stuffed animals. Thank you for pretending like you didn't know any of the answers or lessons, so I could actually play teacher. Thank you for appreciating the updates, for being proud of your "Sis," and for teasing that you'll buy two books, even though you are trying to de-clutter.

MY COLLEAGUES AND FRIEND SUPPORTERS.

It didn't matter when or where I shared that I was writing a book, each one of you gave me your love, support, and encouragement. Dozens and dozens of you celebrated me, cared about this project, connected me with someone you knew, and encouraged me to keep going. Thank you. So much. I needed it more than you ever could know, and each time I experienced your support, I was uplifted. I am lucky to have so many people I can call friends. When I had my finger on the "Stop" button, one of you, undoubtedly, would find me and say, "How's your book? What's the update?! I can't wait to get a signed copy!" Your words of encouragement and your support moved me along. I am so grateful for all the love I got to experience from you in writing this book. Please accept my apology that I cannot name you all because I am lucky enough to work with so many people and to live in a community with so many people who treat those around them like family. Please know I know who you are, and that each conversation we shared pushed me to finish this and to give it to the world. I am eternally thankful for you. I am so very lucky.

MY ESPECIAL THANKS TO:

Leah Ellert: for your absolute joy in all things life and for supporting me early on when this was part complete, part dream. Thank you for your genius and creativity and for helping me to manifest my cover idea into a draft that I could share with Rachel Moore, the book designer. I didn't realize when I asked you for advice with my book cover and logo that you were in the home-buying process and were helping two colleagues in need, while also balancing your own teaching schedule and personal life. You never mentioned it…because you give freely, and we are so lucky to have you. Your humor, your love, your thoughtfulness are full of the brightest lights.

Laura Hughes: for being a huge support to me and for caring about the latest updates. You always believe in me, and I am so lucky. You also always sing my name, which is by far one of the best parts of my teaching day. I love you!

Jim Shields: for letting me use your amazing, fancy Podcast equipment to record the audio version of my book and for all your patience with setting me up and teaching me how to use the equipment. Thank you for your encouragement and advice as you told me to stick with it. You motivated me and illustrated the importance of consistency and sincerity. I am so lucky to have your friendship, and we are all so lucky to have someone in our school who can do everything!

Tammy VanSteenburgh: for your help with my website and for graciously giving me your time within a busy schedule. Thank you for catching my novice error in my website, and for understanding, despite the time we spent together, that I decided to have Rachel Moore take care of the website, after all. Thank you for being such a good person—a light in our school.

Sarah Abercrombie, Sabine Armstrong, Drew Berchick, Nancy Butcher-Perez, Michelle Byers, Karen Cassidy, Colleen Costello-Deblieck, Curtis Dunaway, Laura Evans, Bri Gerlach, Jeff and Christina Grosstephan, Elyse Hackman, Karin Halteman, Sharon Havay, Jen Higgins, Rosemary Knouse, Melissa Leonard, Dan and Kendra Luther, Jimmy and Janine Mahar, Charlie Masters, Krissa Mayhew, Gretchen McFarland, Bryan Moore, Lauren Nash, Megan and Marvin Nichols, Jim and Martine Pinto, Aimee Porco, Megan Schell, Kristy Schmidt, Jason Sobieski, Marcey Varano for your above-and-beyond check-ins, belief in me, continual support, online chatting, and high encouragement. Thank you!

My Administration Team. Dr. Scott Eveslage, Dr. Brea D'Angelo, Dr. Dennis Williams, Jr., Mr. John Zuk, Mrs. Sarah Berman, Mrs. Angela Whelan, Mr. Ralph Rapino, and Mr. Bob Waeltz. Thank you so much for your enthusiasm and support, as I shared updates and latest news. Thank you for that day in the main office when I got to show you, and many others, the Advance Reader Copy. You all cheered, wanted to see the book, and asked me for signed copies. That made me feel so good! Thank you for helping me to make connections, and for, overall, believing in me and this project. I am so thankful that I get to work for people who strengthen my confidence. I wrote about personal experiences, some of which you know, because you were part of making those situations easier to manage. Thank you!

MY ESPECIAL THANKS TO:

Sarah Berman: for walking by my room during study hall when I was talking with Stephanie Clinise about my book and for being so incredibly excited and proud. Thank you for connecting me with Suzanne Dailey, who has given me invaluable encouragement, advice, and support. Thank you, Sarah, for making me feel so good about myself as a person and teacher. I appreciate your support and encouragement and your beautiful, shining light!

Brea D'Angelo: for being excited for me, for telling me you couldn't wait to read my book, for meeting with me during busy days, and for offering me the opportunity to speak to our new teachers. Thank you for understanding the realities of teaching and for being the person who works very hard to move everything that comes your way to a better, more purposeful place.

Scott Eveslage: for being the Superintendent, who welcomes teachers into your office, who takes the time to listen, and who supports your teachers. You are approachable and open. I am so lucky to work for you! Thank you for dedicating time to read my book and thank you for believing in me and my idea.

Dennis Williams: for the many meetings (and emails) you gave to me when you were incredibly busy. Thank you for being excited about this project, for loving the title, and for supporting me when I was still on shaky ground. Thank you for your help with professional advice and for connecting me with Tom Murray, who has been gracious to give me, despite an insanely busy schedule, invaluable advice on business, leadership, and remembering the why. Thank you for reading my book so thoroughly. I loved hearing your thoughts when you had it finished. That meeting was the best.

John Zuk: for being a lightyear ahead of me, and then waiting for me to catch up! You believed in this the first time I told you, but I needed a few boxes checked before I could believe in it myself. You were the first administrator I shared my book with, and I was able to do that because of the many conversations we have had over the years about the challenges of teaching. I knew you'd understand my book from start to finish. Thank you for your encouragement, for liking my posts, and for always allowing me to elicit your assistance when needed.

LOVING FRIENDS, MOVING ME ALONG.
MY ESPECIAL THANKS TO:

Doug and Danna Blystone: for celebrating me and being so excited that I was writing a book. I shared with you when it was new for me to share, and you, of course, made me feel the most comfortable. Doug, thank you for your help with the website and offering so much advice with business. I went in a different direction with the website, but I am thankful you gave me time and set me up to see this project from a holistic lens. Thank you! I love you both!

Victoria Geppert: for our chance meeting as you shared valuable ideas with our teacher group, for gifting me empowering language, and for understanding the challenges in teaching. Thank you for being willing to read my book and for believing in me. Your willingness to go above and beyond to support a new friend says so much about you!

Gwynedd-Mercy friends—Amanda Doyle, Jessica Flack, Kelley Glenn, Krista Lynch, Rose Miele, and Jessica Yodis: for your support and love to me. A special thanks to Jess Flack for helping me with the elementary perspective and for being so excited to read my book and to share it with others! Our group has been united for a long time and we pick up mid-sentence. I am so lucky to have you all.

Carrie Henry: for being a beautiful example of the Universe guiding me in this project. You coached me, week after week, as I shared self-doubts and hesitancies. Thank you for the language, for the practicing, for the "deadlines," and for the reminder that we can never go wrong when we are seeking to serve. You are wise. You are loving. You are a deep listener. Thank you to Lauren for connecting us. I cannot wait to hear how you change lives with your coaching and connection.

Rose Miele: for your thorough reading of my book, as you also adjusted to a new job. I devoured your sticky notes filled with agreements, thoughts, and support. These made me feel like a real author! Thank you for taking the time to set up meaningful connections. Thank you for believing in me and for understanding this book on a personal and deep level. You are a most beautiful friend.

Hardika Patel: for allowing me to host you during a most important semester as you prepared to change the world with your teaching abilities. You are ready to shine and soar, and I am so lucky I got to be a part of it. Thank you for believing in this idea and for supporting me more than one could imagine! You championed me to your University professors, opening the door to a treasured opportunity. Thank you for being a great teacher and a great friend! An additional special thanks to Professor Priscilla Jeter-Iles and Ms. Tanna Frank for believing in my message and for the opportunity to speak with your education students at Arcadia University. Your willingness to have me present was a meaningful experience, as I hope to continue expanding this message to educators entering the profession.

Christy Ridgley: for our reconnection and for your outpouring of support in the FB group, for reading my book, for sharing with me how much you loved my book when I was "patiently" waiting a response from teacher leaders. You have accomplished so much in your career and have remained a person we can all rely on for encouragement and help. You are a supportive, enthusiastic friend like no other, and I am so glad we could pick up mid-sentence. Thank you for being proud of me and for understanding how much work this all was. Any teacher is lucky to work for you—for someone who gets it, remembers it, and cares enough to make a difference.

Susan Scherffel: for being just as strong of a teacher as you are a volleyball player. How amazing to reunite with you after so many years! Thank you for being open to read my book, when you were starting a new position and finishing your college semester as a student-teacher supervisor. Thank you for your help with contacts and thank you for believing in my idea. It meant a lot to me that I could share this with you and that you were open to helping me.

Nicole Wagner: for connecting me with Rachel Moore, for being truly excited that I was venturing into this writing world, for understanding the stresses, self-doubt, time-restraints, and fine-balancing of working, mommying, and writing a book. I don't know how we did it, friend! Thank you for devouring my book so quickly, and for sharing all your validations with me! I needed your boost, and you built me right up! Thank you for being an amazing friend and guidance counselor. Your light shines brightest.

Jenny Yankanich: for being a tremendous, supportive friend to me, always willing to step up to help me and to guide me through troubling thoughts. You were there for me years ago and you continue to be there for me whenever I need it. I am so lucky I got to share this book process with you. Thank you for reminding me why I was doing this and for helping me to focus on how good it will feel when finished. I love you, my dear friend. Thank you for understanding me through and through.

Rob Bell friends. I sat amongst "strangers turned friends" in a most special event and shared with some nerves that I had been writing a book to serve teachers. No person could have been given better validation and support at an event than what you gave to me. Thank you for your excitement, your encouragement for me to get this book out there, and for your immense follow through in our FB Group. I love each of you. A special thanks to Rob Bell for guiding each of us to our permission and for your words of wisdom, life understanding, and confidence. Unquestionably, because of you, this book exists. Thank you for connecting with me personally to make this book even more meaningful. Your words are a gift I will hold close to my heart. A special thanks to Elizabeth Varaso for staying connected with me in the summer of 2023 and for thinking of me when your talented, amazing editor friend, Marla Taviano, was looking for a new client. You, Elizabeth, were the catalyst that sent me into a writer's world. A special thanks to Seth Gillihan for reading my book and for sharing your understanding with me. Thank you for being a huge support at the event and for reaching out to your publisher on my behalf. A special thanks to Zach Jackson and Ian Binns for believing in me, and for being supportive, encouraging, smart, funny, and just really, really awesome! I am so lucky I have you all as friends. Thank you forever.

"Teaching is Emotional" Facebook Group. I love our group, and I appreciate that we have a special place to share the emotions of our job. I didn't even know how to create a post when I started the group; yet, you believed in it. You joined, you "liked," you wrote, and you gave me a space to publicly share what I was working on and how it meant a great deal to me. Thank you for it all. I wish I could name you all. Please know how much I appreciate you. The group feels like a close community, though some of us are a plane ride apart. Thank you for being champion-level educators. I admire you all!

Marla Taviano, my first-ever editor. Thank you for taking the chance to work with me, and for building me up and encouraging me early in the process when I was new, vulnerable, and very unsure. I wanted to be your best friend during our initial phone call. I could have talked to you all day! Thank you for believing in my idea, for giving me the language that the pain points are not something to be afraid of, and for encouraging my vulnerability and courage. You were the first person to read my writing. My hands shook as I sent you my document, hoping it was "good enough." What a relief when you emailed me back with a huge "WOW!" I needed that, and you were the reason I kept going. If I had another editor who was all business and no human connection, my doubt would have won. You nurtured me and cared for my story as if it were your own story. Thank you, a million times. If it weren't for you, I would not have a published book. Thank you so very much, Marla. You empower people all over the planet. Now I get to be one of them. You will forever be special to me.

Rachel Moore. Thank you so much for your masterful genius of perfection! When the printer representative said, "That book designer is 'perfection,'" I exclaimed, "That's what I've been saying!" You are immensely talented, experienced, easy to communicate with, patient, and aware that each project is delicate to its creator. Thank you for working with me through so many changes and so many long Zoom calls. Thank you for figuring things out and knowing exactly what I needed and when. A special thank you to Nicole Wagner for connecting us. Rachel, you treated this entire book experience like it were your own. You guided me through complicated processes and gave me advice that pushed me farther and faster along the timeline. You have been with me in all the hard work. Thank you for your gentleness and enthusiasm. Thank you for being just as excited as I was when the book started to take shape. That was such a special phone call! I LOVE my book design, my cover, and my logo. How lucky I have been to work with someone like you, who gets it through and through. Thank you! Now, for our next project…

Girl Gang on Fire & My Lincoln Woods friends. I was in the debating stage uncertain if I'd even tell people about writing a book, feeling quite unsure if people would understand the intent of my message, when I took that leap to share, and you all cheered and celebrated me—as I knew you would because that is the friendship you have always given to me. Thank you, Liz Cawley, Jess King, Julie Walter, and Erin Wascavage for your enthusiasm for the next update, belief in me, and continual encouragement, most notably when I was feeling regretful and overwhelmed. Thank you for the gifs and uplifting messages and the anticipation for what's to come. I can't thank you enough for your continual encouragement and belief in me, sometimes with daily messages coming through pushing me along. There were so many times when I needed it. You knew I did, and you always stepped up. Thank you, Liz, for reading the early draft and for loving it! Thank you for your notes and for giving it to your mom to read. That made me feel so good. Thanks to each of you for your love, for liking my posts, and for being friends I can rely on when anything in life is happening. To share mom-life, friendship, ups and downs, and career updates with you is a priceless gift that I get to be a part of every day. I am so, SO very lucky.

Aimee Dashkiwsky: Thank you for celebrating me each step of the way, and for truly caring about this project. You made me feel like I was doing something amazing, and I am so lucky I've gotten to share it with you. Thank you for our late-night hangouts and for always letting me come over to chat! Thank you for being a best friend.

Becky White: Thank you for your deep listening and for reminding me to pause and to celebrate all the accomplishments, so I didn't rush too quickly into the next step. You have the ability to make me feel like I am the only one in the room, even when we are surrounded by tons of children all wanting juice boxes. You are such a dear and important friend to me. Thank you!

Daryn White: Thank you for your videos (truly, they are a highlight to my day), prayers, advice, and wisdom. Sometimes you'd do a "Take 2" video, just to get it right for me. I have felt your belief and love with every step, and you helped me to remember that this isn't meant to be easy, but that is what makes it great. Thank you! Ice blue, my friend.

An extra heartfelt thanks to my dear neighbors-turned-best-friends who have given me big hugs, who have supported me in all ways life, including with this project, and who have made my beautiful neighborhood a home: Jamie Cawley, Mike and Yung Cho, Ben Dashkiwsky, Mark Digian, Cindy Donald, Jacky and Domingo Isasi, Jon King (also for fixing my tech woes), Matt and Amy Maloney, Kevin and Melissa Ruth, Matt and Sandy Samarco, Bill and Emily Sasser, Travis and Sandrina Shive, Mike and Alecia Sroka, Eric and Kristey Viscardi (also for liking all my posts), Stephen and Nicole Wagner, Rob Walter, Tim Wascavage.

Lauren Kratz. My best and deep friend, who I've gotten to hog as my best friend for 25 years (and counting). I know you live across the country, and I know I want you to move back. It doesn't matter. We are connected in deeper ways. Thank you endlessly for the hundreds of hours you've given to me, truly wanting to know the latest updates and happenings, always ready with key advice and suggestions that have helped me in ways of business (which I knew nothing about) and social media (which I knew nothing about). Thank you for listening when I was so doubtful and for talking it through with me…again and again. Thank you for celebrating me and cheerleading me on. Thank you for your reminders to be easy on myself as I was doing a lot of new things all at once. Thank you for thinking about my project in your off hours, only for our next conversation to begin with, "Hey! I found this really cool thing that I think will help you with your book!" Thank you for your printing help and for delivering a book and for being steps ahead, so I can learn and catch up. Thank you for holding space for me when I felt doubtful about this project and thank you for reminding me to remember my WHY and to just focus on that as everything else would work out. Thank you for believing in me, way more than I've believed in myself. Thank you for being my marble jar friend. My treasure. You were the one who introduced me all those years ago to the brilliant Brené Brown and the empowered Glennon Doyle, sending me down a path of self-understanding and realization through which you've guided me. I am so lucky to have you in my life. We all are. All your friends—we are all so lucky to have you.

Kristina Ulmer. You had a new baby when you swooped me up, taking me to Starbucks to teach me all things 9th grade. I'll never forget it—your excitement for teaching and you telling me how much I was going to love 9th grade. You were right, but it would have taken me longer to get there if it weren't for you shining a light on everything you touch. I sat amazed at your materials as you walked me through unit designs and curriculum mapping, and I remain blown away at your work and your talent and your efforts. All of us are awe-struck with your brilliance as a teacher and content creator. I have learned so much from you, forever reaching to design and create as you do; my teaching is better because of you. Thank you for helping me with social media and for reading the final draft of my book. Thank you for your book notes and for rushing to my room to hug me so tightly and say, "I loved it. Diane, I loved it!" It was a build-up I needed, and it meant more than words can say coming from you. More than all this, you are my best friend, and you know the struggles and the hard and the expectations and the disappointments, and you understand them all without too much explanation and never with any disclaimers. Disclaimers don't exist with us. We already know the thing under the thing, and that feels so good, so solid, and so trusting. Thank you for letting me send long texts that I know will be read and understood and for being that trusted friend I can lean on whenever I need. This life is a lot better because you are my close and loving friend. Thank you and I love you.

Stephanie Clinise. There isn't a person who is not your best friend and when you called me your new best friend in the first ten minutes of meeting you, I knew we'd be friends forever. You make everyone feel like an all-star, a champion, a model, a masterpiece. I have been so lucky to be the benefit of your energy and your celebration. You have given me great one-liners, reminders to hold power, and necessary reassurances. I handed you my first draft a lot nervous and a lot unsure, and within a day, you came rushing to my room, exclaiming that you loved it and that it is exactly what teachers need. Then I handed you my second draft. Then I asked you to read this change and that change. Then I asked you to review my back-of-book blurb. Then I asked you to write a review. Then I asked if you'd take pictures of me holding the book. Then I asked you for additional reassurance and advice. I asked for so much, and each time, you told me how thankful you were to be part of this process with me. Thank you for all of it. You now shout this book and idea to everyone you meet and have championed me in school and on social media. You know exactly what to say and you say it so well. Thank you for your love, for believing in me, and for your excitement. Thank you for making me feel like an MVP. You, my friend, are the MVP!

Carolyn DeLuca. Your life amped up right when I asked you if you'd be willing to read my book as a non-teacher, but with all the knowledge of what it means to be a teacher. Thank you for reading my book, with so much else going on, and for giving me your time and your friendship. Your viewpoint on some key details helped me to adjust my perspective, and I feel it shows in this final draft. I don't see you as often as I'd like, but when I do, we catch up mid-sentence, and that makes me so very happy. Thank you for being a loving friend.

Sean DeLuca. Thank God in high Heaven for you. You were in the mod 1. I was in the mod 4. How many hours did you give me during my first year of teaching, when everything was overwhelming and new? Thank you for letting me walk the path to your room and for letting me sit with you after a long school day and for listening to me share about the day and the struggles. Thank you for your humor and your reassurance. You always make me laugh, and that is a treasure unlike any other treasure. Thank you for our ice cream dates and for your support and celebration. I could never feel anything but good when with you! Every new teacher needs their version of Sean DeLuca. Each person in the world needs their version of a friend like Sean DeLuca. Thank you for reading the second draft of my book, which happened to be the longest. But you read all of it and you gave me key advice. Thank you!

Ed Doran. You are my treasured school neighbor, who I have admired for nearly twenty years. Thank you

I DIDN'T SIGN UP FOR THIS

for the many, many times you've allowed me to share some frustration or struggle, all the while knowing that you'd understand and would make me feel better. Thank you for your funny memes and videos and jokes. Thank you for letting me just walk into your room when you are obviously busy working, so I can share some news from home or from the school day. Thanks for giving me your time and advice. And thanks for being a phantom because it wouldn't be the same if our conversations didn't end with me talking to myself! Thank you for listening to that crash, and for smelling that burn. Thank you for reading my book two times (!) and for showing up to my classroom door holding it to your chest and saying, "I loved it. I am so proud of you. I loved it." That meant the world to me. You were a big test, and I passed. I have endless respect for you, and I am so lucky to have learned teaching, parenting, and life from you. You deserve all the certificates.

Kim English-Murphy. You saved me all those years ago when I was in a struggle and since then you have been my emotional go-to. Your listening and depth are unmatched, and I am so lucky to have you in my life. I cannot repay all you've given to me, but I can assure you I will never forget how you helped me when I most needed it. That was one tough time—a tough time that was made better because of you seeing me and giving me guidance only you could give. Thank you for my beautiful foreword. Thank you for being so excited to read my book and for having meaningful suggestions that made the draft much stronger. Thank you for the many things I asked, up until the very end. Thank you for your many layers of help with this project that came, of course, when you had your own things going on. Thank you for your life guidance. Our names will forever be connected in print. How cool is that? How lucky am I?

Pat Hagenkotter. You guessed I was writing something without me even saying a word. You always message me when it seems I most need a pick-me-up, an encouragement, and a reassurance. How do you do it? How do you know? Thank you for being a great blend of understanding and pushing. Thank you for your surprise gifts in the mail that inspired me to continue. Thank you for telling me I'm doing a great job and for understanding that less than eight hours of sleep is a personal hell for me. Thank you for reading two drafts of my book and for caring about each new excitement. You are a gift and a loyal friend, who saved me from an unfocused sub-title and many minor typos that my eyes didn't catch. You take your job as a friend and as a teacher seriously and all those who get the gift of your friendship are very lucky. I cannot wait to see what that secret prediction letter holds. Only two more years to wait…

Nalene Hilker. You are an inspiration to me in all things life, and I aim to be you forever and forever. You squeeze every drop out of everything life, and you pave the way for the rest of us to see that there is so much life to live and so much to enjoy and explore. Thank you for being my first school neighbor and for inviting me into the department and taking me under your wing with curriculum and school systems. I love to walk by your classroom and receive some nugget of intelligence you are relaying to your students or to catch a glimpse of them working so hard on their writing because you challenge them, which means you work tirelessly to hold a high standard for our highest level students. Thank you for our hang-outs and for always including me in the good that you do. Thank you for reading my first draft and for finishing it so quickly, giving me the assurance that it was "good" and worthy of next steps. Thank you for being a loving friend, asking me how things were going and sincerely being excited about the updates. I am the President of your fan club, and I absolutely love you.

Meryl Lightstone. It has been wonderful reuniting with you, and I am so appreciative of your years of teaching service and expertise. Thank you for teaching my children and encouraging them to know and love the library. Thank you for your huge support to me and my endeavor, in every way. Thank you for supporting all of us in the FB chat and for being one of the first ones to join and to tell me it was a great idea. Thank you for being my final reader, catching all the mistakes that somehow got through the sieve and for your belief and encouragement. I loved going through your sticky notes to read your thoughts and validations. You are always open to helping others. Thank you for giving me that gift and for believing in this book being much, much more than only a book. I am so lucky to still be connected with you!

Matt Ulmer. My writing hero. You have written multiple books and stories, which is a feat like no other. It is as impressive to me as someone who has run multiple marathons, has competed in Iron Mans, and has been in the Olympics. You are amazing! Thank you for being willing to give your writing and editing talents to me. Thank you from the bottom of my heart. Your advice to refocus, restructure, and expand was exactly what that first book draft needed. You shared it all with kindness and understanding, knowing I was new at this and knowing that it would be a lot of revision work. You helped guide me through what to expect in this writing and publishing process. The words you wrote to me at the end of the last draft made me soar. Thank you for your anticipation texts and for being with me every step of the way. Thank you for your talent. Thank you for sharing it with me. Thank you for your friendship, support, and guidance. This book would not be anywhere near where it is if it weren't for you.

FINALLY, THANK YOU TO ALL THE TEACHERS.

At first, I wrote to get some experiences off my chest and to bring some understanding. Then, I wrote for all of us. To the new teachers and to the veteran teachers: our jobs have, honestly, never been easy. Our teaching profession exposes more about life and ourselves than we could ever imagine. Aren't we incredibly brave and giving to keep showing up, every day, with every intention of offering the best of ourselves? I think so. Thank you for believing in this idea, for sharing it with others, and for reading this book. I assert no profession encompasses better people than the teaching profession. You are all awesome. Absolutely awesome. I am so lucky to be a part of it.

ABOUT THE AUTHOR

 Diane Manser is a devoted high school English teacher in the Philadelphia suburbs, focusing most of her teaching career in the ninth grade. She is the founder of Teaching is Emotional™, which encourages educational leaders, current teachers, and emerging teachers to support teachers' emotional strength as they navigate a challenging profession. Diane loves to be the sunshine in people's days and to find joy in the simplest of moments. She relishes summertime at the beach, self-discovery podcasts and non-fiction books, TV watching with her husband, and playing with her kids. She lives in the Philadelphia suburbs and can be found at www.teachingisemotional.com or on almost everything social @TeachingisEmotional. For more intimate conversations, join the private TeachingisEmotional Facebook Group, or consider sharing your thoughts about the book and your teaching experiences in the "I Didn't Sign Up For This" Facebook Page.

@TeachingisEmotional

BIBLIOGRAPHIC END NOTES

1. Fincher, David. *The Curious Case of Benjamin Button*. Paramount Pictures, 2008.

2. Fuller, Ed. *Pennsylvania Teacher Staffing Challenges*. Penn State College of Education Center for Education Evaluation & Policy Analysis, Fall 2022, https://ed.psu.edu/sites/default/files/inline-files/CEEPA_report_V2.pdf.

3. Chanel, Hill. "Shapiro Plan Tackles Pa. Teacher Shortage." *The Philadelphia Tribune*, 17 Apr. 2023, www.phillytrib.com/news/local_news/shapiro-plan-tackles-pa-teacher-shortage/article_c06253be-f5da-563c-b2bf-ebe6e68adae8.html.

4. Snyder, Dan, and Casey Kuhn. "Pennsylvania Lawmakers, Educators Look for Ways to Fix Teacher Shortage." *CBS Philadelphia*, 26 Feb. 2024, www.cbsnews.com/philadelphia/news/pennsylvania-teacher-shortage-solutions-lawmakers-philadelphia/.

5. Cohen, Gabe. "Doubling up on Classrooms, Using Online Teachers and Turning to Support Staff: How Schools Are Dealing with the Ongoing Teacher Shortage." *CNN*, 11 Sept. 2023, www.cnn.com/2023/09/11/us/ongoing-teacher-shortage-creative-solutions/index.html#:~:text=Lowering%20qualification%20standards&text=With%20fewer%20college%20graduates%20training. Accessed 18 Sept. 2023.

6. Gibson, Padraic. "Human Communication: Connection and Disconnection." *Psychology Today*, 27 Nov. 2023, www.psychologytoday.com/us/blog/escaping-our-mental-traps/202311/human-communication-connection-and disconnection#:~:text=What%20it%20means%3A%20Every%20behaviour.

7. "Social Media and Youth Mental Health — Current Priorities of the U.S. Surgeon General." *www.hhs.gov*, May 2023, www.hhs.gov/surgeongeneral/priorities/youth-mental-health/social-media/index.html.

8. Klein, Alyson. "1,500 Decisions a Day (at Least!): How Teachers Cope with a Dizzying Array of Questions." *Education Week*, 6 Dec. 2021, www.edweek.org/teaching-learning/1-500-decisions-a-day-at-least-how-teachers-cope-with-a-dizzying-array-of-questions/2021/12.

9. Gordon, Deb. "The Kids Are Not Alright: New Report Shows Pediatric Mental Health Hospitalizations Rose 61%." *Forbes*, 30 Sept. 2022, www.forbes.com/sites/debgordon/2022/09/30/the-kids-are-not-alright-new-report-shows-pediatric-mental-health-hospitalizations-rose-61/?sh=6edbe8f67eb7.

10. Natanson, Hannah. "Her Students Reported Her for a Lesson on Race. Can She Trust Them Again?" *Washington Post*, 18 Sept. 2023, www.washingtonpost.com/education/2023/09/18/south-carolina-teacher-ta-nehisi-coates-racism-lesson/.

11. Ratson, Moshe. "How to Manage Expectations." *Psychology Today*, 23 Sept. 2023, www.psychologytoday.com/us/blog/the-wisdom-of-anger/202309/how-to-manage-expectations#:~:text=Expectations%20are%20normal%2C%20but%20the.

12. Hess, Frederick. "Grade Inflation Is Not a Victimless Crime." *Forbes*, 5 Sept. 2023, www.forbes.com/sites/frederickhess/2023/09/05/grade-inflation-is-not-a-victimless-crime/?sh=5371e0417b20.

13. Frost, Robert. "A Servant to Servants" in *North of Boston*. David Nutt, London, 1914.

14. Angelou, Maya. "A Quote by Maya Angelou." *Goodreads.com*, www.goodreads.com/quotes/7273813-do-the-best-you-can-until-you-know-better-then.

15. Brown, Brené. *Daring Greatly: How the Courage to Be Vulnerable Transforms the Way We Live, Love, Parent, and Lead.* New York, Ny, Gotham Books, 2012.

16. Roosevelt, Theodore. "A Quote by Theodore Roosevelt." *Goodreads.com*, www.goodreads.com/quotes/7295676-it-is-not-the-critic-who-counts-not-the-man#:~:text=The%20credit%20belongs%20to%20the.

17. "The Adult Chair Model – Michelle Chalfant | the Adult Chair." *The Adult Chair*, theadultchair.com/adult-chair-model/.

18. Winfrey, Oprah. *The Path Made Clear: Discovering Your Life's Direction and Purpose.* Macmillan Publishers, 2019, us.macmillan.com/books/9781250307507/thepathmadeclear.

19. Angelou, Maya. "A Quote by Maya Angelou." *Goodreads.com*, www.goodreads.com/quotes/518149-when-people-show-you-who-they-are-believe-them-the.

20. Fortin, Jim. Episode 253: *What Makes You Matter?* 18 Jan. 2023, disc 253. Podcast.

21. Shetty, Jay. "How to Learn Faster, Remember More & Find Your Superpower." *Jay Shetty*, jayshetty.me/podcast/jim-kwik-on-how-to-learn-faster-remember-more-find-your-superpower/.

22. "A Quote by Mother Teresa." *www.goodreads.com*, www.goodreads.com/quotes/8204875-people-are-often-unreasonable-and-self-centered-forgive-them-anyway-if.

23. Oliver, Mary. "The Summer Day." *Library of Congress, Washington*, D.C. 20540 USA, www.loc.gov/programs/poetry-and-literature/poet-laureate/poet-laureate-projects/poetry-180/all-poems/item/poetry-180-133/the-summer-day/.

24. Collins, Billy. "Days." *JSTOR and the Poetry Foundation*, Dec. 2021. Source: Poetry Magazine, Sept. 1994, www.poetryfoundation.org/poetrymagazine/browse?contentId=39048.

25. Winfrey, Oprah. "What Oprah Knows for Sure about Hope and Finding Peace." *Oprah.com*, May 2018, www.oprah.com/inspiration/oprah-on-hope-and-peace.

26. Bell, Rob. "Rob Bell / an Introduction to Joy." *Rob Bell*, 20 July 2020, www.youtube.com/watch?v=sA7LmEn3xyc.